DATE DUE

LABOR RELATIONS

LABOR RELATIONS

Millie Allen Beik

Major Issues in American History
Randall M. Miller, Series Editor

GREENWOOD PRESS
Westport, Connecticut • London

Library of Congress Cataloging-in-Publication Data

Beik, Mildred A.
    Labor relations / Millie Allen Beik.
        p.   cm.—(Major issues in American history, ISSN 1535–3192)
    Includes bibliographical references and index.
    ISBN 0–313–31864–6 (alk. paper)
        1. Strikes and lockouts—United States—History.   2. Labor movement—United
States—History.   3. Labor unions—United States—History.   4. Industrial relations—
United States—History   I. Title.   II. Series.
HD5324.B39   2005
331.892′973—dc22   2004028235

British Library Cataloguing in Publication Data is available.

Library of Congress Catalog Card Number: 2004028235
ISBN 0–313–31864–6
ISSN: 1535–3192

First published in 2005

Greenwood Press, 88 Post Road West, Westport, CT 06881
An imprint of Greenwood Publishing Group, Inc.
www.greenwood.com

Printed in the United States of America

The paper used in this book complies with the
Permanent Paper Standard issued by the National
Information Standards Organization (Z39.48–1984).

10 9 8 7 6 5 4 3 2 1

For Bill, Eric, and Carl

Contents

Series Foreword

This series of books presents major issues in American history as they have developed since the republic's inception to their present incarnation. The issues range across the spectrum of American experience and encompass political, economic, social, and cultural concerns. By focusing on the "major issues" in American history, the series emphasizes the importance of an issues-centered approach to teaching and thinking about America's past. *Major Issues in American History* thus reframes historical inquiry in terms of themes and problems rather than as mere chronology. In so doing, the series addresses the current, pressing need among educators and policymakers for case studies charting the development of major issues over time, so as to make it possible to approach such issues intelligently in our time.

The series is premised on the belief that understanding America demands grasping the contentious nature of its past and applying that understanding to current issues in politics, law, government, society, and culture. If "America" was born, and remains, as an idea and an experiment, as so many thinkers and observers have argued, issues inevitably have shaped whatever that America was and is. In 1801, in his presidential inaugural, Thomas Jefferson reminded Americans that the great strength of the new nation resided in the broad consensus citizens shared as to the rightness and necessity of republican government and the Constitution. That consensus, Jefferson continued, made dissent possible and tolerable, and, we might add, encouraged dissent and debate about critical issues thereafter. Every generation of Americans has wrestled with such issues as defining and defending freedom(s), determining America's place in the world, waging war and making peace, receiving and assimilating new peoples, balancing church and state, forming a "more perfect union," and pursuing "happiness." American identity(ies) and interest(s) are not fixed. A nation of many peoples on the move across space and up and down the socioeconomic ladder cannot have it so. A nation charged with ensuring that, in Lincoln's words, "government of the people, by the people, and for the people shall not perish from the earth" cannot have it so. A nation whose heroes are not only soldiers and statesmen but also ex-slaves, women reformers, inventors, thinkers, and cowboys and Indians cannot have it so. Americans have never rested content locked into set molds in thinking and doing—not so long as dissent and difference are built into the character of a people that dates its birth to an American Revolution and annually celebrates that lineage. As such, Americans have been, and are, by heritage and habit an issues-oriented people.

We are also a political people. Issues as varied as race relations, labor organizing, women's place in the work force, the practice of religious beliefs, immigration, westward movement, and environmental protection have been, and remain, matters of public concern and debate and readily intrude into politics. A people committed to "rights" invariably argues for them, low voter turnout in recent elections notwithstanding. All the major issues in American history have involved political controversies as to their meaning and application. But the extent to which issues assume a political cast varies.

As the public interest spread to virtually every aspect of life during the twentieth century—into boardrooms, ballparks, and even bedrooms—the political compass enlarged with it. In time, every economic, social, and cultural issue of consequence in the United States has entered the public realm of debate and political engagement. Questions of rights—for example, to free speech, to freedom of religion, to equality before the law—and authority are political by nature. So, too, are questions about war and society, foreign policy, law and order, the delivery of public services, the control of the nation's borders, and access to and the uses of public land and resources. The books in *Major Issues in American History* take up just those issues. Thus, all the books in this series build political and public policy concerns into their basic framework.

The format for the series speaks directly to the issues-oriented character of the American people and the democratic polity and to the teaching of issues-centered history. The issues-centered approach to history views the past thematically. Such a history respects chronology but does not attempt to recite a single narrative or simple historical chronology of "facts." Rather, issues-centered history is problem-solving history. It organizes historical inquiry around a series of questions central to understanding the character and functions of American life, culture, ideas, politics, and institutions. Such questions invariably derive from current concerns that demand historical perspective. Whatever determining the role of women and minorities and shaping public policy, or considering the "proper" relationship between church and state, or thinking about U.S. military obligations in the global context, to name several persistent issues, the teacher and student—indeed, responsible citizens everywhere—must ask such questions as "how and why did the present circumstance and interests come to be as they are" and "what other choices as to a policy and practice have there been" so as to measure the dimensions and point the direction of the issue. History matters in that regard.

Each book in the series focuses on a particular issue, with an eye to encouraging readers and users to consider how Americans at different times engaged the issue based on the particular values, interests, and political and social structures of the day. As such, each book is also necessarily events-based in that the key event that triggered public concern and debate about a major issue at a particular moment serves as the case study for the issue as it was understood and presented during that historical period. Each book offers a historical narrative overview of a major issue as it evolved; the narrative provides both the context for understanding the issue's place in the larger American experience and the touchstone for considering the ways Americans encountered and engaged the issue at different times. A timeline further establishes the chronology and place of the issue in American history. The core of each book is the series of between ten to fifteen case studies of watershed events that defined the issue, arranged chronologically to make it possible to track the development of the issue closely over time. Each case study stands as a separate chapter. Each case study opens with a historical overview of the event and a discussion of the significant contemporary opposing views of the issue as occasioned by the event. A selection of four to nine critical primary documents (printed whole or in excerpts and introduced with brief headnotes) from the period under review presents differing points of view on the issue. In some volumes, each chapter also includes an annotated research guide of print and non-print sources to guide further research and reflection on the event and the issue. Each volume in the series concludes with a general bibliography that provides ready reference to the key works on the subject at issue.

Such an arrangement ensures that readers and users—students and teachers alike—will approach the major issues within a problem-solving framework. Indeed, the design of the series and each book in it demands that students and teachers understand that the crucial issues of American history have histories and that the significance of those issues might best be discovered and recovered by understanding how Americans at different times addressed them, shaped them, and bequeathed them to the next generation. Such a dialectic for each issue encourages a comparative perspective not only in seeing America's past but also, and perhaps even more so, in thinking about its present. Individually and collectively, the books in *Major Issues in American History* thereby demonstrate anew William Faulkner's dictum that the past is never past.

Randall M. Miller
Series Editor

Preface and Acknowledgments

My keen interest in the labor movement and the history of labor relations stems from my earliest years. As a young child growing up in Mine 40, a coal mining settlement outside of Windber, Pennsylvania, I overheard my father and other rank-and-file union miners talking, angrily, about a new "slave labor" statute, the Taft-Hartley Act. Then, in a newsreel at a local movie house, I saw John L. Lewis, whose big, bushy eyebrows fascinated me, emphatically denounce the new measure in the same strong language. I was mystified and intrigued at the time and had no idea then that I would ever become a historian who would write about such events. But these were formative years, and in a sense, I have to admit, I first learned about the inequalities that have so often prevailed in U.S. labor relations at my father's knee.

My general goal in this book has been to provide a useful introduction, valuable primary documents, and bibliographical information to students, teachers, and researchers who are interested in the important subject of labor relations. By exploring eleven watershed events, I have tried to highlight many of the continuities and changes that have occurred in U.S. labor relations throughout its history. The choice of events that cover this time span was difficult, if only because so many others are also significant. In the end, my biggest regret is that time restraints did not permit me to include a chapter on the United Farm Workers' Strike, that is, the Grape and Lettuce Boycotts that took place from 1965 to 1970.

My choice of events was informed by the belief that labor and labor relations constitute the essence of American history and are not separate or isolatable subjects divorced from the nation's overall past. Working people have been instrumental in the building of America, and U.S. labor relations have been shaped by a wide variety of broad historical happenings. The selected events are all nationally significant. All necessarily deal with the primary issue of the power and class relationships that existed in a developing capitalist society. My general aim was to tell important stories about labor relations and interrelate essential issues of class, race, ethnicity, gender, and culture into those stories.

I might add that strikes figured prominently but not exclusively in this selection of watershed events for several reasons. For one thing, strikes, related violence, and government repression have characterized much of U.S. labor and industrial history. More than many other "events," strikes often highlighted major national issues or had a significant impact in spurring on progressive or reactionary changes in society at large. Also, large numbers of working people, nonunion workers as well as union members, have historically taken part in this form of protest and challenged existing power relations. African Americans, Hispanics, immigrants, men, women, children, people born in the United States, those with high skills, and those with little skill have gone on noteworthy work stoppages. For organized labor and diverse working people, the strike has traditionally been considered a last resort but a cherished weapon they needed to have at their disposal when other means of rectifying social and economic injustices and inequalities failed.

I am especially grateful to Gary Bailey and Irwin Marcus of Indiana University of Pennsylvania for encouraging me to undertake this project. After I decided to do so, Dr. Marcus, Elizabeth Ricketts, Janet Greene, Gregg Andrews, Michael Honey, and Jonathan Prude provided good suggestions about the topics I might cover. Later Dr. Greene also offered valuable advice about the documents I might use in the chapter on the Taft-Hartley Act.

The impressive library collections and resources I used at Emory University, Georgia Perimeter College, and Georgia State University proved essential to the completion of this work. I also benefited from the professional assistance of archivists at the Baker Library at Harvard University; the Catholic University of America in Washington, D.C.; the National Archives at College Park, Maryland; the Reuther Library of Labor and Urban Affairs at Wayne State University; the Southern Labor Archives at Georgia State University; and the University of Memphis. Arvil Adams, Dennis Dickerson, Thomas Dublin, Victoria McGoey, Ray Marshall, and Lawrence S. Root generously responded to specific queries from me. And I certainly want to thank Hattie Elie Jackson for sharing her thoughts and her memoir, *65 Dark Days in '68: Reflections: Memphis Sanitation Strike* (2004), with me.

Two individuals in particular stand out for the qualitative and generous support they have rendered throughout this project. One is Randall Miller, who has been an excellent and consistently admirable editor. His critical insights and suggestions have made this a stronger and better book as a result. The other is William Beik, my husband, who has lived with this project as long as I have and who, unlike me, has maintained rare good humor throughout it. From time to time, he has generously interrupted his own scholarly work to encourage me, offer suggestions, or provide needed computer help.

Working on *Labor Relations* has been a meaningful and moving experience that has, for me, underscored how far working people have come in this country and how far we have yet to go. I thank all those who directly or indirectly contributed to its completion. I alone am responsible for the interpretations contained in this book and for any errors that escaped my attention. I sincerely hope that students, teachers, researchers, working people, and others will find it of interest and value.

Chronology of Events

1789	U.S. Constitution takes effect.
1806	In first "conspiracy case," Philadelphia Journeymen Cordwainers' Union is found guilty of "criminal conspiracy" for trying to obtain higher wages.
1827	Mechanics Union of Trade Associations, the first city central federation, founded in Philadelphia.
1828–1829	Workingmen's parties founded in Philadelphia, New York City, and other places.
1831	Nat Turner leads slave rebellion in Virginia.
1834	First "turnout" of factory women in Lowell, Massachusetts. National Trades Union, the first and ephemeral national labor federation, founded.
1835	Growth of ten-hour movement in East. General strike for ten-hour day in Philadelphia.
1842	In *Commonwealth v. Hunt* decision, Massachusetts Supreme Court rules that labor unions, as such, are not criminal conspiracies.
1860	New England Shoemakers' Strike.
1863	Emancipation Proclamation.

1865   Civil War ends.
         Thirteenth Amendment to the Constitution outlaws slav-
         ery.

1866   National Labor Union founded in Baltimore, Maryland.

1869   Colored National Labor Union founded in Washington, D.C.
         Noble Order of the Knights of Labor founded in Philadel-
         phia.

1877   National wave of railroad strikes, with some put down by
         federal and state troops.

1882   Chinese Exclusion Act passed.
         First Labor Day celebration held in New York City.

1886   Haymarket Square bombing during a rally for the eight-hour
         day in Chicago.
         Seven anarchists later convicted; five hung.
         American Federation of Labor (AFL) founded, with Samuel
         Gompers as its first president.

1890   Sherman Antitrust Act passed.
         United Mine Workers of America (UMWA) founded.

1892   Homestead Strike and Lockout at Carnegie Steel in Pennsyl-
         vania.

1894   Pullman Strike and Boycott.

1896   In *Plessy v. Ferguson*, U.S. Supreme Court upholds Jim Crow
         segregation laws under principle of "separate but equal."

1898   Erdman Act provides for mediation and arbitration of labor
         disputes on the railroads.

1902   Anthracite Strike in Pennsylvania leads to presidential inter-
         vention and arbitration.

1903   National Women's Trade Union League founded at AFL con-
         vention to organize women.

1905   Industrial Workers of the World (IWW) founded in Chicago.

1909   National Association for the Advancement of Colored People
         (NAACP) founded.

1912   Lawrence ("Bread and Roses") Strike in Massachusetts.

1913   U.S. Department of Labor created.
         Ludlow Massacre in Colorado during coal strike.

1914   Clayton Antitrust Act limits injunction and affirms that labor is not a commodity.

1917   Great Migration of African Americans from the South to northern cities grows.

1918   National War Labor Board created. Government takes over railroads.

1919   Unprecedented wave of strikes, including the Great Steel Strike.
        Red Scare begins.
        UMWA delegates unanimously pass the "Miners' Program" at the union's convention.

1922   National coal strike and national railroad shopmen's strike.

1924   National Origins Act establishes quotas and selectively restricts immigration.

1925   Brotherhood of Sleeping Car Porters organized by A. Philip Randolph and others.

1926   Railway Labor Act ensures collective bargaining rights for railroad workers.

1933   National Industrial Recovery Act (NIRA), with Section 7 (a), passed.

1934   Wave of strikes throughout the United States
        The General Textile Strike fails.

1935   U.S. Supreme Court declares the NIRA unconstitutional.
        Congress passes the National Labor Relations Act (NLRA) and the Social Security Act.
        The United Auto Workers (UAW) union founded.
        The Committee for Industrial Organization formed within the AFL.

1937   UAW wins sit-down strike against General Motors in Flint, Michigan.
        U.S. Supreme Court declares the NLRA (Wagner Act) constitutional.
        American Federation of State, County, and Municipal Employees (AFSCME) founded.

1938   Fair Labor Standards Act establishes minimum wage and 40-hour week.
        The Congress of Industrial Organizations (CIO) becomes independent federation.

1941   A. Philip Randolph's threat to march on Washington leads to establishment of Fair Employment Practices Committee (later the Fair Employment Practices Commission).
AFL and CIO adopt no-strike pledges for the duration of the war.

1942   National War Labor Board established. It regulates wages using "Little Steel" Formula.

1943   Smith-Connally Act restricts unions and prohibits wartime strikes.

1946   Unprecedented wave of strikes throughout the United States after World War II.

1947   Taft-Hartley Act passed.

1949–1950   CIO expels eleven unions for alleged communist domination.

1955   AFL and CIO merge.

1959   Labor-Management Reporting and Disclosure Act (Landrum-Griffin Act) passed.

1962   Executive order gives collective bargaining rights to federal employee unions.

1963   March on Washington for jobs and justice.
Equal Pay Act prohibits wage differentials based on sex.

1964   Civil Rights Act of 1964.
Title VII prohibits discrimination in employment based on race, color, religion, sex, and national origin.

1965   Voting Rights Act passed.
United Farm Workers Organizing Committee founded by César Chavez.
Strike of California grape workers begins. Strike and boycott last for five or more years.

1968   Memphis Sanitation Strike and assassination of Dr. Martin Luther King Jr.

1970   Postal Strike, first national strike by a public employee union, occurs.
Occupational Safety and Health Act (OSHA) passed.

1974   Coalition of Labor Union Women (CLUW) founded.

1981   Professional Air Traffic Controllers Organization (PATCO) Strike.

1992   North American Free Trade Agreement (NAFTA) passed.

1993   Executive order lifts ban on rehiring of PATCO strikers.

1999   Seattle protests against World Trade Organization (WTO) policies.

2002   President Bush invokes Taft-Hartley Act against longshoremen during lockout.

2005   President Bush proposes vast changes in existing Social Security, Medicare, and federal pension programs.

LABOR RELATIONS

Introduction

Workers' rights have been an important, persistent, and contentious issue throughout the entire history of the United States. The critical issue arose, with fateful consequences, at the nation's founding when the elite framers of the Constitution considered, and then adopted, a series of compromises that protected slavery and left slavery a local institution that was largely immune from legal interference by the federal government. Much has happened since then. The experience of work and the world of the workers have undergone significant changes from 1790 to the present, but workers' rights, broadly defined, remain as contested as ever.

Throughout these centuries, U.S. labor relations have been shaped by a wide variety of broad historical happenings, including wars, depressions, government policies, labor unrest, and global competition. For example, it took the Civil War and the Thirteenth Amendment, not good will, to end slave labor, and it was the mobilization for victory in World War I that brought about the enormous political and social changes that set a precedent for New Deal labor policies. Such major events often had contradictory results, depending on the specific circumstances of the time. Thus, depressions in 1837 and throughout the nineteenth century damaged or destroyed the labor movements that were in existence then, while the Great Depression of 1929 spawned a labor upsurge, reform, and new social programs in the 1930s. Strikes and labor unrest often sparked massive government repression from 1877 on, but such unrest, political mobilization, and cross-class alliances also prompted calls for mediation and occasional progressive reforms. In any case, the nation's labor laws and policies generally favored the rights of business over labor except for the period from 1933 to 1947, while other of its policies, including its acceptance or rejection of racial segregation, women's inequality, and immigration exclusion or restriction had a significant impact of their own on civil rights and labor relations. And today, despite protests, global competition has become the new rationale for business and government to adhere to a free market economy that critics believe undercuts workers' rights in the United States and undermines human rights around the globe.

These examples suggest, correctly, that labor relations are not static and that they entail power relations between capital (or business), labor, and government that have rarely, if ever, been in equilibrium. It is important to note that, from 1790 to the present, U.S. labor relations have evolved within the framework of a capitalist economy, whether it be an emerging or more fully developed industrial, post-industrial, or global one. It is also important to note that capitalism is a dynamic, historical, and even a revolutionary economic system that is motivated, first and foremost, by the notion of profit, not human needs. Although its proponents have argued that it benefits the working class in the long run, no one has ever claimed that it is egalitarian or places human needs above profits. In its twenty-first-century variant as well as its nineteenth- and twentieth-century ones, the assumption is that a minority of individual or corporate private property owners rightfully holds the preponderance of wealth and the means of production in its hands while the majority of people, middle- and lower-class wage or salaried workers, remain dependent on their labor, their jobs, for a livelihood. Although the relative balance or imbalance of power between labor, business, and the government has shifted from time to time, the unequal power and class relations that are characteristic of capitalism have historically prevailed in the United States, and at any given time, the state of labor relations has reflected the existing balance of power within those limits. Working people, their unions, and their allies have faced an uphill struggle for workers' rights, higher wages, and better working conditions even in the best of times.

This book seeks to explore eleven watershed events that highlight the continuities and changes that have occurred in U.S. labor relations throughout its history. Each of these events is of national importance and illuminates some of the major issues in vogue during a particular period in the nation's past.

Chapters 1 and 2 cover events that occurred during the antebellum period when at least two distinct labor systems, free and unfree, and two vastly different regional economies coexisted. During this formative and transitional period in the republic, much of the northern half of the country underwent vast economic and social changes that were gradually transforming it into an industrial center based on wage labor, while the southern half continued to rely, primarily, on agriculture and slave-produced cash crops to sell on the world market.

Meanwhile, as the growth of cities, banks, railroads, commerce, large-scale manufacturing, and factories expanded in the North during the early nineteenth century, Thomas Jefferson's vision of a stable agrarian republic of relative equality (for whites), with yeoman farmers and self-sufficient, independent producers as its social base, was dissipating. Instead, capitalist economic development gradually and dynamically transformed the social and class relationships that had existed at the time of the Revolution. By the late 1820s, inequality was rising; wealth and power were becoming increasingly concentrated in the hands of "monopolies," merchant capitalists, factory owners, financiers, and large property owners; and more and more yeomen farmers, journeymen craftsmen, and other women and men were losing their economic independence and being drawn into a larger pool of wage labor. In this context, working people who saw themselves as members of the "producing and useful classes" drew radically different lessons from the American Revolution than their bosses and entrepreneurs did. Their adherence to the republican ideals of "equal rights," "civic virtue," and "community" stood in sharp contrast to their employers' belief in the values of "self-interest," "individualism," and an uncontrolled "market." They began to ask questions about the type of society that was being created and the future of the Republic. And, from 1827 to 1837, in cities and in the region where free or wage labor predominated, skilled workers led efforts to forge an American labor movement that is the subject of Chapter 1. Suffice it to say here that the existence of the slave-labor system, laws that defined labor unions as "criminal conspiracies," and an economic depression placed severe limitations on the growth and durability of that pioneering movement.

Despite these developments, slavery remained the preeminent labor issue of the nation throughout the antebellum period. Until the Civil War led to emancipation, no section of the country could escape its impact. When women mill workers referred to themselves as "daughters of free men" during a strike in Lowell, Massachusetts, in 1834, and when female stitchers and binders in Lynn, Massachusetts, carried a banner that proclaimed "AMERICAN LADIES WILL NOT BE SLAVES" during the New England shoemakers' strike of 1860, they were drawing upon an invidious and familiar comparison. And when Abraham Lincoln supported the shoemakers' cause during a speech in New Haven, Connecticut, in March 1860, he did so on the grounds that the right to strike was not only essential but one of the major distinctions that made free labor superior to slave labor.

That New England shoemakers' strike is the subject of Chapter 2. This strike, the largest work stoppage to take place in the United States before the Civil War, was a harbinger of things to come, of future labor and

industrial relations. On the one hand, it marked the demise of the traditional artisanal and hand-making era of the shoe industry, an era characterized by skilled work and the workers' relative independence. On the
other hand, it signaled the onset of a new industrial era in which a permanent class of wage laborers carried out mechanized shoe production in
factories owned by others. The unprecedented strike that involved men,
women, children, immigrants, and those who were born in the country
also revealed the deep divisions that existed within the working class and
the importance of incorporating gender and other types of social analysis
into labor history. Male artisans espoused "equal rights" and considered
the work of *all* women shoemakers as subordinate in importance to theirs
in a family-based economy they took for granted, while the female strikers were divided.

Until the Civil War ended slave labor and removed other obstacles to
national industrial development, economic growth was primarily a local
and regional affair. Throughout this time, local and state authorities
oversaw labor relations. It was the Massachusetts Supreme Court and
not the U.S. Supreme Court that ruled that unions were legal entities.
Southern states and other states were thus free to ignore the court's decision. Also, organizations such as the Lowell Female Reform Association
petitioned their state legislatures, not Congress, on behalf of the ten-
hour day, and reformers in Pennsylvania and several other states won
passage of ineffective laws limiting child labor. On constitutional
grounds, the national government limited its role in labor relations to
matters involving interstate commerce and the employment of federal
workers.

The beginning of the government's expansion of its role in U.S. labor
relations dates from 1877, when a massive wave of spontaneous railroad
strikes erupted and federal and state troops helped break the strikes.
Chapter 3 covers the railroad strikes of 1877, and Chapter 4 the Pullman
strike and boycott of 1894. These two important events occurred in the
late nineteenth century when the triumph of industrial capitalism was
being achieved and the United States was emerging as an industrial
power on a national scale. The rise and consolidation of big businesses,
the growth of national labor unions, and violent labor and class conflict
were characteristic of the period. Railroads epitomized the new industrial
structure in many ways, and the two strikes highlight the changing class
and labor relations of the period.

From 1865 to 1900, big businesses and large-scale factories gradually
assumed an importance that small businesses and agriculture once had.
Population growth, mass immigration, and the rise of more and larger
cities accompanied the industrial expansion. New inventions like the telephone and transatlantic cable facilitated communication; electricity, new
methods of forging steel, and technological developments revolutionized

industry. In the process, formerly independent "producers" such as yeomen farmers and skilled craftsmen whose skills were debased or eliminated by technological changes found themselves in the status of permanent wage workers. Many immigrants, women, children, and former slaves were already in that position. At emancipation, African Americans received nothing that enabled them to achieve economic independence, and many continued to work in agriculture as sharecroppers.

Working people began to form unions and take part in broad political reform movements to improve their lot. But they faced an uphill battle. The economic depressions that occurred in 1873, 1886, and 1893 created massive unemployment and weakened unions while employers experimented with new policies such as "judiciously mixing the nationalities" to retain control over their work forces. The working classes were divided by race, sex, skill, and ethnicity that limited solidarity, and the labor movement even led racist efforts to obtain passage of the Chinese Exclusion Act in 1882.

Meanwhile, Congress passed a number of reforms, including the Interstate Commerce Act of 1887, a measure to eliminate abusive railroad practices; and the Sherman Antitrust Act of 1890, a law designed to prohibit business combinations, trusts, and conspiracies in restraint of trade; but such measures proved ineffective. By 1892, dissatisfaction with the existing situation led a new independent political party, the Populist Party, to make government ownership and operation of the railroads, telegraph, and telephone system a top priority in its platform. Railroads were pioneers in the new business consolidations and questionable practices that the public often condemned. During this era of industrial expansion, the rights of the public, as well as labor, versus the rights of corporations and trusts emerged as a significant issue.

In many ways, the 1890s were a critical turning point in U.S. history. By then, a small portion of the population had consolidated a massive amount of wealth and power in its private hands, and the nation's courts were siding with big business against labor and the public. Industrial capitalism was being consolidated. The U.S. Supreme Court's decision to uphold the applicability of the Sherman Antitrust Act against labor combinations and thus authorize a sweeping labor injunction against the American Railway Union during the Pullman strike set a striking precedent that lasted until the New Deal. Its legalization of Jim Crow practices in 1896 in the *Plessy v. Ferguson* decision strengthened inequality and racial division that lasted until the 1960s. Such decisions were made at a time when Social Darwinism was the dominant ideology of the day, when so-called experts reported that inequalities of all sorts were "scientific" and part of the "natural" order. Thus, the capitalist class's domination over working people, the "natural" supremacy of Anglo-Saxon and Nordic peoples over all other racial and ethnic groups, and man's presumed "natural" rights over women's rights at home or in the workplace acquired valuable respectability and an aura of inevitability.

It is significant to note that, until the mid-1890s, none of the major national labor organizations that were founded after the Civil War accepted the capitalist system or the notion of a class of permanent wage earners. The ultimate goal of the craft-based National Labor Union (1866–1872) and the all-inclusive Knights of Labor (1869–1890s), the most important labor organization in the nineteenth century, was a cooperative commonwealth of producers. Both established cooperatives and engaged in political actions to change laws. A fundamental change in the nature of the U.S. labor movement took place in the mid-1890s when the American Federation of Labor (AFL), a federation of existing craft unions headed by a former socialist, Samuel Gompers, rose to prominence. Unlike its predecessors, the AFL accepted the permanence of capitalism and pursued "pure and simple unionism," that is, direct bargaining with employers, to obtain gains within the system. Its primary political goal was to keep the federal government out of industrial relations for fear of its formidable police powers and judicial injunctions. It eschewed radicalism and focused on representing the interests of skilled workers, the strongest members of the working class. Unlike the earlier unions, it discriminated against African Americans, women, immigrants, and all unskilled labor.

The labor problem remained a central public concern into the Progressive Era, when workers, the middle classes, and segments of business sought all sorts of social reforms. For example, in 1900 Ralph Easley, a Chicago journalist, and Senator Mark Hanna, an Ohio Republican, founded the National Civic Federation (NCF), a private organization of business, labor, and public representatives that sought to undermine popular support for socialism by promoting collective bargaining and social reforms designed to create industrial peace, stability, and efficiency. AFL President Samuel Gompers joined the NCF and served as one of its vice presidents.

In 1900, a presidential election year, Hanna and the NCF did work behind the scenes to help secure a settlement of the anthracite coal strike that established the United Mine Workers of America (UMWA) in the hard-coal region, but the NCF's efforts to conclude the more important anthracite strike in 1902 failed. The region's monopolistic and adamantly anti-union coal-carrying railroads refused to negotiate with the UMWA miners, who remained on strike for five months. Only active intervention by President Theodore Roosevelt, who established a new federal precedent by his efforts to mediate the conflict and represent the public's interest, ultimately led to a somewhat nebulous resolution of the dispute. Although the union made important gains in membership, wages, hours, and working conditions, the strikers did not achieve their main goal of union recognition, and the Anthracite Arbitration Commission that subsequently emerged from the strike later proved disappointing to them.

The National Association of Manufacturers (NAM) and many other businesses in the United States, like the anthracite coal-carrying railroads, never accepted the reformist goals of the NCF and were unwilling to recognize, let alone cooperate, with unions, however conservative they might be. Most followed the example of the steel industry. The violent and disastrous Homestead strike and lockout of 1892, followed by a strike in 1901, had destroyed the Amalgamated Association of Iron, Steel, and Tin Workers and made steel a bastion of the open shop until the New Deal.

From about 1900 on, large-scale corporations also began to adopt the policies of "scientific management" espoused by Frederick W. Taylor to control labor, reduce costs, and avert unionization. Through the use of time-and-motion studies, Taylor was able to subdivide tasks, thus undermining skills and reducing the labor force while increasing productivity. Managerial reorganization of the labor process and the pace of work, along with the introduction of new machinery, payment plans, and increased supervision of the work force, threatened the traditional measures of workers' control that skilled workers especially valued. The assembly line became a reality, and the demand for unskilled labor increased.

Nevertheless, workers continued to organize unions. In 1903 middle-class and working women founded the Women's Trade Union League, an organization that supported protective legislation that limited the working hours of women and children. Reformers did win successful passage of a number of child labor, workers' compensation, and other labor-related laws on the state and national levels during this period. The most important legislation, by far, for the AFL was the Clayton Antitrust Act, a measure it hailed as a "Magna Carta" for labor in 1914. The law was designed to exempt organized labor from the provisions of the Sherman Antitrust Act. Within a short time, however, the courts reinterpreted the law and again allowed labor injunctions to be issued against strikes under the older law.

During the Progressive Era the Socialist Party and the radical Industrial Workers of the World (IWW) provided workers with viable political and economic options, and it is significant that both organizations achieved the height of their influence in the United States from 1900 to 1916. In 1912 the Socialist Party's presidential candidate, Eugene Debs, received over 900,000 votes, and 1,000 socialists were elected to public offices. Meanwhile, the IWW's notions of "one big union" and the restructuring of society, along with its focus on direct action and support of industrial unions that included all those who worked in a given industry, appealed to segments of the immigrant and American working classes who were overlooked by the AFL. The IWW became known in the East when it came to the aid of the strikers in Lawrence, Massachusetts, in 1912. That "Bread and Roses" strike highlighted major issues of the time and embodied labor's highest ideals. It is the subject of Chapter 5.

The entry of the United States into World War I brought about enormous social changes. The institution of the military draft and the sharp decline in immigration opened up opportunities for women, who took on factory and other jobs that were once closed to them, and for African Americans, who continued the Great Migration from the South to northern cities where they took jobs in meatpacking, steel, mining, and other industries. Meanwhile, organized labor was growing in numbers and in strength. By the end of the war, 20 percent of the nation's nonagricultural workers were members of a union. Government policies had aided that growth. Union representatives joined business representatives and government officials on the various wartime boards that oversaw the economy. And the National War Labor Board, a federal agency established to ensure efficient war production by fostering harmonious labor relations, set a precedent for the New Deal by recognizing the right of workers to organize and bargain collectively, even though it had no power to enforce employers to comply. The federal government's involvement in the economy was such that, at President Woodrow Wilson's directive, the Railroad Administration even took the railroads out of private hands and ran them for the duration.

At the war's end, the United States was not immune from the profound political and economic changes that were turning the world upside down. It was a rare and fluid moment in U.S. history when socialists, progressives, the general public, and the labor movement were discussing the possibility of reconstructing American society in fundamental ways and extending democracy at home. In this context in 1919, 4 million workers, further fueled by rampant inflation and postwar unemployment, went out on strikes throughout the country. Strikers were seeking higher wages and better working conditions, but many were also seeking to obtain or maintain "workers' control" that displaced management's prerogatives. The notions of the nationalization and the socialization of industries were not new ideas either, and the war experience had stimulated pragmatic thoughts on these subjects. The railroad brotherhoods adopted the Plumb Plan for nationalization of the railroad industry, and, in 1919, members of the United Mine Workers of America (UMWA), the largest union in the country, unanimously adopted resolutions endorsing a "Miners' Program" that included nationalization of the coal industry with democratic management, the formation of a labor party, a six-hour day and five-day work week, and other measures.

The Miners' Program, a classic example of the class-conscious labor radicalism that characterized the post–World War I era, is the subject of Chapter 6. Although never implemented, it did enjoy some public support and represented an important alternative course that the U.S. labor movement and the U.S. government might have pursued but did not. Instead, the conservative UMWA president, John L. Lewis, consolidated his power within the union, eschewed radicalism, and became a leading exponent of "business unionism," that is, a form of unionism that accepted capitalism, employed business methods, and relied on collective bargaining to ensure modest gains for union members.

For the most part, throughout the 1920s, businesses aided by government continued to hold the upper hand in labor relations. The decade began with a drive by many anti-union employers for the open shop and ended in growing unrest during the Great Depression. In many ways, as the historian Irving Bernstein has argued, these were labor's "lean years," a time when judicial injunctions, blacklists, and private police prevailed in many industrial quarters, a time when economic depressions created miserable conditions in such industries as coal and textiles long before the stock market crash in 1929. Major national strikes occurred in coal and railroads in 1922 and 1923, and in 1929 a textile strike in Gastonia, North Carolina, foreshadowed the resurgence of labor militancy in the 1930s. Congress had sought to defuse radicalism by passing racially based legislation to restrict immigration from southern and eastern Europe and Asia in 1924. This decade was also marked by anti-radical, anti-foreign-born "cultural wars" that included the expansion of the Ku Klux Klan into northern states, where it was directed against labor, immigrants, and Catholics; and by a lengthy but unsuccessful international crusade to save two Italian immigrant anarchists, a shoe cutter and a fish peddler, Nicola Sacco and Bartolomeo Vanzetti, from execution for a dubious crime committed in South Braintree, Massachusetts, in 1920. Meanwhile, union membership in the United States declined from a high point of 5.1 million in 1920 to 3.6 million in 1929.

At the same time, during this era of triumphant business values, some progressive reformers continued the effort to achieve industrial peace and stability through government and business cooperation. Herbert Hoover, U.S. Secretary of Commerce from 1921 through 1929, pursued the elusive goal by advocating the establishment of national trade associations that were to serve as self-regulating agencies that set industrywide standards and ended the cutthroat competition that fueled unrest and misery. Such associations subsequently provided a direct link to New Deal recovery policy in the 1930s. And many corporations used a carrot-and-stick approach in their approach to labor. In addition to the repressive measures at their disposal, General Motors and Ford Motor Company were among those employers who sought to secure the loyalty of their workers and avert unionization by offering them a variety of company-controlled employee representation plans, pension plans, savings plans, and other welfare measures. However, neither government–business cooperation nor corporate welfare policies could avert the Great Depression, which undermined the prestige of big business and set the stage for the New Deal and the revival of the labor movement.

The most fundamental shift of labor relations in U.S. history outside of the ending of slavery occurred in the context of the Great Depression. During the New Deal era the U.S. government used its power to shift the balance of power between capital and labor. From 1933 to 1947, it actively supported the workers' right to organize and engage in collective bargaining through inclusion of section 7 (a) in the National Industrial Recovery Act of 1933 (NIRA) and then the passage of the Wagner or National Labor Relations Act of 1935. It also established important social programs such as Social Security in 1935 and passed laws such as the Fair Labor Standards Act of 1938 to regulate hours and wages for workers engaged in interstate commerce. Throughout this time the labor movement expanded and grew in membership and influence. Industrial unionism emerged as a major issue, and John L. Lewis led workers to form the Congress of Industrial Organizations (CIO). The rival alternative to the craft-based AFL helped organize the automobile, steel, and other major industries. Union membership increased from 4 million at the end of 1933 to nearly 15 million in 1945.

Chapters 7 and 8 cover two strikes that emphasize the ambiguities, strengths, and limitations of New Deal labor policy. Like other New Deal policies, its labor ones were pragmatic, not planned in advance, and they evolved over time. The historian Irving Bernstein has noted that the inclusion of section 7 (a) in the NIRA was a mere afterthought designed to win labor's support for the recovery plan, the government's top priority. He has also suggested that no other Congress in U.S. history but the one in 1935, with its peculiar political alignments and divisions, would have passed the Wagner Act. In this context, the failure of the textile strike of 1934 can be seen as a test of the ongoing influence and power of business and a test of the early New Deal's commitment to workers' rights. The successful General Motors sit-down strike of 1936–1937 occurred at a later date, after President Franklin D. Roosevelt's landmark reelection and the passage of the Wagner Act, but it, too, tested the administration's labor policies and business's clout. Taken together, the two strikes exemplify an evolving national pattern of labor relations in which the North and mass-production industries emerged as the centers of union strength while the South remained a bastion of the open shop and an ongoing threat to organized labor.

That many businesses never accepted organized labor or the changed labor relations policy of the 1930s became evident in the 1940s when the National Association of Manufacturers led a vigorous movement to change the nation's labor laws and restore the balance of power between business and labor that predated the New Deal. Wildcat strikes during

World War II, despite the AFL and CIO's no-strike pledges, and an impressive wave of postwar strikes in 1946, comparable only to those in 1919, contributed to a conservative political climate that made enactment of the Taft-Hartley Act possible. That controversial law that business said would "equalize" labor relations and that labor considered a "slave-labor" statute is the subject of Chapter 9. The Taft-Hartley Act stressed the rights of employers and individual workers; prohibited closed shops, union shops, and other forms of union security; and legalized the rights of states to enact "right to work" laws that undercut the right to organize. Its passage over President Harry Truman's veto marked the beginning of the gradual demise of New Deal labor policy.

The shift in the political balance of power to business during the post-war period, the new labor legislation, the Cold War, and the anti-communist witch hunts of the late 1940s cast a large shadow over the labor movement. Throughout the New Deal, communists and other radicals had actively championed labor and civil rights. But unions were required by the new law to sign non-communist loyalty affidavits to enjoy the rights of the National Labor Relations Board, and all but two unions did so. The CIO had linked its fate to reform, not broader social change, and to the Democratic Party, which was under siege. In 1948 and 1949 it succumbed to pressures to purge eleven communist-led unions, including the United Electrical Workers, from its ranks. As the historian Ronald Filippelli has noted, for the first time in U.S. history, the radical voices that had been present in the mainstream American labor movement throughout its existence were missing or effectively silenced.

In this context, corporations and unions, purged of dissent, reached an accommodation. General Motors and the United Auto Workers (UAW) set the example. During a strike in 1946, Walter Reuther, an important UAW leader, and then the government, demanded that General Motors open up its books. The huge corporation refused the demand but ultimately granted employees a significant pay raise that satisfied everyone. This incident illustrates management's intent on jealously retaining its "right to manage" as well as the union and government's compliance. Postwar unions stressed economic gains, not workers' control. Collective bargaining, grievance procedures, and contracts became the basis of a labor relations system in which private enterprise tolerated unions that restrained militancy and left capitalism unchallenged. The system was bolstered by the absence of significant international economic competition from the late 1940s to 1970 and by a prospering economy in which many workers, nonunion as well as union ones, made gains in real wages and "fringe benefits." The government's role was crucial, too. The extension of social programs, reforms, and lucrative government contracts granted in the pursuit of a global war against communism underlay the accommodation that was perhaps two-edged. After World War II, union gains and government benefits enabled many working people to achieve home ownership, increased education for their children, and a middle-class status. Over time, some began to identify themselves, not as workers, but as middle-class citizens who no longer saw the need for, or the value of, unions.

Meanwhile, from the New Deal on, racial equality and civil rights emerged as critically important issues in labor relations as well as in other arenas of American society. A. Philip Randolph, an African American socialist who had helped black workers form the Brotherhood of Sleeping Car Porters in 1925, led a relentless uphill fight from then on to end widespread racial discrimination within the AFL and the labor movement, to secure equal access to jobs for minorities, and to extend the rights of all working people.

The formation of the CIO, an industrial union that admitted members of all races, in 1935, encouraged Randolph and other black workers who were unhappy that Congress had defeated an amendment to the Wagner Act that would have barred racist unions or employers from discriminating against them. Consequently, in 1936 hundreds of individuals and representatives of African American organizations held the National Negro Congress in Chicago to unite all Negro organizations in the quest for civil rights and equality, in the workplace and elsewhere. Randolph emphasized that economic equality was essential to the attainment of social and political equality. From then on, an alliance between the CIO and the civil rights movement was forged. Imperfect as it was, the alliance enabled the CIO to organize mass-production industries where black labor was important.

In 1941 ongoing racial discrimination led Randolph to threaten to lead a march on Washington to demand equal access for minorities to jobs in the growing defense industry. In return for his acquiescing to President Franklin D. Roosevelt's request to call the march off, Roosevelt issued Executive Order No. 8802, which established the Fair Employment Practices Committee and prohibited the government from awarding contracts to those firms that practiced racial discrimination in hiring. Civil rights was an issue that was here to stay.

The culmination of the Civil Rights Movement for legal equality occurred in the 1960s with the passage of the Civil Rights Act of 1964 that barred discrimination in employment on the basis of race, color, religion, sex, or national origin, and the Voting Rights Act of 1965. Enforcement of the law, and attaining economic opportunity and equality, was another matter. The ongoing quest of minority workers for dignity was aptly demonstrated in 1968 when African American sanitation workers in Memphis went out on strike for higher wages, improved working conditions, and recognition of their public union, Local 1733 of the American Federation of State, County, and Municipal Employees (AFSCME). In 1962, President Kennedy had issued an executive order that permitted government employees to form unions and engage in collective bargaining, and the explosive growth of public unions that followed soon surpassed that of private-sector unions. An impressive labor and civil rights coalition supported the Memphis strikers in a conflict in which many of the turbulent decade's quintessential issues—civil rights, the rights of public unions, and poverty—converged. The Memphis strike is the subject of Chapter 10.

At the same time, in California, César Chavez was leading Mexican-American and other farm workers in a strike and broad-based grape and lettuce boycott to achieve dignity and fundamental rights. Farm workers were not covered by the National Labor Relations Board. But, in 1970, the United Farm Workers won a contract with growers, and, in 1975 passage of a California state law that required growers to bargain collectively with the union.

The federal government's new legal commitment to equal opportunity extended to women. The Equal Pay Act of 1963 outlawed wage differentials based on race, color, religion, sex, or national origin, and Title VII of the Civil Rights Act prohibited discrimination based on gender. Meanwhile, a broad-based women's rights movement emerged in the 1960s and 1970s. Issues such as equal pay for equal work, day care, and abortion rights entered public consciousness. In this context, women who were members of labor unions formed the Coalition of Trade Union Women in 1974 to represent their particular gender and class-based interests. But economic equality and opportunity proved elusive. In 1979, as in 1959, women earned 59 cents for every dollar a man earned, and occupational segregation was still widespread.

Congress passed other reforms that affected labor relations. In 1970 the Occupational Safety and Health Act (OSHA) became law, as did the Employment Retirement Income Security Act (ERISA), a measure to regulate private pension plans, in 1974. But the severe economic recessions of the 1970s were setting the stage for critical changes in existing labor relations and the status of organized labor. Stagflation—a combination of high inflation and high unemployment—combined with greater foreign competition, deregulation of key industries, plant relocations to southern states or other countries, the introduction of new technology, and the growth of diversified international business conglomerates, reduced organized labor's clout in collective bargaining. Terms like "concessions" and "rust belt" became commonplace in the 1970s.

In this setting the tragic strike by the Professional Air Traffic Controllers' Association (PATCO) in 1981 is far more than the story of an elite public union of controllers challenging the federal government and losing decisively when President Ronald Reagan fired them. This strike, the subject of the final chapter of this book, marked a significant turning point in U.S. labor relations. It changed the parameters of acceptable behavior and contributed to the demise of a labor relations system that had existed since the New Deal.

After PATCO, employers in the private sector, backed by the government, felt freer to wage bitter fights against unions they had once tolerated and against collective bargaining. They broke established custom and exercised their legal right to hire permanent replacement workers during strikes. Meanwhile, the combination of repressive labor policies and the hardships of economic recessions throughout the 1980s left their mark. Strike activity and union membership steadily declined. In 1983, 20.1 percent of U.S. workers belonged to unions, but in 2004 only 12.5 percent did. Plant closings and plant relocations decimated the nation's industrial heartland and union base, while public unions in the service and white-collar industries became the source of organized labor's strength. The labor movement's loss of political clout was evident in the 1990s when it failed to stop the passage of the North American Free Trade Agreement (NAFTA) in 1993 or make enforcement of various side agreements on labor's rights effective. Nor could it redeem President Bill Clinton's pledge to revise the nation's labor laws.

At any given time, the state of organized labor is one important standard for measuring the basic character and quality of life in a modern democratic society. Its relative rise or decline reveals something about whether a country is taking a direction toward greater social equality or inequality. Unions have historically been the primary instrument working people have used to assert their rights, their dignity, and their citizenship. Even though only a minority of American workers have ever belonged to them, their status has had significant implications for *all* workers. That the labor movement has historically led the battles to gain workers' rights against hostile employers and hostile state and federal governments is an important reality. The value of labor and the place of working people in American society have been contentious issues throughout U.S. history, and they remain so today, as much as they ever did.

Outsourcing, privatization, health care, the future of Social Security, Medicare, and retirement plans are only a few of the many problems facing middle-class and working-class people today. Meanwhile, enforcement of laws such as the Occupational Safety and Health Act (OSHA) remains lax, and many of the historic protections for workers are being modified or abolished. For example, in 2004, changes in the Fair Labor Standards Act eliminated overtime pay for millions of workers, although some gained from the revision. Indeed, the alliance between government and business that became manifest in the aftermath of the PATCO strike increasingly resembles that of the pre–New Deal era, when no balance of power, no equilibrium, in labor relations seemed to exist.

The next chapter on U.S. labor relations is being written in the context of the triumph of global capitalism upon the ending of the Cold War and the simultaneous emergence of fundamental issues of workers' rights and human rights around the globe. Perhaps an event like the protests in Seattle in 1999 against the World Trade Organization by the American labor movement and many other progressive organizations from the United States and other countries marks the beginning of a movement that will substantially change labor relations. Perhaps not. Whether the alliance between government and business that is so heavily weighted against labor will continue indefinitely in this new environment remains to be seen. Whether the U.S. labor movement can renew itself, cooperate with broad coalitions to support environmental and social justice causes, and develop new strategies and directions that effectively shift the balance of power in labor relations once again remains an open question.

1

The Uneven Emergence of a Labor Movement, 1827–1837

At its inception in 1789, the new American republic under the Constitution was a diverse, multiracial, multiethnic society of 4 million people whose various classes and populations derived dissimilar legacies from the American Revolution. The elite framers of the Constitution had taken fateful decisions that excluded Native Americans from the civic polity, perpetuated the subordinate status of women, and preserved the slave-labor system, largely by leaving it the subject of local law beyond the reach of federal authority. Thus, in an important sense, at birth, the new nation was both free and unfree. It had inherited distinctive regional economies from the colonial era, and those differences grew even more marked in the nineteenth century. Consequently, when the labor movement emerged in the United States in the 1820s, it was shaped by the realities of social inequality and the coexistence of disparate "free-labor" and "slave-labor" systems.

Throughout the early nineteenth century, cities, commerce, transportation, and industry developed at a greater rate in the North than in the South. Although remnants of slavery and indentured servitude continued to survive in the North into the early nineteenth century, yeomen farmers, independent urban artisans, and laborers formed the bulk of the region's "producing classes." As time went on and the economy developed, however, class structures changed. More and more, journeymen mechanics (craftsmen) found it impossible to achieve the independence of master craftsmen, and women, skilled and unskilled immigrants, factory workers, and outworkers (those workers who sewed clothing or performed other work at home for an outside employer) were increasingly drawn into the paid wage-labor force. "Free labor," another term for wage labor in a capitalist economy, fueled northern industrial development during the nineteenth century.

By contrast, slave labor was the foundation of the antebellum southern economy. The wealth and political power of the minority of white slave owners made them dominant. Big planters derived their wealth from the profits they made when they sold slave-produced commodities such as cotton, tobacco, and rice on the capitalist world market. But the owners of slaves also used men and women to perform a wide variety of other skilled and unskilled jobs, including those in the region's sparse industries. Both northern and southern free white workers had reason to fear slave-labor competition.

FREE LABOR AND THE BIRTH OF A LABOR MOVEMENT

It was not accidental that the modern American labor movement emerged during the period from 1827 to 1837 in the North, where free labor prevailed and capitalist economic development was expanding. Vast social and economic changes were occurring there. Many people sensed, at least vaguely, that inequality was rising, reforms were needed, and class structures were changing in a way that undermined their traditional rights as American citizens. In the 1820s, most of the region's working people still thought of themselves as members of the "producing and useful classes," not as a permanent wage-labor class, but something rotten seemed to be destroying their livelihoods and the Republic. In their view, they were the producers of the nation's wealth, but few were receiving the full product of their labor, and many were not able to earn a living wage. Labor was degraded, and the emerging class-based inequalities in wealth, education, and political power seemed excessive and unjust. As a result, white journeymen craftsmen or mechanics who had found it increasingly difficult to become independent master artisans began to organize labor unions and form independent political parties, while disgruntled artisans, dissatisfied women workers, and poor unskilled workers took part in numerous strikes.

From the late 1820s on, disparate workers turned to the Declaration of Independence as a source for their rights and began to use the term "equal rights" to justify their various demands. The term itself is often confusing or unclear. "Equal rights" meant different things to different people. Some labor leaders and workers used it when they made moderate demands for a larger share of the pie through greater economic opportunity, greater educational access, and increased political rights. Other, more radical working people used it as an implicit, if not explicit, critique of capitalism by identifying the problems of "wage slavery" and economic dependence. Whatever was meant in specific instances over time, the emerging labor movement's diverse calls for "equal rights" linked the struggles of ordinary working people to the country's revolutionary traditions and brought to the nation's attention the inordinate inequalities they believed were corrupting the ideals of the American Revolution.

Traditionally, Philadelphia has been considered the birthplace of the labor movement in the United States. In June 1827, journeymen carpenters in the city launched a strike to reduce and limit the working day to ten hours, a popular working-class goal opposed by master artisans and most employers. Although the strike failed, it prompted new and broader efforts for reform and precipitated a meaningful series of events. In 1828 wage-earning carpenters, weavers, printers, and other skilled artisans mobilized and established the country's first citywide federation of labor, the Mechanics Union of Trade Associations, and then founded a working-men's political party. Soon other cities were following the Philadelphia example. In the late 1820s, for the first time in the nation's history, an active labor movement that transcended trades, occupations, and cities was visible and on the scene.

From 1828 to 1832, skilled white journeymen mechanics established independent workingmen's political parties in other major eastern cities and numerous smaller cities and towns throughout the northern states. The founding and evolution of each of these parties differed somewhat, but what happened in New York City suggests the promise, problems, and fate of many of the short-lived parties.

On April 28, 1829, in New York City, 5,000 to 6,000 mechanics, concerned about retaining the ten-hour day against an employer effort to extend the working day, met and passed resolutions that ultimately resulted in the formation of the New York City Working Men's Party. Historians have attributed the origins of the independent party to the influence of the radical machinist Thomas Skidmore, who supported the idea of "equal property for all." The workers did successfully retain the ten-hour day, and on the eve of the 1829 November elections, a printer, George Henry Evans, founded a labor newspaper, *The Working Man's Advocate*, to support the new party. It was one of many labor papers founded in the country around this time.

The New York Working Men's Party enjoyed great success in the November municipal elections, but its very success precipitated its undoing. It polled an impressive 6,000 votes out of the total 21,000 votes cast throughout the entire city. Alarmed politicians from other political parties immediately reacted, entered the party, and ousted Skidmore. The promising independent party soon split into three factions, each of which survived only briefly.

During their brief existences, workingmen's parties throughout the nation demanded significant reforms related either to their members' specific livelihoods or to the broader welfare of society at large. Thus, they sought passage of a mechanics' lien law to ensure payment for work they had done, the regulation of prison labor, and the abolition of imprisonment for debt. But they also championed the establishment of a public educational system, paid for by the public and free from the stigma attached to "charity" schools, and they supported the abolition of state-chartered monopolies that granted banks, insurance companies, and corporations exclusive legal privileges. The 1830s and 1840s were an age of reform not confined to workers alone, and such measures enjoyed support from other classes besides the working classes. For various reasons, the parties quickly disintegrated, but, in time, many of their specific reforms were achieved.

The labor upsurge continued into the mid-1830s. Union organization reached a high point in 1834 when workers formed an ephemeral but precedent-setting national organization, the National Trades Union, that lasted from 1834 to 1836. Meanwhile, craftsmen in Philadelphia and the New England Association of Farmers, Mechanics, and Other Working-men took remarkable steps toward labor unity when they sought to incorporate factory workers and unskilled laborers into labor's fold, despite the serious national, religious, and skill differences that divided them. And when rising prices and wage reductions made serious inroads into workers' livelihoods during these years, diverse workers in many industries engaged in strikes.

Women workers, including New York tailoresses, Lynn shoe binders, and Lowell textile workers, engaged in such "turn-outs" (strikes). The teenagers and single young women who had been recruited from New England farms and villages to work in the new cotton textile factories in Lowell, Massachusetts, in the 1820s "turned out" (struck) for the first time in February 1834 to protest a 25 percent wage reduction. The strike at the Lawrence Manufacturing Company in Lowell began immediately after William Austin, a company agent, fired a popular leader, who responded by throwing her scarf into the air as a signal to the other workers to walk out. About 800 women took part.

Because visitors and entrepreneurs had touted Lowell as a leading example of genteel and modern economic development, the unprecedented work stoppage by women who had achieved some degree of financial independence was shocking. Austin, who informed the company's absentee Boston officers about the turn-out, described the women who took part in the day's procession as "Amazons." For him, the very notion of female protest was almost incomprehensible and a betrayal: "Notwithstanding the friendly and disinterested advice which has been on all proper occassions [sic] communicated to the girls of the Lawrence mills a spirit of evil omen . . . has prevailed, and overcome the judgment and discretion of too many, and this morning a general turn-out from most of the rooms has been the consequence."[1]

Perhaps most shocking to observers was that these pioneering Yankee women workers were proudly proclaiming themselves the "daughters of free men" and justifying their strike on the basis of the revolutionary republican tradition, much as male workers did. Many of these pioneering female strikers were not totally dependent on their wages for a living and were able to exercise their option to leave Lowell and return to ties to their families in the countryside. Although Austin found it easy to hire new recruits from Vermont and other places, and although the turn-out failed to avert the wage cut, the Lowell women's novel job action signaled noteworthy dissatisfaction with the emerging economic order. In 1836, in response to another wage cut, the women textile workers there again "turned out."

In an effort to halt the broadening labor upsurge of the 1830s, employers turned to the courts. Because the U.S. Constitution had limited the role of the national government in labor relations, specifically authorizing it to set policies for its employees and to intervene in labor affairs when they had a direct impact on interstate or federal commerce, it had left the broader subject of labor relations to state and local jurisdictions. Thus, the employers turned to state and local courts, as they had done before.

In 1806, for the first time in U.S. history, master artisan employers had gone to court in Philadelphia to sue the journeymen shoemakers' society there for forming "a combination and conspiracy to raise their wages."[2] Upon a judge's instructions, a jury found those "cordwainers" or shoemakers guilty, as charged. This important precedent-setting case helped establish the legal framework underlying labor relations in the United States for nearly a century.

From 1806 on, various state and local courts ruled that English common law applied in the new nation and that labor unions were a criminal conspiracy, especially when a union's purpose was to raise wages or hinder commerce. Moreover, such labor combinations were presumed to injure the community as a whole, cause general economic damage, and infringe on the rights of individuals. Despite some dissent and the ineffectiveness of some of the imposed restraints, these early court rulings placed the weight of the government on the side of employers who were trying to impede the development of labor unions and hinder the collective action of their workers. The judiciary's advocacy of the conspiracy doctrine, as applied to labor unions, also undermined labor's prestige with the public and facilitated acceptance of capitalist values during a critical era of the nation's economic and industrial development.

In all, nineteen conspiracy cases were brought to trial from 1806 to 1842; workers were acquitted in three of the cases. Then, in 1842, in the case of

Commonwealth v. Hunt, Chief Justice Lemuel Shaw of the Massachusetts Supreme Court issued a ruling that is often considered a turning point in U.S. labor relations. A bootmakers' union had gone on strike to enforce its traditional right to work in a closed shop, that is, a shop where only union members were employed, and a lower court had found the union guilty of criminal conspiracy. Shaw reversed that court's decision and, on narrow grounds, ruled that the common-law conspiracy doctrine did not apply to labor unions. In effect, his decision legalized them. It meant that, henceforth, workers had the legal right to organize and strike or use other peaceful means to raise wages or compel a closed shop. Although Shaw's landmark decision was of immediate and historic importance to the labor movement, its subsequent impact was measured and not lasting. The Massachusetts judge's findings were not binding outside the Bay State. Its principles were never applied to the South, and corporate and governmental interests revived the conspiracy doctrine on new grounds later in the century.

Employers did not hesitate to wield the weapon of the conspiracy doctrine against workers during the labor upsurge of the 1830s, and workers protested. For example, in 1836, a combination of New York City's master tailors sued striking journeymen tailors in a sensational court case, *People v. Faulkner*. A jury reluctantly convicted twenty journeymen for conspiracy on May 31, 1836, after an extremely partial judge, Ogden Edwards, ordered them to do so. For wealthy merchants and the business classes, the verdict was welcome; for the journeymen who paraded with a coffin, distributed handbills, and called for a workingmen's party, the verdict symbolized the death of "equal rights" and the Republic.

"Equal rights" remained the overriding theme of northern workers even as the depression of 1837 undermined the labor upsurge. The craftsmen of many trades increasingly used the term to express their belief that labor was the source of all wealth and value, along with the notion that egalitarian rights of citizenship derived from the American Revolution. At the same time, disgruntled white journeymen and other northern workers were beginning to speak of "wage slavery." In voicing complaints that their descending status and dependent condition resembled that of the slaves, they were reflecting fear of a degraded status that was readily apparent to them.

SLAVE LABOR AND ITS IMPACT

The slave-labor system that prevailed in the southern half of the nation was a major obstacle to the formation of a labor movement in the South and in the nation as a whole. The unique experience of the unfree populations who represented a large portion of the country's workers precluded their taking part in the emergence of a labor movement initiated by free labor in the North. It was impossible for slaves, who possessed no rights, either as human beings or as citizens, to share in the "equal rights" artisanal traditions of white northern workers. For them, "freedom" itself became the essential and all-encompassing goal.

The coexistence of two such disparate labor systems entailed distinctive sets of labor relations. Despite certain similarities, the slave-labor system differed qualitatively from the wage-labor system in important respects. Unlike the "free-labor" system of the North, under slavery human beings were considered property or "chattel." Slaves could be, and were, bought and sold like inanimate commodities on an auction block. Mothers could be sold apart from their children, husbands from their wives. Unlike "free wage labor," which many Americans then considered a temporary condition, slavery was automatically a life sentence—and more. It extended into perpetuity, involving the lives of a slave's children and all posterity, except for the small portion of fortunate ones who could escape or purchase their own freedom. Although both systems involved hardships for those who worked, the sheer brutality of slave labor, characterized by arbitrariness, disciplinary whippings, and corporal punishment, was unsurpassed. Slaves had absolutely no rights to protest, vote, form unions, strike, or advocate reforms. Even their voluntary movement from place to place was prohibited by law.

Under such circumstances, slaves recognized—and resisted—their exploitation, however and whenever they could. The Nat Turner rebellion, conspiracies to revolt, and the frequency of runaways are well known, but less spectacular instances of resistance occurred on a day-to-day basis and took different forms. Planters themselves complained about their slaves' procrastination, feigned illnesses or pregnancies, property damage, and thefts. Murder and suicide were other ways of protesting. Even the dreaded auction block could be an arena of contestation between slaves and their masters. At the sales, owners often sought to sell their unruly or unproductive slaves to unwitting buyers, while slaves tried to influence the outcome of the sales in their own interest. Resistance was not always successful, by any means, but, in many different ways, slaves tried to increase their sphere of well-being and daily freedom within the context of slavery, when outright freedom was an impossibility.

Throughout its existence, this racially based slave-labor system proved to be a formidable obstacle to the formation of an effective antebellum southern white working-class labor movement. Artisans and other white workers in cities in the antebellum South had joined in the labor upsurge of the 1830s. For example, Baltimore workers had founded unions and engaged in strikes that easily matched the number, intensity, and levels of such labor activity in Philadelphia. But free workers in southern states confronted obstacles that their northern counterparts did not. Southern employers could—and did—successfully use the slave-labor system to prevent the emergence of a powerful free white labor movement. In fact, an employer's use of slave labor emerged as the chief issue in one of the South's major antebellum labor-capital conflicts, a strike that occurred in 1847 in Richmond, Virginia, at the Tredegar Iron Works. The issues and outcome of the conflict at this important ironmaking plant illustrate the likely prospects for any such endeavor in the region.

For a number of years preceding the strike, both whites and blacks had worked at Tredegar, in their respective occupations, with whites occupying the skilled positions. Serious management–labor problems began to arise after 1844, when Joseph R. Anderson, the owner, consciously adopted a policy of employing slaves to reduce the power, wages, and numbers of skilled white workers. In 1847 he expanded the Tredegar operations, doubled his work force, and then ordered white mechanics to train slaves in the various ironmaking skills. Skilled white workers, fearful of losing their jobs, responded by going out on strike on May 23, 1847. The strikers originally asked for higher pay and termination of slave labor but soon dropped the wage demand. Anderson wrote his "late" workers: "If I were to yield to your demands, I would be giving up the rights guarantied [sic] to me by the constitution and laws of the State in which we live."[3] By June, the strikers were defeated, discharged, and subsequently replaced by slave labor. The community of Richmond had almost unilaterally supported Anderson, who continued to confront labor problems in the next decade.

As time went on, free white northern and southern workers were increasingly forced to face the challenges posed by the existence of the slave-labor system. Some became active participants in the abolition movement; others did not. But by 1849, mechanics and other working men in Louisville, Kentucky, were among those citizens who were meeting together and advocating emancipation. As the wording of a resolution they passed at a meeting in May 1849 suggests, these workers understood the significant negative impact that the coercive labor system had made on *their* lives. In their view, slavery degraded *all* labor; it was not only prejudicial to the interests of working people but to those of the broader community and the state as well.

Meanwhile, throughout the antebellum era, free blacks who lived and worked in the North or South faced their own special difficulties. Frederick Douglass, one of the nineteenth century's leading spokesmen for abolition and for equality for blacks, had experienced life in the two regions under the two different labor systems. Born a slave in Maryland in 1817, he escaped to freedom in 1838. In 1845 he published the *Narrative of the Life of Frederick Douglass, an American Slave*, in which he revealed the prejudice and discrimination he had encountered from white workers in both sections of the country. As a slave who had been "hired out" by his master to work as a ship caulker in the Baltimore shipyards, he confronted skilled white carpenters who refused to work with him and threatened his life. But when he sought employment at his craft in the New Bedford, Massachusetts, shipyards shortly after his escape, skilled white workers there refused to work with the new "free laborer" also, and he was forced to take low-paying, unskilled jobs thereafter. Although he found northern freedom far preferable to southern slavery, he quickly learned that racial prejudice and harsh discrimination were not confined to the slaveholding states.

The emergence of the American labor movement was necessarily uneven; it was also primarily local or regional, as were the economies of the time. Significantly, free white workers in the northern states were able to draw upon the legacy of egalitarian republican ideals derived from the American Revolution and shape its birth from 1827 to 1837 during a critical era of capitalist economic expansion, while the slave-labor system deterred or aborted a parallel development in the South. The combination of depressed economic conditions, the prevalence of the conspiracy doctrine, and the pervasive impact of the slave-labor system sharply limited the extent, magnitude, and duration of that initial labor upsurge. Two distinctive labor systems and two sets of labor relations continued to exist in the nation. Only a bloody civil war, followed by the Thirteenth Amendment, formally ended the coercive system that had prevailed in half the nation and made a significant impact on *all* American workers in *all* regions of the country.

NOTES

1. Thomas Dublin, "Women, Work, and Protest in the Early Lowell Mills: 'The Oppressing Hand of Avarice Would Enslave Us,'" *Labor History* 16 (1975): 108.

2. John R. Commons et al., eds., *A Documentary History of American Industrial Society*, with preface by Richard T. Ely and introduction by John B. Clark, 11 vols. (Cleveland: Arthur H. Clark Company, 1910–1911), 3:59.

3. "Difficulties at the Tredegar and Armory Iron Works," *Richmond Times and Compiler*, May 28, 1847.

DOCUMENTS

**1.1.   Journeymen Carpenters in Philadelphia Demand a
Ten-Hour Day, June 14, 1827**

---

*This resolution from a meeting of Philadelphia journeymen
carpenters on June 14, 1827, expressed their view that a ten-
hour work day was desirable, necessary, and in the public's interest as well as their own. Although their strike failed, it
prompted the craft unions to form the first citywide labor federation in the nation.*

Whereas, all men have a right to assemble in a peaceable and orderly
manner, for the purpose of deliberating on their own and the public good:
And, whereas, the Journeymen house carpenters, of the city and county
of Philadelphia, have for a long time suffered under a grievous and slave
like system of labour, which they believe to be attended with many evils
injurious alike to the community and the workmen; they believe that a
man of common constitution is unable to perform more than ten hours
faithful labour in one day, and that men in the habit of labouring from
sun rise until dark, are generally subject to nervous and other complaints;
arising from continued hard labour and they believe that all men have a
just right, derived from their Creator, to have sufficient time in each day
for the cultivation of their mind and for self improvement; Therefore, resolved, that we think ten hours industriously employed are sufficient for
a day's labour.

The above resolution being unanimously adopted, it was resolved, that
it be carried into effect from this day . . .

WILLIAM LOUCK   Chairman
CHARLES FERRIS, Secretary

Philadelphia, June 13th, 1827

Source: "Preamble and Resolutions adopted at a meeting of journeymen house
carpenters, June 14, 1827, from the *Democratic Press* (Phila.), June 14, 1827, p. 2,"
quoted in John R. Commons et al., eds., *A Documentary History of American Industrial Society*, with preface by Richard T. Ely and introduction by John B. Clark,
11 vols. (Cleveland: Arthur H. Clark Company, 1910–1911), 5:80.

1.2.   Master Carpenters in Philadelphia Resist the Journeymen's Demand, June 15, 1827

On June 15, 1827, master carpenters in Philadelphia met and passed this resolution to express their opposition to the journeymen's demand for a ten-hour work day. Note that they solicited the support of their employers.

Whereas, the journeymen House Carpenters of the city and county of Philadelphia have entered into a combination and passed certain resolutions, not to labour longer than from six o'clock in the morning to six o'clock in the evening, thereby depriving their employers of about one fifth part of their usual time:

Therefore, resolved, that in the opinion of this meeting it is inexpedient and altogether improper to comply with the resolutions passed by the Journeymen House Carpenters, at their late meeting, held at the Mayor's court room.

RESOLVED, that we view with regret the formation of any society that has a tendency to subvert good order, and coerce or mislead those who have been industriously pursuing their avocation and honestly maintaining their families.

RESOLVED, that the present price per day given to Journeymen Carpenters, is as high as can be afforded by their employers, when the whole time of the workman is given.

RESOLVED, that we will not employ any Journeyman who will not give his time and labour as usual; inasmuch as we believe the present mode has not been, and is not now, oppressive to the workmen.

RESOLVED, that we mutually pledge ourselves to support and fully carry into effect the foregoing resolutions.

RESOLVED, that the Master Carpenters composing this meeting, request of their employers a co-operation in the above measure.

RESOLVED, that the Master Carpenters composing this meeting give their names to the Secretary; when the following was the result: (Number of Signatures—122.)

RESOLVED, that a committee of 12 persons be appointed to call on the Master Carpenters who were unable to attend this meeting to procure their signatures . . .

JOSEPH SMITH, Chairman—JOSEPH MOORE, Secretary.

Source: "Preamble and resolutions adopted at a meeting of master carpenters, June 15, 1827, from Poulson's *American Daily Advertiser* (Phila.), June 18, 1827, p. 3," quoted in Commons et al., *Documentary History*, 5:81–82.

1.3.   "Prospectus," *The Working Man's Advocate,* October 31, 1829

George Henry Evans's "Prospectus" for The Working Man's Advocate *vividly captures the spirit and goals of the overall labor movement of the 1830s. The language of "useful classes," "equal rights," "republic," "happiness," and "community" reveals working people's values that were in conflict with those of the new entrepreneurial capitalists who glorified "self-interest," the "market," and uncontrolled "individualism."*

We have long thought it very desirable, that the useful and industrious classes of this populous city should have at least a weekly, if not a daily, paper devoted to their interests, which should freely and fearlessly discuss all questions of importance to them, and assist them in ascertaining the best and most effectual remedies for the evils and deprivations under which they are suffering; and we have as long lamented our own limited means of supplying the deficiency. Having, however, at length determined to make the attempt, we shall briefly explain the course we intend to pursue.

In the first place we would premise, that we think we see, in the state of society existing around us, something radically wrong. We observe one portion of society living in luxury and idleness; another, engaged in employments which are useless, or worse than useless, to the community at large; while the numerous portion to which we profess to belong, and of which we are to be the humble advocate, are groaning under the oppressions and miseries imposed upon them by the two former divisions—and all are suffering from the effects of vice, produced, on the one hand, by luxury and indolence, and by the ignorance consequent on poverty on the other.

While, then, these divisions in society exist, it will be our object to draw the line as distinctly as possible between them, in order to prevent any further encroachments on our equal rights by those whose interests are in opposition to them, and who now fatten on the labor of the industrious. But it shall be our ultimate aim to develop, as far as in us lies, the means by which all may be placed, as we think they ought to be, on an equal footing; so that those who now vainly seek for happiness by oppressing and trampling on the rights of their fellow beings, may be brought to a knowledge of the truth that all men *ought* to be equal, and that the only way to enjoy true happiness ourselves, is by endeavoring to promote the happiness of those around us.

In furtherance of these views, we shall oppose the establishment of all exclusive privileges, all monopolies, and all exemptions of one class more than another from an equal share in the burdens of society; all of which, to whatever class or order of men they are extended, we consider highly anti republican, oppressive, and unjust.

We consider it an exclusive privilege for one portion of the community to have the means of education in colleges, while another is restricted to common schools, or, perhaps, by extreme poverty, even deprived of the limited education to be acquired in these establishments. Our voice, therefore, shall be raised in favor of a system of education which shall be equally open to *all*, as in a real republic it should be.

We will oppose every thing which savors of a union of church and state; particularly the daring advances now making toward that union under cover of the *sabbath mail question*.

To a free discussion of any subject of general interest to the useful classes, our columns shall ever be open, provided our correspondents adapt the length of their communications to the importance of the subject, and clothe them, in the language of courtesy.

An ample summary of foreign and domestic intelligence will be given, when not excluded by more important matters.

Source: George Henry Evans, "Prospectus," *The Working Man's Advocate*, October 31, 1829.

1.4.   "[Proclamation of Lowell Women Strikers]," *The Man*, February 22, 1834

> At the outset of the Lowell strike of 1834, prompted by a proposed 25 percent wage cut, the "daughters of free men" issued this proclamation. To justify their strike, they cited their "patriotic ancestors" and the importance of independence. They also asserted their "equal rights" against the new Tories—the mill owners.

UNION IS POWER.—Our present object is to have union and exertion, and we remain in possession of our own unquestionable rights. We circulate this paper, wishing to obtain the names of all who imbibe the spirit of our patriotic ancestors, who preferred privation to bondage and parted with all that renders life desirable—and even life itself—to produce independence for their children. The oppressing hand of avarice would enslave us, and to gain their object they very gravely tell us of the pressure of the times; this we are already sensible of and deplore it. If any are in want of assistance, the ladies will be compassionate and assist them, but we prefer to have the disposing of our charities in our own hands, and, as we are free, we would remain in possession of what kind Providence has bestowed upon us, and remain daughters of freemen still.

All who patronize this effort we wish to have discontinue their labor until terms of reconciliation are made.

Resolved, That we will not go back into the mills to work unless our wages are continued to us as they have been.

Resolved, That none of us will go back unless they receive us all as one.

Resolved, That if any have not money enough to carry them home that they shall be supplied.

> Let oppression shrug her shoulders,
>   And a haughty tyrant frown,
> And little upstart Ignorance
>   In mockery look down.
> Yet I value not the feeble threats
>   Of Tories in disguise,
> While the flag of Independence
>   O'er our noble nation flies.

Source: "[Proclamation of Lowell Women Strikers]," *The Man*, February 22, 1834, quoted in U.S. Bureau of Labor, *Report on Condition of Woman and Child Wage-Earners in the United States*, vol. 10: *History of Women in Trade Unions*, by John B. Andrews and William Dwight Porter Bliss (Washington, DC: GPO, 1911), p. 28.

1.5.   William Austin to Henry Hall, February 15, 1834

> *Austin, a Lawrence Manufacturing Company agent in Lowell, wrote this descriptive letter to the company's treasurer in Boston to tell him about the turn-out. In it, he unwittingly tells us something about how the women organized the protest as well as how he viewed it. Especially note his denigrating references to a "dictatress," "Amazons," and "combinations" [unions]. For clarity, the paragraphs have been indented but are not in the original text.*

I send you herewith one of the inflammatory preambles, resolutions, & poetic effusions, which have been distributed among the females employed in the various mills.

It appears certain that a general turn out had been determined, on the taking effect of the reduced wages, now assumed to be the 1st of March, and that the commotions of yesterday & today were premature movements, produced by occurrences in our mills on Thursday.—During the time for dinner, the watchman reported to me that a large num[ber] of girls were holding a caucus & passing resolutions in the spinning room of no. 1 & it appeared that they had required him to leave the room on his going into [it] to examine it.

I felt it proper to ascertain the purposes of their assembling & went into the room for this purpose. I stated to them what were my own views of the course they were pursuing, advised them to wait patiently untill [sic] it should be known what the reduction would amount to, & to refrain from such combinations. It appeared that before I entered the room, they had appointed a dictatress & voted to be governed by her in all cases. This woman, whose name is Julia Wilson, retorted upon me, with no little vehemence, & declared that there was no cause for any reduction whatever, that the causes assigned for it were without foundation in fact, that she had to pay as much for a yard of cloth as ever, & that convinced her that there was no truth in the assertions of the agents. Perceiving that this woman had a great sway over the minds of the other females, I deemed it advisable to persuade her if possible to leave the mills, to receive her pay, and she should be honorably discharged. She would not do it, and waiting 'till evening & perceiving that she continually had a crowd around her, & having the opinion of the overseer, that it would be necessary to discharge her in order to preserve the order of the room, & also the opinion of Mr. Means, that she ought to be "got rid of," I ordered her discharged & to leave the mill, forthwith. She declared that every girl in the room should leave with her, made a signal [threw a scarf in the air], & the bell ringing, it being half past 7 o'clock, they all marched out, & very few returned the ensuing morning who had been subject to her influences.

During the same afternoon, I received a note from Mr. Wright, Superintendent of the Lowell Mills, stating that a girl name H. Lawson who worked in Lawrence No. 2 had visited the Lowell mills to urge the girls to turn out, that she had been employed in those mills, previous to October last. Was a "decidedly mischievous girl & unworthy of employment."

She [H. Lawson] was sent for, & requested to leave the mills, stating, to her, that I had received information, making it proper for me to discharge her, & she was accordingly discharged. This event raised a good deal of steam in that room (Dressing room no. 2). So that five of the girls employed in it returned the next morning, and about 8 o'clock, about three fourths of the other girls from both mills turned out, & then commenced the Amazonian parade, stump oratory, marching & countermarching about the other mills, & soon a feminine phalanx of about 700 were seen in procession perambulating the streets & which continued through the day. Julia Wilson, it appears, delivered several extempore addresses, with great effect . . . being elivated [sic] to the top of pumps, &

figures as the heroine of the disgraceful drama "then being enacted." This afternoon we have paid off many of these Amazons, & presume that they will leave town on Monday, & let the reign of peace & order be restored among us.

In the mean time several girls have arrived from the country, & who have been urged to return, & insulted by the malcontents, for persevering in the fulfillment of this engagement.—I have a proposition to employ 12 girls from Vermont this evening, & have engaged them. There shall be employed also about 50 weavers, from a factory which is about to stop, in Pembroke, N.H., making about 300, with those mentioned this morning, & showing that our mills will soon be full. Manned, and womaned, again, and, that there will be no necessity for soliciting the return of those who left so abruptly. I have however given them the opportunity to do so untill Monday evening, especially those who did not expose themselves in the Amazonian procession.

I have thus employed a few minutes this evening in giving details which the labors of the day did not permit.

Source: Lawrence Manufacturing Company Collection, Baker Library, Harvard Business School, Boston, Massachusetts. I am grateful to Thomas Dublin, who generously searched his attic to supply me with a photocopy of this letter.

**1.6.   Resolution of Louisville, Kentucky, Workers on
            Slavery, May 1849**

---

*At a meeting in May 1849, Louisville mechanics and other
working men passed this resolution in support of emancipation.
Their arguments that slavery degraded all labor and that it inevitably damaged the general community and the state as well
are especially noteworthy.*

VOICE OF THE WORKING MEN

The mechanics and working men of Louisville, Ky., recently adopted the following resolution at a public meeting; and, at the same time, ordered the publication of 20,000 copies of an address on emancipation:

Resolved, That the institution of slavery is prejudicial to every interest of the State, and is alike injurious to the slaveholder and non-slaveholder; that it degrades labor, enervates industry, interferes with the occupations of free laboring citizens, separates too widely the poor and the rich, shuts out the laboring classes from the blessings of education, and tends to drive from the State all who depend upon personal labor for support. That while we recognize the right of property in slaves under existing laws, we hold that the laboring man has as full a right to his occupation and the profits of his labor, as the master to his slaves; and as slavery tends to the monopoly of as well as the degradation of labor, public and private right require its ultimate extinction.

Source: "Voice of the Working Men," *The North Star*, May 25, 1849.

1.7.   **"[Editorial]," *Richmond Times and Compiler*, May 28, 1847**

As this editorial from the Richmond Times and Compiler *insists, the community of Richmond opposed the Tredegar strikers and supported the ironmaker owner, Joseph R. Anderson, in 1847. The issues were critical and straightforward. The strikers had dared to challenge not only the managerial prerogatives of business but also the property rights of slave owners—the basis of the southern economy.*

It is obvious that these proceedings have raised a very grave question in our community; and it remains to be decided whether Mr. Anderson shall be sustained or discountenanced, in the firm, yet temperate, course which he has pursued. The principle is advocated, for the first time we believe in a slave-holding State, that the employer may be prevented from making use of slave labor. This principle strikes at the root of all the rights and privileges of the master, and, if acknowledged, or permitted to gain foothold, will soon wholly destroy the value of slave property. When such must be the results of the precedent now sought to be established, it becomes every citizen who respects the institution of slavery, and desires its protection, to protest against this alarming innovation. It is a question about which there ought not to be two opinions.

Source: "[Editorial]," *Richmond Times and Compiler*, May 28, 1847.

1.8.   **Frederick Douglass, "My Escape to Freedom," *The Century Illustrated Monthly Magazine*, November 1881**

In this excerpt from a November 1881 article in The Century Illustrated Monthly Magazine, *Frederick Douglass expanded on comments he had made in his famous narrative, published in*

1845, about the occupational discrimination he confronted in the North soon after his escape. As his experience suggested, such problems would persist in the nation—North and South— after slavery's demise.

Mr. Ruggles was the first officer on the "Underground Railroad" whom I met after coming North, and was, indeed, the only one with whom I had anything to do till I became such an officer myself. Learning that my trade was that of a calker [*sic*], he promptly decided that the best place for me was in New Bedford, Mass. He told me that many ships for whaling voyages were fitted out there, and that I might there find work at my trade and make a good living. . . . Thus, in a fortnight after my flight from Maryland, I was safe in New Bedford, a citizen of the grand old commonwealth of Massachusetts. . . .

The fifth day after my arrival, I put on the clothes of a common laborer, and went upon the wharves in search of work. On my way down Union street I saw a large pile of coal in front of the house of Rev. Ephraim Peabody, the Unitarian minister. I went to the kitchen door and asked the privilege of bringing in and putting away this coal. "What will you charge?" said the lady. "I will leave that to you, madam." "You may put it away," she said. I was not long in accomplishing the job, when the dear lady put into my hand *two silver half-dollars*. To understand the emotion which swelled my heart as I clasped this money, realizing that I had no master who could take it from me,—*that it was mine—that my hands were my own*, and could earn more of the precious coin,—one must have been in some sense himself a slave. My next job was stowing a sloop at Uncle Gid. Howland's wharf with a cargo of oil for New York. I was not only a freeman, but a free working-man, and no "master" stood ready at the end of the week to seize my hard earnings. . . .

Notwithstanding the just and human sentiment of New Bedford three and forty years ago, the place was not entirely free from race and color prejudice. The good influence of the Roaches, Rodmans, Arnolds, Grinnells, and Robesons did not pervade all classes of its people. The test of the real civilization of the community came when I applied for work at my trade, and then my repulse was emphatic and decisive. It so happened that Mr. Rodney French, a wealthy and enterprising citizen, distinguished as an anti-slavery man, was fitting out a vessel for a whaling voyage, upon which there was a heavy job of calking and coppering to be done. I had some skill in both branches, and applied to Mr. French for work. He, generous man that he was, told me he would employ me, and I might go at once to the vessel. I obeyed him, but upon reaching the float-stage, where others calkers were at work, I was told that every white man would leave the ship, in her unfinished condition, if I struck a blow at my trade upon her. This uncivil, inhuman, and selfish treatment was not so shocking and scandalous in my eyes at the time as it now appears to me. Slavery had inured me to hardships that made ordinary trouble sit lightly upon me. Could I have worked at my trade I could have earned two dollars a day, but as a common laborer I received but one dollar. The difference was of great importance to me, but if I could not get two dollars, I was glad to get one; and so I went to work for Mr. French as a common laborer. The consciousness that I was free—no longer a slave—kept me cheerful under this, and many similar proscriptions, which I was destined to meet in New Bedford and elsewhere on the free soil of Massachusetts. For instance, though colored children attended the schools, and were treated kindly by their teachers, the New Bedford Lyceum refused, till several years after my residence in that city, to allow any colored person to attend the lectures delivered in its hall. Not until such men as Charles Sumner, Theodore Parker, Ralph Waldo Emerson, and Horace Mann refused to lecture in their course while there was such a restriction, was it abandoned.

Becoming satisfied that I could not rely on my trade in New Bedford to give me a living, I prepared myself to do any kind of work that came to hand. I sawed wood, shoveled coal, dug cellars, moved rubbish from back yards, worked on the wharves, loaded and unloaded vessels, and scoured their cabins.

Source: Frederick Douglass, "My Escape to Freedom," *The Century Illustrated Monthly Magazine* 23 (November 1881): 129–31.

SELECTED ANNOTATED BIBLIOGRAPHY

Books

Andrews, John B. and William Dwight Porter Bliss. *History of Women in Trade Unions*. 1911. Reprint, New York: Arno Press, 1974. Reprint of vol. 10, U.S. Bureau of Labor, *Report on Condition of Woman and Child Wage-Earners in the United States*. 19 vols. Washington, DC: GPO, 1910–1913. Contains valuable primary material on the strikes, unions, and protests of nineteenth-century working women, including Lowell mill workers.

Berlin, Ira. *Generations of Captivity: A History of African-American Slaves*. Cambridge, MA: Belknap Press of Harvard University Press, 2003. Acclaimed history focuses on the regional differences that characterized slavery from 1620 through the Revolution and the unique aspects of slavery in the South through the Civil War, with special emphasis on the ways slaves resisted bondage.

Blassingame, John W., ed. *Slave Testimony: Two Centuries of Letters, Speeches, Interviews, and Autobiographies*. Baton Rouge: Louisiana State University Press, 1977. Good collection, with excellent introductory essay on the critical use of slave sources.

Commons, John R., Ulrich B. Phillips, Eugene A. Gilmore, Helen L. Sumner, and John B. Andrews, eds. *A Documentary History of American Industrial Society.* Preface by Richard T. Ely and introduction by John B. Clark. 11 vols. Cleveland: Arthur H. Clark Company, 1910–1911. Excellent source for primary documents on the labor movement.

Commons, John R., David J. Saposs, Helen L. Sumner, E. B. Mittelman, H. E. Hoagland, John B. Andrews, and Selig Perlman. *History of Labour in the United States.* Introduction by Henry W. Farnam. 4 vols. New York: Macmillan Company, 1918–1935. See especially, Sumner's "Citizenship (1827–1833)," 1:167–332, and Mittelman's "Trade Unionism (1833–1839)," 1:333–484.

Dew, Charles B. *Ironmaker to the Confederacy: Joseph R. Anderson and the Tredegar Iron Works.* New Haven, CT: Yale University Press, 1966. Good material on the Tredegar strike.

Douglass, Frederick. *Narrative of the Life of Frederick Douglass, an American Slave, Written by Himself.* 1845. Reprint, New York: New American Library, 1968. Classic and essential narrative.

Dublin, Thomas. *Women at Work: The Transformation of Work and Community in Lowell, Massachusetts, 1826–1860.* New York: Columbia University Press, 1979. The best and most readable study of the work, protest, and experiences of early Lowell mill workers.

Filippelli, Ronald L. *Labor in the USA: A History.* New York: McGraw-Hill, 1984. Useful and highly readable introduction to the U.S. labor movement outside slavery.

Foner, Philip S., ed. *The Factory Girls: A Collection of Writings on Life and Struggles in the New England Factories of the 1840's, by the Factory Girls Themselves and the Story, in Their Own Words, of the First Trade Unions of Women Workers in the United States.* Urbana: University of Illinois Press, 1977. Excellent collection of documents.

———. *History of the Labor Movement in the United States: From Colonial Times to the Founding of the American Federation of Labor.* New York: International Publishers, 1947. A pioneering and useful labor history.

Foner, Philip S. and Ronald L. Lewis, eds. *The Black Worker: A Documentary History from Colonial Times to the Present.* Vol. 1: *The Black Worker to 1869.* Philadelphia: Temple University Press, 1978. Good documents and a useful survey of non-agricultural labor.

Genovese, Eugene D. *The Political Economy of Slavery: Studies in the Economy & Society of the Slave South.* 2nd ed. Middletown, CT: Wesleyan University Press, 1989. Major critical economic study of slavery and its political impact.

Hugins, Walter. *Jacksonian Democracy and the Working Class: A Study of the New York Workingmen's Movement, 1829–1837.* Stanford, CA: Stanford University Press, 1960. Unlike Pessen, author argues that the movement was middle class and Jacksonian.

Jones, Jacqueline. *American Work: Four Centuries of Black and White Labor.* New York: W. W. Norton, 1998. Important chronological survey considers forced labor and racial rationalizations as central to U.S. labor history.

Josephson, Hannah. *The Golden Threads: New England's Mill Girls and Magnates.*

New York: Duell, Sloan and Pearce, 1949. A classic history of the Lowell textile industry.

Kimball, Gregg D. *American City, Southern Place: A Cultural History of Antebellum Richmond*. Athens: University of Georgia Press, 2000. Valuable study provides insights into the Tredegar strike and the complexities of labor and racial relations.

Laurie, Bruce. *Artisans into Workers: Labor in Nineteenth-Century America*. Urbana: University of Illinois Press, 1989. Useful synthesis and survey for advanced students.

Levine, Bruce et al. *Who Built America? Working People and the Nation's Economy, Politics, Culture, and Society*. Vol. 1: *From Conquest and Colonization Through Reconstruction and the Great Uprising of 1877*. New York: Pantheon Books, 1989. Comprehensive social history textbook puts work and working people at the center of U.S. history.

Lewis, Ronald L. *Coal, Iron, and Slaves: Industrial Slavery in Maryland and Virginia, 1715–1865*. Westport, CT: Greenwood Press, 1979. Contains material on the Tredegar strike.

Pessen, Edward. *Most Uncommon Jacksonians: The Radical Leaders of the Early Labor Movement*. Albany: State University of New York Press, 1967. Remains the most readable comprehensive book on the labor movement of the 1830s.

Robinson, Harriet H. *Loom and Spindle: Or, Life Among the Early Mill Girls: With a Sketch of "The Lowell Offering" and Some of Its Contributors*. Introduction by Jane Wilkins Pulz. Rev. ed. Kailua, HI: Press Pacifica, 1976. Idyllic memoir of Lowell's early days.

Rorabaugh, W. J. *The Craft Apprentice: From Franklin to the Machine Age in America*. New York: Oxford University Press, 1986. Essential history and primary documents on the changing work experiences of apprentices from 1720 to 1865.

Skidmore, Thomas. *The Rights of Man to Property! Being a Proposition to Make It Equal Among the Adults of the Present Generation: And to Provide for Its Equal Transmission to Every Individual of Each Succeeding Generation, on Arriving at the Age of Maturity*. New York: Burt Franklin, 1829. Exposition of radical agrarian ideas by the machinist who was the principal founder of the New York Working Men's Party.

Stansell, Christine. *City of Women: Sex and Class in New York, 1789–1860*. New York: Alfred A. Knopf, 1982. Innovative study of poor women's work, culture, and class relationships.

Starobin, Robert S. *Industrial Slavery in the Old South*. New York: Oxford University Press, 1970. A pioneering survey of industrial slavery and its impact on politics.

Sumner, Helen L. *History of Women in Industry in the United States*. 1910. Reprint, New York: Arno Press, 1974. Reprint of vol. 9, U.S. Bureau of Labor, *Report on Condition of Woman and Child Wage-Earners in the United States*. 19 vols. Washington, DC: GPO, 1910–1913. Valuable history contains documents on nineteenth-century women's work.

Wilentz, Sean. *Chants Democratic: New York City & the Rise of the American Working Class, 1788–1850*. New York: Oxford University Press, 1984. Highly readable chronicle on artisanal life, culture, and republicanism in New York City, and the rise of a working class.

Young, Alfred Fabian. *The Shoemaker and the Tea Party: Memory and the American Revolution*. Boston: Beacon Press, 1999. Valuable exploration of the egalitarian legacy of the American Revolution, with a focus on the life of a shoemaker who took part in it.

Web Sites

Thomas Dublin's highly commendable article, "Women, Work, and Protest in the Early Lowell Mills: 'The Oppressing Hand of Avarice Would Enslave Us,'" is available online at http://www.si.edu/lemelson/centerpieces/whole_cloth/u2ei/u2materials/dublin.html.

The 1842 *Commonwealth v. Hunt* decision, 45 Mass. 111, is available through LexisNexis Academic at http://web.lexis-nexis.com/universe/printdoc. For a brief description of the case, its context, and its significance, see "The Boston Bootmakers in the Supreme Judicial Court" at the Massachusetts AFL-CIO site, http://www.massaflcio.org/bootmakers.html.

The Library of Congress National Digital Library Program has released the Federal Writers' Project, Works Progress Administration, Slave Narratives online. The collection, "Born in Slavery: Slave Narratives from the Federal Writers' Project, 1936–1938," is available at the American Memory Web site—http://memory.loc.gov/ammem/snhtml/.

Video

The Lowell strike is the subject of the American Social History Project's excellent production, *Daughters of Free Men* (New York: American Social History Productions, 1987). The 30-minute video is ideal for use in classrooms.

2

The New England Shoemakers' Strike of 1860

The largest strike in the history of the United States before the Civil War occurred in New England in February, March, and April of 1860. It involved more than 20,000 men, women, and children, the native-born and immigrant populations who made shoes by hand in the various stages of the domestic or "putting-out" industry. The center of strike activity was in Massachusetts, where a large percentage of the nation's shoes and boots was produced at the time, and in particular in Lynn, where shoemakers specialized in making women's shoes. The importance of this unprecedented event has sometimes been overlooked, perhaps because it took place in the context of the emerging sectional crisis over slavery on the eve of the Civil War.

In many ways, however, the shoemakers' strike of 1860 was a watershed event in American labor history. In broad terms, it marked the ending of one era and the beginning of another. The conflict between the classes and the changed labor relations associated with the advance of industrial capitalism in the shoe industry were harbingers of things to come for many Americans in the later nineteenth century. Soon after the strike, the century-old artisanal shoemaking and putting-out system, which had once involved relative independence for workers and skilled handwork, was destroyed. What followed was mechanized shoe production carried out by a class of permanent wage laborers in factories. The strike itself has often been viewed as a protest against the factory system, that is, against the capitalist features that system entailed, especially the destruction of the artisanal system and the descent of workers into permanent wage-labor status.

The artisanal system—and the ideal of artisanal independence—had been undermined long before 1860. After 1800, shoemaking had become specialized work involving the entire family. Wives and daughters did the "binding," that is, the hand stitching of the pieces of the upper portion of the shoe. Their journeymen husbands or fathers then attached the "uppers" to the rest of the shoe, which they made. By about 1830, journeymen "cordwainers," the traditional term for shoemakers, could no longer realistically expect to become independent masters of the trade. About then, the shoe bosses—the master manufacturers—also began to establish central shops. These shops physically separated the bosses, who no longer engaged in actual shoe production, from the journeymen who did, and enabled the bosses to exert greater control over working shoemakers. New classes, new values, and less egalitarian relationships emerged.

If the establishment of central shops seriously undermined the male artisanal system, the introduction of the Singer sewing machine in the mid-1850s undermined the livelihoods of female binders and affected their monetary contribution to the shoemakers' family economy. The new technology enabled manufacturers to install the machines in factories and to hire female stitchers and less skilled journeymen wage earners. By 1855 hundreds of women had become factory stitchers. One stitcher working at a machine full-time could do the work of eleven binders at home, and shoe production soared. The depression of 1857 contributed to an over-supply of shoes, lower piece rates, and unemployment for many binders and shoeworkers.

The strike itself was precipitated by the shoe manufacturers' decision in February 1860 to cut piece rates, effective March 1, 1860. In the midst of the ongoing depression, journeymen cordwainers in Natick, Lynn, and other towns in Massachusetts quickly mobilized in response to the wage cut. They shared a long-standing radical tradition of protest dating from the American Revolution, and they already had established unions. Lynn shoemakers had successfully organized the Lynn Mechanic's Association in 1858. A year later, Alonzo Draper initiated publication of a labor news-paper, *The New England Mechanic*, which was read throughout the region. Lynn rapidly became the focal point of organization for the strike.

The journeymen responded by drawing up a list of their own prices (really wages). They then demanded that shoe manufacturers formally sign these lists to signify employer recognition and consent to pay the journeymen rates. If the shoe bosses had not signed by February 22, the men decided to launch a strike with a large procession in Lynn on George Washington's birthday. The consciously chosen date emphasized their republican revolutionary heritage and "equal rights" beliefs. "Equal rights" was the ideology of the craftsmen of many trades, not just shoe-makers. It incorporated a belief that labor was the source of all wealth and value, along with the notion that egalitarian rights of citizenship derived from the American Revolution. On February 22, a massive parade of journeymen, the first of five such processions held in Lynn, marked the onset of the strike.

Initially, violence was rare and relatively minor, despite the large scale of the strike. But violence and the norms of community behavior soon became contested issues. On Thursday, February 23, when manufacturers tried to ship cases of shoe stock to outworkers via wagons or the railroad, striking shoemakers intervened to prevent the movement. The shoe bosses then turned to city officials to request force to suppress all intervention in their business. A reluctant mayor issued proclamations to call out the Lynn Light Infantry and to restrict the assembling of crowds. With less reluctance, other city officials contacted state authorities and asked the Boston police to intervene.

On Friday morning, twenty Boston police arrived to occupy the town. As they moved through the streets, they incurred the wrath of the shoemakers, who viewed them as "outsiders" called in by city hall and the manufacturers to defeat the strike. This outside police intervention, a departure from custom, became an important issue in itself. The vast majority of the Lynn community shared the workers' sentiments that the police presence was a shocking violation of the rights of community self-government. After one day, the police were sent back to Boston, and the strikers organized to discipline themselves. The community's disapproval of the police intervention so upset the mayor that he then retired from public activity for the duration of the conflict.

The strike, which eventually included one-third of all the shoemakers in Massachusetts, was not simply an "American" or "male" affair. Immigrants and women became active participants, too. At the time of the strike, approximately 10 percent of the Lynn shoemakers were Irish, while 50 percent of the Natick shoemakers were German. Female strikers, often considered a novelty at the time, captured the national limelight when they marched with the men in Lynn on March 7. Vivid artistic sketches of that march in *Frank Leslie's Illustrated Newspaper* on March 17, 1860, showed women parading with a banner that read "AMERICAN LADIES WILL NOT BE SLAVES."

The women binders and stitchers of 1860 were drawing upon their own unique, gender-based class traditions. As they had done in 1833, they held their own meetings and voted on what piece rates to demand from the manufacturers for their work. The working women were divided, however, and their meetings were contentious, especially over the issue of *which* specific scale of wage rates to present as demands to the manufacturers. At the time, factory stitchers earned more than binders. Many of these factory workers were single women or widows who enjoyed no family support and were entirely dependent on the wages they earned. Consequently, they endorsed a demand for higher wages than did the majority of women—the wives and daughters of striking journeymen shoemakers—who were an integral part of a family economy in which male wages were considered primary. Both groups of women supported the journeymen's demands for higher wages.

Men and women thus approached the strike from their respective gender, marital, and occupational tasks. Although male shoemakers were eager to have the women's moral and material support, evidence suggests that they never took an interest in raising the rates of the binders. They considered female work subordinate, thought exclusively in terms of a family economy, and merely assumed that raising the men's rates would benefit everybody, without exception. This strike vividly illustrates some of the tensions and divisions that existed within the working class, divisions that hurt the strike. It also highlights the importance of gender in class analysis. Although these female workers were workers, they nevertheless underwent the working-class experience in an entirely different way than male workers did.

Neither strikers nor shoe bosses won an unqualified victory when shoemakers called off their work stoppage in April. Because of the depression, most shoe manufacturers had had a large stock of shoes and boots on hand before the strike and were easily able to withstand it. When the strike began, some said they would pay the higher wage rates but would never sign the shoemakers' list, an important demand of the workers for union recognition. Others adamantly rejected any compromise. Only one ever formally signed the journeymen's list. Many manufacturers did pay higher wages after the strike, but the ongoing depressed state of the trade and economy left numerous less fortunate shoemakers unemployed or underemployed. One direct political consequence of the strike was that Lynn shoemakers subsequently organized a political alternative, a workingmen's party, in time for the municipal election held later that year. They not only defeated those city officials whom they viewed as allies of the business interests, but they elected a working shoemaker for mayor and took charge of Lynn.

In 1860 large strikes were a new and rare phenomenon in the United States. Capitalist industry was in an early stage of development, and slave labor prevailed in half the nation. Yet, at the height of the strike in March, a future president who was campaigning in New England for the new Republican Party did talk, briefly, about the unprecedented labor conflict. In a revealing speech in New Haven, Abraham Lincoln supported the shoemakers and endorsed the right to strike, a right which he emphasized distinguished free labor from slave labor. In his related comments, he forthrightly noted the existence of economic inequalities in the nation but offered a justification for them. As he saw it, labor was still only a temporary condition for workers in the United States. For him, and for many others, before and since then, the preeminent national labor issue of the era was slavery, not the capitalist factory system. Indeed, it was not long after the strike that the New England shoe trade dramatically improved. Shoemakers and shoe manufacturers soon had an unexpected new market—Union soldiers—for their goods.

The broader significance of the impressive 1860 strike became fully apparent only as the years passed. The journeymen shoemakers and female strikers had waged a serious workers' challenge designed to give them a lever of control in the industry, even if that control was traditional and artisanal in form. That they lost that challenge meant that the shoe manufacturers were freer than they had ever been before to develop the dreaded factory system. The largest strike in U.S. history before the Civil War may have been overshadowed by the national crisis over slavery and the Civil War, but it was a harbinger of the numerous massive and serious labor conflicts that would occur once that war ended, and it continues to stand out today for the important issues it raised.

DOCUMENTS

2.1. "[Strike Meeting] At Saugus," *Boston Post*, February 27, 1860

Union leaders from Lynn went to neighboring towns to pub-licize their cause and encourage other shoemakers to join the strike. According to this account of a meeting at Saugus, Lynn's James Dillon recited reasons for the strike, emphasized the de-terioration of the craft system, and made invidious comparisons between slavery and free labor. In particular, he ridiculed a shoe manufacturer abolitionist who paid "slave" wages to his north-ern shoeworkers.

A very large meeting of the shoemakers of Saugus was held at the Town Hall in Saugus Centre on Saturday evening. A.J. Mills presided, and James R. Steele was appointed Secretary. The hall was well filled, and the meeting was composed of a majority of the shoemakers of the town.

The chairman introduced Mr. James Dillon, of Lynn, and he was re-ceived with applause. He proceeded to give an account of the causes of the strike in Lynn and its expected results, and gave the reasons why the movement should be generally extended and Saugus should join in the strike. In speaking of the present system of apprenticeship, he said shoe-makers were made as quick at the present time as shoes are made in En-gland. If no more apprentices are taken for two years, taking out those who will die a natural death, those who will go out West to engage in farming, and those who will starve to death, their numbers will be so re-duced that they cannot enter into competition with the regular journey-men. [Applause.] He referred to a noted manufacturer of Lynn, a man with the largest amount of money and the smallest amount of brains, who, when Anthony Burns [a runaway slave—Au.] was carried away from Boston, came back to Lynn and tried to persuade everybody to go to Boston and make a rescue of the slave, and who, at the present time, is having mock welts made for ten cents a pair [which Dillon considered a slave wage—Au.]. [Applause.] He shouldn't be surprised if within a short time we have an underground railroad to the South to run off the Northern slaves, as we now have an underground railroad to carry the Southern slaves to Canada. [Great applause.]

A Boston paper has recommended that we had better pack up our kits and go West, but we should be in a poor plight with five or six children and two or three at the breast. The only salvation of Lynn is in an organization of the workmen. He hoped that Saugus would cooperate with Lynn, so that each place could strengthen the other in the conflict with capital. Nothing but an organization of the workmen can secure the price for labor consistent with our state of civilization. Figure up the expenses and see if an average of five dollars a week will support your family, educate your children, and pay your honest debts. As honest men, it is our duty to our creditors to demand a remunerative rate for our labor. The object of the Lynn Mechanic's Association is to fix the price of labor. The reductions in prices begin at a point but a few rods from the depot, and the wave reaches West Lynn in about five or six weeks. [Applause.] A manufacturer in West Lynn had told him that a man offered him to make heels for nine cents, which work was better than some that he had paid eighteen cents a pair for, while in his shoe room he had work that cost him a shilling. He was very much surprised when he was told (by Dillon) that the same work was done for four cents at the depot. After speaking of some of the causes of the present hard times, Mr. Dillon proceeded to say that the Saugus shoemakers understood their own affairs well enough. He would only say that the first thing to be done after they were aroused was to prepare a scale of prices, and next to see if the manufacturers will agree to it. Every expedient has been tried to draw the Lynn strikers into a riot, but without effect. On the 22d there were a few acts of violence for which a striker was held in the modest sum of $40.00 at the request of parties in Lynn. The strikers will hold out until they are starved out, and if they are starved out they will all hang together. If they leave Lynn they will take the business with them and settle in the West and Southwest. If they leave Lynn business will leave it.

Source: "At Saugus," *Boston Post*, February 27, 1860, p. 4.

2.2. "Cordwainer's Song," *Lynn Weekly Reporter*, March 3, 1860

During the strike, Alonzo Lewis, a Lynn historian and poet, wrote this song that accurately conveyed the journeymen's belief in "equal rights," their fear of descent into slavery, and their gendered notions of "manliness." Note that this strike anthem completely overlooked the female strikers, whom Lewis and the journeymen considered subordinate and unequal in the struggle. Throughout the strike, the women wrote strike poems and songs of their own.

Shoemakers of Lynn, be brave!
    Renew your resolves again;
Sink not to the state of a slave,
    But stand for your rights like men!
Chorus—Yes, we'll stand for our rights like men!

Resolve by your native soil,
    Resolve by your fathers' graves,
You will live by your honest toil,
    But never consent to be slaves!
Chorus—No, never consent to be slaves!

The workman is worthy his hire,
    No tyrant shall hold us in thrall;
They may order their soldiers to fire!
    But we'll stick to the hammer and awl!
Chorus—Yes, we'll stick to the hammer and awl!

Better days will restore us our right,
    The future shall shine o'er the past;
We shall triumph by justice and right,
    For like men we'll hold on to the last!
Chorus—Yes, like men we'll hold on to the last!

The peaceable people of Lynn
    Need no rifles to keep them at peace;
By the right of our cause we shall win;
    But no rum, and no outside police.
Chorus—No rum, and no outside police.

Source: "Cordwainer's Song," Lynn Weekly Reporter, March 3, 1860.

2.3.   Lynn Mayor's Proclamation to Call up the Lynn Light Infantry, February 23, 1860

This unpopular proclamation, rarely used in internal civic disturbances, was issued by Lynn's mayor, Edward Davis, in response to a couple of minor incidents of strikers disrupting the movement of shoe stock on February 23. Other city officials used those incidents to justify bringing in the "outside" Boston police.

Commonwealth of Massachusetts—Essex, s.s.

To Lieut. GEORGE T. NEWHALL, Commanding Company D, Eighth Regiment, Fourth Brigade, Second Division, M. V. M.:

Whereas, It has been made to appear to us as Mayor, and to the Aldermen of the city of Lynn, County, and State aforesaid, that bodies of men have tumultuously assembled in said city, and have offered violence to persons and property, and have by force and violence resisted and broken the laws of this Commonwealth, and that military force is necessary to aid the civil authority in suppressing the same.

Now, therefore, we command you that you cause the company of infantry under your command, armed, equipped and with ammunition, as the law directs, and with proper officers, to parade at their armory on Friday, the 24th day of February instant, at 9 o'clock, and then and there to obey such orders as may be given them according to law. Hereof fail not at your peril, and have you there this warrant, with your doings returned thereon.

Witness my hand at Lynn on the 23d day of February, in the year 1860.

EDWARD DAVIS,
Mayor of the City of Lynn.

Source: "The Cordwainers' Riots," *New York Times*, February 27, 1860, p. 2.

2.4.   Religious and Community Sentiments, "The Strike of the Shoemakers," *Boston Post*, February 27, 1860

On the first Sunday after the strike began, the Boston Post *surveyed the views of the three Lynn clergymen who had spoken out on the strike in their pulpits that morning. The Congregational minister, who represented a mainstream Protestant denomination, noted the growing importance of labor–capital conflicts. The Roman Catholic priest, whose parish included Irish shoemakers, openly supported the strikers. The minister of the African Methodist Episcopal Church, attended by many of the 226 free blacks who lived in Lynn in 1860, expressed sympathy for the strikers and the oppressed.*

The allusions to the strike were not so general in the Lynn pulpits yesterday as was expected. In most of the churches the subject was not referred to at all, and in some others there was only a casual allusion to the subject. In only three was there anything said worthy of mention.

At the Second Congregational Church, Rev. C. C. Shackford preached from the text—Luke, 12th chapter, 15th verse: "And he said unto them, take heed, and beware of covetousness; for a man's life consisteth not in the abundance of the things which he possesseth." Jesus had been hold-

ing up to view the falsehood, hypocrisy and oppression of those among
his countrymen who claimed to be purer and more righteous than others. He appealed to the infinite realities of love, justice and truth. He was
asked to apply them, authoritatively, to a particular case. His reply was
in accordance with the whole spirit of his teaching. He takes no side, as
of one individual against another, but goes at once to the root of the difficulty, and warns them, against the continual striving for more—more
wealth, more business, more possessions. Christianity today furnishes no
specific directions what measures to adopt in the question between labor
and capital, but it furnishes the spiritual and universal principles which
should pervade all the conduct. The covetous spirit is the same, whether
in rich or poor. . . . He who looks upon his fellow-men only as machines
to be run at the least possible cost, must not be surprised that they shall
regard him as a machine to give them more food and clothing—more and
yet more. The question of labor and capital meets us everywhere today.
It will be settled by science as humanity advances; and it is well if such
events as have recently occurred, should lead to thoughtful consideration,
and to ask what is Christian duty. . . .

At the Catholic Services in Lyceum Hall, Father Strain of Chelsea, offi-
ciated. He spoke of the strike of the shoemakers as a struggle for the compensation for labor to provide nourishment and clothing for themselves
and their children. This they have not had, to his personal knowledge.
He hoped that Catholics would not raise a hammer as long as the Americans held out. He cautioned his hearers to be orderly, not to trouble the
expressmen, and to avoid the use of intoxicating liquors. The movement
should not be made a political one. It is not the movement of any party
or sect, and ought not to become so. All that is desired is a fair compensation for labor. The hall was crowded to overflowing.

Rev. Thomas Driver, at the African Methodist Episcopal church, made
some allusions to the events of the week. He said that his soul was with
the oppressed. If he understood the strikers, he was with them. It is to
make the bosses pay more wages; the bosses to secure higher prices from
the jobbers; the jobbers to make the retailers pay dearer for their shoes,
and the consumer to foot the bill. But this is not all. The laborer is operated upon by another power. Importers are to be affected by this strike.
They, to secure large profits, have demanded and received a larger profit
on their hides than is reasonable. The strike is to cause the bosses to beat
down the prices of hides in the hands of the merchants; and the merchants, the importers. As it has been, the importer has made money out
of the merchant; the merchant, out of the leather maker; the leather maker
out of the bosses; and the boss, to secure himself from loss, cuts down the
journeyman's wages. So the laborer is cut down on both sides. You, my
colored brethren, know how to sympathize with laborers unrequited. . . .
They [the strikers] are in the centre of eight money making powers. The

poor journeyman is the bird picked! He is now the cider juice in the press under the screw. May God grant that the screw may be eased, and men say live and let live.

Source: "The Strike of the Shoemakers," *Boston Post*, February 27, 1860, p. 4.

2.5.   "The Bay State Strike," *New York Times,* **February 29, 1860**

In this excerpt from an article, "Howard," a male New York Times reporter, focused attention on a disorderly women's meeting in which the divisions between factory stitchers and binders became apparent. He reported on the organizers' efforts to unify the cause by making references to Molly Stark, a New England revolutionary heroine and wife of an important revolutionary general. He also noted that, when Clara Brown, a leader of the factory stitchers, used a racial epithet, women in the abolitionist cause shamed her. In subsequent articles, Howard ridiculed the women for changing their minds—and their list of wages— three times at successive meetings. But he also lambasted male strike leaders and claimed the strike was senseless.

About noon, the procession from Lynn, consisting of about 3,500 men, preceded by a brass band, entered the village green, escorted by 500 Marbleheaders. The sight from the hotel steps was a very interesting one. Four thousand men, without work, poor, depending partially upon the charities of their neighbors and partially upon the generosity of the tradesmen of their town, giving up a certainty for an uncertainty, and involving in trouble with themselves many hundreds of women and children, while to a certain extent the wheels of trade are completely blocked, and no immediate prospect of relief appears. Their banners flaunted bravely. Their inscriptions of "Down with tyranny," "We are not slaves," "No sympathy with the rich," "Our bosses grind us," "We work and they ride," "No foreign police," and many others of like import, read very well and look very pretty, but they don't buy dinners or clothing, or keep the men at work or the women at home about their business. By this strike $25,000 *weekly is kept from circulation in Lynn alone,* and who can say what the effect will be on the storekeepers, dealers in articles of home consumption, if such a state of drainage is kept up for any great length of time? . . .

The most interesting part of the whole movement took place last evening, and will be continued tonight. I refer to the mass meeting of the binders and stitchers held by

THE FEMALE STRIKERS AT LIBERTY HALL. . . .

The object of the meeting was the hearing the reports of Committees who had been deputed to make a list of reasonable prices, and to solicit the girls of Lynn and the surrounding towns to join the strike movement.

There are two classes of workers—those who work in the shops and those who work at home—the former use the machines and materials of the bosses, while the latter work on their own machines, or work by hand, furnishing their own materials. It is evident that the latter should receive higher pay than the former, and the report not having considered this fact, was subjected to severe handling. The discussion which followed was rich beyond description—the jealousies, piques and cliques of the various circles being apparent as it proceeded. One opposed the adoption of the report because, "the prices set were so high that the bosses wouldn't pay them." Cries of "Put her out," "Shut up," "Scabby," and "Shame" arose on all sides; but, while the reporters were alarmed, the lady took it all in good part, and made up faces at the crowd. The Chairman stated that, hereafter, Pickleeomoonia [a type or shape of?—Au.] boots were to be made for three cents a pair less, which announcement was received with expressions of dismay, whereupon he corrected himself, and said they were to be three cents higher; and this announcement drew forth shouts and screams of applause. "There! didn't I *say* so?" said an old lady behind me. "You shut up," was the response of her neighbor; "you think because you've got a couple of machines you're some [one]; but you ain't no more than anybody else." At this point some men peeped in at the window—"Scat, scat, and put 'em out," soon drove them away, and the meeting went into a Committee of the Whole, and had a grand chabbering for five minutes. Two ladies, one representing the machine interest, and the other the shop girls, became very much excited, and were devoting themselves to an *exposé* of each other's habits, when the Chairman, with the perspiration starting from every pore, said in a loud and authoritative tone of voice: "Ladies! look at me; stop this wranglin'. Do you care for your noble cause? Are you descendants of old MOLLY STARK or not? Did you ever hear of the spirit of '76? [Yes, yes, we've got it.] Well, then, do behave yourselves. There ain't nobody nowhere who will aid you if you don't show 'em that you're regular built Moll Starks over agin." [Cheers, clappings, &c.]

"Here comes the Boston police;" "Pitch 'em in the river;" "Who's afraid?" "We'll put 100 girls at the dépot, and *then* see if the police dare arrest anybody." What could the Chairman do? He hammered and yelled "Order," but had to succumb and let the girls talk it out, when they again came to order and resumed business.

A proposition to march in the procession was the next topic which drew forth discussion. Some thought that proper minded women would better stay at home than be gadding about the streets following banners and music. To this there was some assent, but when a younger girl asked the last speaker what she meant by talking that way, when everybody in Lynn knew that she had been tagging around on the sidewalks after the men's processions the last week, the uproar was tremendous, and the pit of the Bowery never at any performance of "The Three Fast Men" so resounded with screams and whistles and hurrahs as did that well named Liberty Hall.

Some of the statements were quite interesting. A Mrs. MILLER said that she hired a machine on which she was able to make $6 per week—out of that she paid—for the machine, $1; for the materials, $1.50; for her board, $2; for bastings, $1;—making $5.50 in all, which left her a clear profit of only fifty cents a week. One of the bosses says, however, that if a woman is at all smart she can make $10 per week with her machine, which would be clear $3, sure. In fact, from remarks which were dropped around I judge that Mrs. MILLER's estimate is rather low. The leading spirit of the meeting, Miss CLARA BROWN, a very bright, pretty girl, said that she called at a shop that day and found a friend of hers hard at work on a lot of linings. She asked what she was getting for them, and was told *eighty cents for sixty.* "Girls of Lynn," said CLARA, "*Girls* of Lynn, do you hear that and will you stand it? Never, *Never,* NEVER. Strike, then—strike at once; DEMAND 8½ cents for your work when the binding isn't closed, and you'll get it. Don't let them make niggers of you; [Shame, there are colored persons here.] I meant Southern niggers:—keep still; don't work your machines; let 'em lie still till we get all we ask, and then go at it, as did our Mothers in the Revolution."

This speech was a good one; it seemed to suit all parties, and they proposed to adjourn to Tuesday night, when they would have speeches, and be more orderly. Canvassing Committees were appointed to look up female strikers and to report female "scabs." And with a vote of thanks to the Chairman, the meeting adjourned to meet in Lyceum Hall.

Source: "The Bay State Strike," *New York Times*, February 29, 1860, p. 8.

2.6.   "The Shoemakers' Strike," *Boston Post*, April 10, 1860

This newspaper article accurately conveyed the mixed terms on which the strike ended.

THE SHOEMAKERS' STRIKE.—We are about hearing the last of this great movement as a matter of the present, although it will long be remembered as constituting one of the most powerful demonstrations ever made by labor in its conflict with capital. No formal announcement is made of a compliance on the part of the manufacturers with the demands of their employés—neither is there any intelligence received of a return to work of the latter at old prices. But a relinquishment of the demand that "bosses" should *sign* the bill of wages agreed upon, and a willingness to resume labor at prices acceptable—each individual regulating the matter for himself—have paved the way to a profitable and honorable compromise. Haverhill came first into line, and the other towns following rapidly, we have now from Lynn—the stronghold of the revolution and the headquarters of its leaders—this report: "A majority of the best workmen are now employed at good prices, and others commence work this week. Owing, however, to the limited demand for goods, a large number of shoemakers will necessarily be out of work for some time to come."

Source: "The Shoemakers' Strike," *Boston Post*, April 10, 1860, p. 4.

2.7.   Abraham Lincoln, Speech at New Haven, Connecticut, March 6, 1860

Of the many divergent responses to the strike, Lincoln's was one of the most interesting and significant. As this excerpt from a campaign speech indicates, he considered free labor superior to slave labor, the right to strike critical, and the use of the shoemakers' strike by southern politicians a mere ploy in their efforts to ambush the Republicans. That his strike-related comments were only a minor portion of a speech devoted to the issue of slavery also shows that he viewed the strike as subordinate to the preeminent national labor issue of the day—slavery.

MR. PRESIDENT AND FELLOW CITIZENS OF NEW HAVEN: If the Republican party of this nation shall ever have the national house intrusted to its keeping, it will be the duty of that party to attend to all the affairs of national housekeeping. Whatever matters of importance may come up, whatever difficulties may arise, in the way of its administration of the government, that party will then have to attend to: it will then be compelled to attend to other questions besides this question which now assumes an overwhelming importance—the question of slavery. It is true that in the organization of the Republican party this question of slavery was more important than any other; indeed, so much more important has it become that no other national question can even get a hearing just at present. . . . For whether we will or not, the question of slavery is the question, the all-absorbing topic, of the day. . . .

Look at the magnitude of this subject. One sixth of our population, in round numbers—not quite one sixth, and yet more than a seventh—about one sixth of the whole population of the United States, are slaves. The owners of these slaves consider them property. The effect upon the minds of the owners is that of property, and nothing else; it induces them to insist upon all that will favorably affect its value as property, to demand laws and institutions and a public policy that shall increase and secure its value, and make it durable, lasting, and universal. The effect on the minds of the owners is to persuade them that there is no wrong in it. The slaveholder does not like to be considered a mean fellow for holding that species of property, and hence he has to struggle within himself, and sets about arguing himself into the belief that slavery is right. The property influences his mind. . . .

But here in Connecticut and at the North slavery does not exist, and we see it through no such medium. To us it appears natural to think that slaves are human beings; men, not property; that some of the things, at least, stated about men in the Declaration of Independence apply to them as well as to us. I say we think, most of us, that this charter of freedom applies to the slave as well as to ourselves; that the class of arguments put forward to batter down that idea are also calculated to break down the very idea of free government, even for white men, and to undermine the very foundations of free society. We think slavery a great moral wrong, and while we do not claim the right to touch it where it exists, we wish to treat it as a wrong in the Territories, where our votes will reach it. We think that a respect for ourselves, a regard for future generations and for the God that made us, require that we put down this wrong where our votes will properly reach it. We think that species of labor an injury to free white men—in short, we think slavery a great moral, social, and political evil, tolerable only because, and so far as, its actual existence makes it necessary to tolerate it, and that beyond that it ought to be treated as a wrong. . . .

. . . I see the signs of the approaching triumph of the Republicans in the bearing of their political adversaries. A great deal of this war with us nowadays is mere bushwhacking. . . . [Lincoln then cited several examples of bushwhacking, including the Democratic Party's efforts to blame Republicans for John Brown's uprising. He then turned to the shoemakers' strike.]

Another specimen of this bushwhacking—that "shoe strike." Now be it understood that I do not pretend to know all about the matter. I am merely going to speculate a little about some of its phases, and at the outset I am glad to see that a system of labor prevails in New England under which laborers can strike when they want to, where they are not obliged to work under all circumstances, and are not tied down and obliged to labor whether you pay them or not! I like the system which lets a man quit when he wants to, and wish it might prevail everywhere. One of the reasons why I am opposed to slavery is just here. What is the true condition of the laborer? I take it that it is best for all to leave each man free to acquire property as fast as he can. Some will get wealthy. I don't believe in a law to prevent a man from getting rich; it would do more harm than good. So while we do not propose any war upon capital, we do wish to allow the humblest man an equal chance to get rich with everybody else. When one starts poor, as most do in the race of life, free society is such that he knows he can better his condition; he knows that there is no fixed condition of labor for his whole life. I am not ashamed to confess that twenty-five years ago I was a hired laborer, mauling rails, at work on a flatboat—just what might happen to any poor man's son. I want every man to have a chance—and I believe a black man is entitled to it—in which he can better his condition—when he may look forward and hope to be a hired laborer this year and the next, work for himself afterward, and finally to hire men to work for him. That is the true system. . . .

Now to come back to this shoe strike. If, as the senator from Illinois asserts, this is caused by withdrawal of Southern votes, consider briefly how you will meet the difficulty. You have done nothing, and have protested that you have done nothing, to injure the South; and yet to get back the shoe trade, you must leave off doing something that you are now doing. What is it? You must stop thinking slavery wrong. Let your institutions be wholly changed; let your State constitutions be subverted; glorify slavery; and so you will get back the shoe trade—for what? You have brought owned labor with it to compete with your own labor, to underwork you, and degrade you. Are you ready to get back the trade on these terms?

But the statement is not correct. You have not lost that trade; orders were never better than now. . . .

Another bushwhacking contrivance—simply that, nothing else!

Source: Abraham Lincoln, "Speech at New Haven, Connecticut, March 6, 1860," in *Complete Works of Abraham Lincoln*, ed. John G. Nicolay and John Hay (New York: The Tandy-Thomas Company, 1894), 5:339–40, 343–45, 357, 360–63.

SELECTED ANNOTATED BIBLIOGRAPHY

Books

Andrews, John B. and William Dwight Porter Bliss. *History of Women in Trade Unions*. 1911. Reprint, New York: Arno Press, 1974. Reprint of vol. 10, U.S. Bureau of Labor, *Report on Condition of Woman and Child Wage-Earners in the United States*. 19 vols. Washington, DC: GPO, 1910–1913. Contains valuable primary material on the unions and protest activities of female shoemakers and other working women in the nineteenth century.

Blewett, Mary H. *Men, Women, and Work: Class, Gender, and Protest in the New England Shoe Industry, 1780–1910*. Urbana: University of Illinois Press, 1988.

This significant corrective to previous studies on Lynn incorporates women into the shoemakers' strike of 1860 and brings gender into the analysis of shoemaking and labor protest.

————. *We Will Rise in Our Might: Workingwomen's Voices from Nineteenth-Century New England*. Ithaca, NY: Cornell University Press, 1991. Valuable excerpts of primary documents, with historical context, that cover the themes, scope, and material in *Men, Women, and Work*.

Cantor, Milton, ed. *American Workingclass Culture: Explorations in American Labor and Social History*. Westport, CT: Greenwood Press, 1979. See especially Alan Dawley and Paul Faler, "Workingclass Culture and Politics in the Industrial Revolution," pp. 61–75; and Paul Faler, "Cultural Aspects of the Industrial Revolution: Lynn, Massachusetts, Shoemakers and Industrial Morality, 1826–1860," pp. 121–48.

Commons, John R. *Labor and Administration*. New York: The Macmillan Company, 1913. See the labor economist's essay, "American Shoemakers, 1648 to 1895," pp. 219–66; it is noteworthy for its omission of the 1860 strike.

Cumbler, John T. *Working-Class Community in Industrial America: Work, Leisure, and Struggle in Two Industrial Cities, 1880–1930*. Westport, CT: Greenwood Press, 1979. Covers Lynn shoemakers in the decades following the strike.

Dawley, Alan. *Class and Community: The Industrial Revolution in Lynn*. Cambridge, MA: Harvard University Press, 1976. This winner of the 1977 Bancroft Prize in American History is especially valuable for its treatment of male artisans, artisanal culture, the ideology of "equal rights," and the 1860 strike.

Essex Institute Historical Collections 115 (October 1979). Entire issue is devoted to the history of Lynn and its shoemakers in all eras.

Faler, Paul. *Mechanics and Manufacturers in the Early Industrial Revolution: Lynn, Massachusetts 1780–1860*. Albany: State University of New York Press, 1981. Traces vast social, economic, and cultural changes. Argues that the Lynn journeymen shoemakers who had belonged to a community of mechanics and producers in 1790 became a distinctive working class by the time of the 1860 strike.

Filippelli, Ronald L., ed. *Labor Conflict in the United States: An Encyclopedia*. New York: Garland Publishing, 1990. See, especially, Paul Faler's excellent account, "Shoemakers' Strike of 1860," pp. 480–83.

Foner, Philip S. *History of the Labor Movement in the United States*. Vol. 1: *From Colonial Times to the Founding of the American Federation of Labor*. New York: International Publishers, 1947, pp. 241–45. A useful brief account of the strike.

Frank Leslie's Illustrated Newspaper, March 17, 24, and 31, and April 7, 1860. Excellent for artistic sketches of the women strikers and detailed information on piece rates.

Hazard, Blanche Evans. *The Organization of the Boot and Shoe Industry in Massachusetts Before 1875*. Cambridge, MA: Harvard University Press, 1921. Traces the stages of the industry's development over time but is highly inaccurate and misleading about labor protest.

Huston, James L. "Facing an Angry Labor: The American Public Interprets the Shoemakers' Strike of 1860." *Civil War History* 28 (September 1982):

197–212. Indispensable article on the diverse reactions of the American public to the strike.

Johnson, David N. *Sketches of Lynn, or the Changes of Fifty Years.* c. 1880. Reprint, Westport, CT: Greenwood Press, 1970. A useful local history.

Sumner, Helen L. *History of Women in Industry in the United States.* 1910. Reprint, New York: Arno Press, 1974. Reprint of vol. 9, U.S. Bureau of Labor, *Report on Condition of Woman and Child Wage-Earners in the United States.* 19 vols. Washington, DC: GPO, 1910–1913. Contains valuable primary material on nineteenth-century women's work, the sexual division of labor, and technological change in various industries, including boot and shoemaking.

Ware, Norman. *The Industrial Worker, 1840–1860: The Reaction of American Industrial Society to the Advance of the Industrial Revolution.* c. 1924. Reprint, Gloucester, MA: Peter Smith, 1959, pp. 38–48. A brief pioneering history of the strike.

Young, Alfred Fabian. *The Shoemaker and the Tea Party: Memory and the American Revolution.* Boston: Beacon Press, 1999. Valuable for information on the prominent role cordwainers played in the American Revolution, their militant traditions, and the ideology of "equal rights."

Web Site

"Women and Social Movements in the United States, 1775–2000," edited by Kathryn Kish Sklar and Thomas Dublin and produced by the Center for the Historical Study of Women and Gender at the State University of New York at Binghamton, contains valuable primary documents and is available online at http://womhist.binghamton.edu/about.htm. For materials on the 1860 strike, see, specifically, "How Did Gender and Family Divisions among Shoeworkers Shape the 1860 New England Strike?"

Video

Alfred Young was also a consultant for an important historical video project, *Tea Party Etiquette*, produced in New York by the American Social History Productions, 1987, distributed by the American Social History Project Film Library. This 30-minute video depicts the American Revolution from the viewpoint of a Boston shoemaker and is an ideal length for use in classrooms and workshops.

3

The Railroad Strikes of 1877

The sudden and spontaneous railroad strikes that occurred in 1877 in major cities throughout the nation from July 16 through August 5 were a watershed event in the history of the United States. They had a profound impact on American consciousness. For the first time, American workers had engaged in widespread strikes and riots that led many to fear that the United States was not really unique, that it was in fact becoming more like Europe, where rigid classes and class conflict were presumed to prevail.

The strikes began in Martinsburg, West Virginia, on July 16, when indignant railroad workers on the Baltimore and Ohio Railroad protested the imposition of a 10 percent wage cut and refused to allow trains to run. Their example was contagious. Like a conflagration, the Great Strike quickly spread to Baltimore, Cumberland, Pittsburgh, Buffalo, Chicago, St. Louis, Reading, Cincinnati, Omaha, and many other urban centers in all regions of the country except New England and the South. Before the strikes were over, and often at the urgent request of railroad officials, the governors of nine states wired President Rutherford B. Hayes for U.S. troops, who effectually served as strikebreakers. To get the federal troops, Hayes insisted that the governors had to maintain, accurately or inaccurately, that their states were undergoing a domestic "insurrection" that local authorities and state militias were unable to quell. In fact, the strikers often enjoyed broad visible support among the laboring and business classes. Tearing up railroad tracks, destroying railroad property, and defying troops were community-based activities in many places where urban rioting occurred. At least 100 people, 42 in Pittsburgh alone and another 11 in Baltimore, died as a result of the industrial violence that accompanied the strikes. The sheer scale of the protests, the violence, and the unfolding of events was unprecedented.

The strikes took place during the fifth year of a severe, ongoing depression. The many American and immigrant working families who now lived in cities instead of the countryside faced especially hard times. Craft unions were devastated, and workers were basically forced to confront wage cuts, layoffs, slack work, and hunger, alone, as best they could. They found little comfort in the philosophical notions that had accompanied industrial expansion after the Civil War. Big business and sympathetic economists now viewed workers as mere commodities subject to the immutable laws of supply and demand. The policy of "laissez-faire" meant the federal government was to keep "hands off" the regulation of business, even though it had generously aided railroads and other corporations with public funding and public lands. Many of the nation's 3 million unemployed workers, who were vilified as vagrants and tramps in the newspapers, wandered from town to town in search of work.

By the 1870s, railroad corporations had come to symbolize Big Business, a new era in capitalist industry, the first monopolies. The names of Jay Gould, Thomas Scott, Cornelius Vanderbilt, and other railroad magnates were well known to the public. Their political influence in Congress and state legislatures was great. Thomas Scott, a United States Senator and president of the Pennsylvania Railroad, was widely perceived to have been the kingpin behind the highly disputed and questionable selection of Republican Rutherford B. Hayes as president of the United States in 1877, even though the Democratic candidate, Samuel Tilden, had won the popular vote in a hotly contested presidential election characterized by fraud in several southern states. Other notorious scandals of the era included the Crédit Mobilier affair, which involved corrupt railroad officials and prominent congressional politicians. Thus, railroad workers were not the only citizens with grievances against the railroads. A wide variety of citizens, including farmers, workers, and business people, were angered by such things as discriminatory or monopolistic freight rates, government grants and subsidies, watered stock, the railroads' political influence, and the high number of accidents.

All railroad corporations were not financially successful, but it is probably not accidental that most of the strikes occurred on large, profitable trunk lines that continued to pay annual dividends of 6 to 8 percent to their stockholders throughout the depression. Such railroads had also discovered ways to eliminate "survival of the fittest" among themselves. Five eastern corporations—the Pennsylvania Railroad, the Baltimore and Ohio, the New York Central, the Erie Railroad, and the Grand Trunk—were among the pioneers who created "pools," informal agreements in which former competitors agreed to set uniform rates and divide the rail traffic among themselves. During the spring of 1877, the managers of these five railroads decided to offset business losses by cutting the wages of their employees once again. That decision ultimately provoked the strikes.

The Pennsylvania Railroad led the combination's effort to reduce wages by imposing a 10 percent wage cut on its employees, effective June 1. In response, on June 2, disgruntled engineers, brakemen, firemen, and conductors transcended the narrow limits of their individual craft brotherhoods and met in Pittsburgh to form a Trainmen's Union, a new industrial union that included all those who worked on the railroads. Organizers spread news of the organization to railroad workers in other states in preparation of a general railroad strike set for June 27, but the strike effort fizzled and the organization collapsed. The railroad strikes of 1877 did not begin until July 16, when the Baltimore and Ohio announced a similar 10 percent wage reduction that its workers spontaneously protested.

The common thread of all the disparate strikes was the railroad workers' opposition to imposed wage cuts. But each strike was unique in that particular circumstances influenced the timing and magnitude of local work stoppages, the response of authorities, the degree of violence, and the outcome of events. In Cleveland, events were relatively peaceful. In Louisville, black sewer workers enlarged the strike and achieved wage gains. In Chicago and St. Louis, the Workingmen's Party of the United States, a small, recently founded, Marxist organization, sought to provide leadership of the uprisings and begin citywide general strikes. In San Francisco, a workers' movement that had favored the eight-hour day and nationalization of the railroads degenerated into an anti-Chinese riot, which helped to pave the way for the first Chinese Exclusion Act in 1882, a pivotal event itself in American labor history.

Pittsburgh witnessed the worst violence and urban rioting that took place anywhere in the nation during the strike. The immediate impetus for the local job action was the Pennsylvania Railroad Company's issuance of a new order mandating that, as of July 19, all trains running east be double-headers, that is, two trains run by one engine and a lesser crew. The new order meant that many jobs would be eliminated and that more work would be created for those workers left on the job. It also came in the context of the company's recent wage cut and news of the ongoing B&O workers' strike in West Virginia and Maryland. The order sparked the outbreak of the local strike. It was initially peaceful.

In the meantime, Pennsylvania Railroad Company officials rejected the notion of making any compromises. Once the strike began, they immediately launched a campaign to get local and state authorities to suppress the peaceable work stoppage by military force. But local units of the National Guard proved to be unreliable in Pittsburgh, and the strike itself enjoyed great support in the city. The railroad then sent appeals for state troops through Allegheny County Sheriff R. H. Fife to Adjutant General Robert Latta, who acted for Governor John F. Hartranft in his absence. At the time, Hartranft was touring the West at the Pennsylvania Railroad's expense in Tom Scott's private railroad car. Latta ordered the Philadelphia militia to Pittsburgh.

These unwelcome strangers from a rival city that was also the headquarters of the hated rail corporation arrived in Pittsburgh on the morning of Saturday, July 21. When ordered to clear the tracks, they fired into a jeering and stone-throwing crowd, thereby killing many, few of whom had any direct connection to the railroad strike. The shooting intensified the population's anger and precipitated widespread rioting. The troops themselves came under siege when they retired to the roundhouse. Groups of young boys and men sent flaming oil-drenched railroad cars toward the roundhouse in an effort to set it on fire. Women provided arsonists with food and drink and participated in the looting of standing railroad cars before crowds set those cars and other railroad properties on fire. On Sunday morning, July 22, the Philadelphians had to fight their way out of the roundhouse when it went it up in flames. The soldiers escaped with their lives and marched out of the city to the town of Allegheny.

News of such events and the ongoing spontaneous strikes that were occurring throughout the country sparked lively outcries. One of the most notable responses came from Henry Ward Beecher, a controversial but nationally prominent clergyman who took to the pulpit to denounce the strikers. In two well-publicized sermons he preached at Plymouth Church in Brooklyn, New York, during the strikes, he angered working people by bluntly stating that any workers (and their families) who could not live on $1.00 a day were not fit to live. He also blasted unions as un-American and communistic. By making such pronouncements during events that the public considered shocking, Beecher helped popularize the notion of Social Darwinism, the belief that Darwinian concepts such as the "survival of the fittest" should apply to society. Henceforth, many wealthy industrialists and middle-class Americans adopted the pseudo-scientific idea to justify the glaring inequities that existed in American society during the late nineteenth century.

The impressive spontaneous strikes also inaugurated a new era in labor relations in the United States. One major result was that government—especially state and federal governments—assumed a new, repressive role in those relations. Although the mass of strikers allowed passenger trains and mail cars to move in a futile effort to avert federal intervention, the federal judiciary intervened on the side of the railroad companies and propertied interests. Resulting court injunctions, federal troops, and state militias helped the railroads break the strike. Injunctions and troops would be used against labor in future strikes.

After the strikes were over, anti-union corporations fired strikers, cre-ated blacklists, and revived conspiracy laws. Allan Pinkerton, the famous detective who had worked with Reading Railroad president Franklin Gowen to defeat the Molly Maguires (an Irish-American secret society and union) in the anthracite coal fields of Pennsylvania, blamed the entire railway uprising on communists and tramps but especially on the Broth-erhood of Locomotive Engineers, which had played no role in it. Thomas Scott called for federal injunctions, a large increase in the standing army, and the stationing of that army at regional sites so that it could more eas-ily put down rebellions such as that his railroad had just experienced. *The Nation*, one of the nation's leading journals, endorsed his proposals.

Meanwhile, the moderate *National Labor Tribune*, a labor journal based in Pittsburgh, was one of a number that placed the sole blame for the strike and subsequent rioting on the railroads. Its editorial, "Fact vs. Fancy," published on July 28, 1877, maintained that the greatest lesson of the strike was that it proved that "there is a point beyond which endurance ceases to be a virtue, a point beyond which it is unsafe to press the workingmen of America."[1] Subsequently, although the journal contin-ued to fear that emerging class divisions were endangering the Republic's future, it noted that the strike had aroused hope, a sentiment later shared by Samuel Gompers, the founding president of the American Federation of Labor. In his memoirs, written many years after the event, Gompers described the railway strike as a tocsin that had heralded hope. Indeed, the strikes had rejuvenated the labor movement. Once the depression ended, railroad and other workers began to join new unions in greater numbers, and the main beneficiary—the emerging Knights of Labor—soon became the most important labor organization of the nineteenth cen-tury.

In general, the American public was confused and shocked by the unex-pected outbreak of the 1877 railroad strikes, whose meaning was unclear and contested. It was a national trauma of sorts. The final report of the committee of the Pennsylvania State Legislature that investigated the Pennsylvania strikes reflected the confusion and contradictions of the larger society. It first blamed labor, and then capital, for the conflict; it applauded the actions of the Philadelphia troops but understood the sen-timents of local militias; and although it left no doubt as to the cause of the strike, it offered no remedies. The report concluded by carefully distin-guishing the strikes from the riots and by insisting that the strikes were not an insurrection, that is, an uprising against civil or political authority. By placing blame for the riots on nondescript tramps and idle vagrants instead of the railroad workers or the unemployed in general, it sought to reassure a shocked public that such massive strikes and violence were an aberration in the United States.

Were the strikes a genuine insurrection, an attempt to form a commune similar to the Paris Commune of 1871, as some commentators wildly charged at the time? Were they an act of sheer desperation? Did they mark the end of the youth of the American Republic, as one British journalist noted? Whatever diverse Americans thought, the strikes brought to the center of the nation's attention debatable issues such as the relationship between capital and labor in an emerging industrial capitalist society. They also evoked new concerns about what a society with entrenched class divisions—permanent wage laborers and wealthy capitalists— might mean for the future of the Republic. These were serious contested issues and concerns that would remain long after the strikes ended.

NOTE

1. "Fact vs. Fancy," *National Labor Tribune*, July 28, 1877, p. 4.

DOCUMENTS

3.1. *New York Times* Report on the Beginning of the Pittsburgh Strike, July 19, 1877

The Pittsburgh strike, ultimately the most violent, began peacefully on July 19, 1877. This report from the New York Times *outlined the strikers' grievances, adopted at a meeting of the Train Men's Union.*

PITTSBURG [*sic*], Penn., July 19.—A large and very enthusiastic meeting of the Train Men's Union was held at Phoenix Hall, on Eleventh street, tonight. Nearly all of the strikers were present, and the meeting was addressed by many speakers. But one sentiment was expressed—a determination to continue the strike. The meeting was very orderly. The strikers were joined at the meeting by the engineers and firemen of the Western Division and it was determined to have the fight on the reduction of wages which went into effect on June 1, and against the doubling of trains. The following resolutions were unanimously adopted as their ultimatum:

First—We, the undersigned committee appointed by the Western Division of the Pennsylvania Railroad Company, do hereby demand from said company, through its proper officers, the wages as per departments of engineers, firemen, conductors, and brakemen received prior to June 1, 1877.

Second—That each and every employe who has been dismissed for taking part or parts in the present strike or meetings held prior to or during said strike be restored to their positions as held prior to the strike.

Third—That the classification of each of said departments be abolished now and forever, and that hereafter engineers and conductors receive the same wages as received by engineers and conductors of the highest class prior to June 1, 1877.

Fourth—That the running of double trains be abolished, excepting coal trains.

Fifth—That each and every engine, whether road or shifting, shall have its own fireman.

The officers of the road claim that the double train arrangement is simply a pretext for the strike. They state that for three months past the freight business has been very low, and that many crews have been kept in the employ of the company in anticipation of better business. During the last two weeks the decrease of freight has been so heavy that the company only had work for 15 or 18 of the 26 crews in their employ. They further state that the strike was gotten up because a large number of men expected to be thrown out of work by the new order.

Source: "The Pennsylvania Railroad," *New York Times*, July 20, 1877, p. 1.

3.2.   Major General Robert Brinton's Testimony before a Committee of the Pennsylvania State Legislature, 1878

In 1878 a committee of the Pennsylvania State Legislature investigated the strikes. In his testimony before that committee, Major General Robert Brinton, commander of the Philadelphia troops who had been sent to Pittsburgh, offered this description of the violent events of July 21, 1877.

General Pearson [Commander of the Sixth Division of the National Guard, headquartered in Pittsburgh] ordered me to have the troops ready to move to Twenty-eighth street. At that time, I told them in coming up, I had seen the hills covered with people, and I asked them in the event of their ordering me out, to go out with me, and look over the ground. I was an entire stranger there, and I thought they must be misinformed in regard to having cleared the hill, as they said General Brown's brigade had. I also met Mr. Cassatt [vice-president of the Pennsylvania Railroad] at the depot, and I said in the event of our going down and clearing the tracks, can you move your trains. He said we can; we have crews already engaged to take out double-headers. General Pearson then ordered me down to Twenty-eight street. I ordered one brigade to go down Liberty street. General Pearson then told me to go down the railroad, which I did, dragging the Gatling guns. We arrived at the crossing near Twenty-eight street, going through rows of men, who were hooting and howling at us. Previous to this, while I was yet in the Union depot, I had been approached by several parties, who wanted to know if I would fire on poor workingmen. I didn't give any decided answer, not desiring any conversation with them. I called the brigade companies and several of the regimental companies together, and told them no matter what was done to us—even if they spit in our faces—I didn't want a shot fired, but if they attempted any personal violence, we had the right to defend ourselves, and we should do it. That was the order from which the firing commenced. We got down near to the Twenty-eight street crossing. There was a large concourse of people there, far back as you could see, back on the railroad, and we were stopped. Sheriff Fife and his posse were ahead of us, and I believe he attempted to read the riot act, at least I heard him saying something; but he disappeared, and I didn't see any more of him or his deputies. General Pearson was with us. We could not force our way through without using some force, and I asked General Pearson whether he had any instructions to give. He hesitated a moment, and then said that the tracks must be cleared. The crowd then had pressed in between the column of fours, and I ordered the fours put into lines backward, and face the rear rank, about to push the crowd back from either side, and from a hollow-square.

By Senator Yutzy:

Q. How did you march?

A. The right in front—the First regiment was in front. The crowd gave back. We had a little difficulty in getting them back to the line of the cars. Quite a number of cars were there—the Twenty-eighth street crossing was blocked. The men standing there had evidently made up their minds to stay, saying that the railroad company had nothing to do with it, that they were not occupying anything but public ground. I then ordered two small companies, but finding them insufficient, I ordered up another command with arms aport, and attempted to push the crowd back but finding it impossible, I gave orders to charge bayonets, which they did, and I saw one or two men bayoneted. The crowd at that time commenced firing on us, not only stones but pistol balls, and the men, acting on the orders already given to defend themselves, commenced firing—firing a few shots at first, which gradually went along the whole line. At that time, I had not over three hundred men. The second brigade had been left back, to guard the yard where the engines were to start from. . . .

The firing lasted about a minute—not over that, and the crowd, the moment the firing commenced, or shortly afterwards, dispersed and went in every direction. I gave the order to cease firing, and my staff officers had the firing stopped, and the ranks, which were somewhat broken, were reformed, and I sent a staff officer to report to General Pearson. I thought he was on the ground, because it was not certainly—my opinion is, that in three minutes after he gave me the order to clear the tracks, the firing commenced. In the meantime, the Pittsburgh troops on the hill—I had not discovered them before—quite a number of them threw down their arms and left. I went up the hill a very short distance, and I saw what was going on there, and I hunted for General Pearson; finally, I received a note from him, saying he was at Mr. Pitcairn's office at the outer depot, and, that if I wished to communicate with him, to send a staff officer, which I did—Colonel Wilson—and he came back and said that General Pearson desired to see me. I turned the command over to General Matthews, and reported to General Pearson at the office of the Pennsylvania railroad at the outer depot—Mr. Pitcairn's office. I said to General

Pearson at the time, that I thought we ought to continue to drive the crowd. I understood that they had gone to the arsenal. Several men came up to me and said that the crowd had gone to the United States arsenal to arm themselves, and I thought, when I found that they had gone away, that they would probably get arms and ammunition, and I proposed to General Pearson that we should follow the crowd. He hesitated some time about it, and finally I grew more imperative in my question, and I said, you must do something, I cannot allow my men to stand on the track with the crowd pushing around me, and not be allowed to fire. We will either have to move from there or attack the crowd. Finally, he said that the Second brigade had been moved into the round-house and machine shops, because he was afraid that they would be burned, and then he told me to move my whole force in, amounting to six hundred men, which I did just at dusk in the evening. We moved in there . . . [Continuing on the siege] About two o'clock in the morning Colonel Snowden, of the Third regiment, called into the round-house, and directed my attention to what he considered a piece of artillery. It was quite dark at the time. We watched it for probably fifteen minutes, when a cloud cleared away, and we decided it was a piece of artillery, around which were quite a number of men who were training the piece. I immediately ordered Colonel Snowden to get fifty men out, and told him to lower their pieces and fire low, and I gave the order. They had got the piece finally into a position to suit themselves, and a man had hold of the lanyard. I gave the order to fire, and when the smoke cleared away eleven of them were lying there.

By Mr. Lindsey:

Q. The mob had it?

A. Yes; it was a brass field-piece that they had captured from Hutchinson's battery, I believe. During the whole night we had a skirmish with those people. They ran cars down loaded with oil, and attempted to set fire to the building, but fortunately some jumped the track and blocked the others. The next morning they ran down cars from the Allegheny side, which came down with their own gravity, but we finally threw a pile of car wheels on the track, and upset the cars. They were burning. They were loaded with whisky, or the most of them with high wines. We put out those fires by fire extinguishers, and also by a hose that we had there. We finally discovered that the building part of the Sixth division was on fire, and it communicated with the building we were in by the oil sheds. They got on fire, and the building we were in got on fire. During the night I had communication with General Latta, finding General Pearson did not return, and told him my situation, and received orders from him—or suggestions they were afterwards styled—in the first place to hold on vigorously, but in case I was obliged to leave there, to go out Penn avenue east towards Torrens station, and that there would be reinforcements sent to us not later than six o'clock in the morning; that part of the command—

three hundred—who had failed to join, were at Walls station, and would join Colonel Guthrie at Torrens, and that they would join us. We waited until ten minutes of eight o'clock, when the smoke got so great that the men could scarcely breathe, and we went through the machine shops. We couldn't go out of the gate, the regular gate, on account of the cars that had been upset there and were burning, and I went out, I think, Twenty-third street—I am not very familiar with the streets—with the intention not to leave Pittsburgh, but to go to the United States arsenal, where I certainly could get ammunition and possibly something to eat, as we had nothing but a sandwich and a cup of coffee since leaving Philadelphia, and through the excitement and the loss of two nights' sleep, the men were very much fatigued and thoroughly worn out. We went out towards the arsenal, and probably had gone a quarter of a mile out Penn avenue, when we were attacked. I was at the head of the column, and didn't see the force that was attacking us, but I sent a staff officer immediately to the rear. The firing was all at the rear, and I think four men were killed and some ten or twelve wounded.

Q. On your retreat from the round-house?

A. Yes; these men were shot from street cars, and from out of houses, and from behind chimneys. There was not any regular organized body, or a body sufficiently large to attack, until we got nearly to the arsenal, when—the Gatling guns I had placed between the two brigades, so that we could use them either in rear or at the front—when we opened with one of them, and dispersed the mob.

Source: Pennsylvania, General Assembly, Committee Appointed to Investigate the Railroad Riots in July, 1877, *Report of the Committee Appointed to Investigate the Railroad Riots in July, 1877* (Harrisburg: Lane S. Hart, 1878), pp. 907–10.

3.3.   "Military Blunder—Uncalled-for Bloodshed," *Pittsburgh Critic*, July 22, 1877

The vast majority of Pittsburgh newspapers condemned the Pennsylvania Railroad, the governor, or the Philadelphia troops for the tragic shooting and subsequent rioting that began on July 21, 1877. This excerpt is from the Pittsburgh Critic's *editorial, one such typical response.*

Even at the moment of this writing, it is not difficult to perceive that a fearful blunder has been committed by the Governor and his ill-timed military advisers. It is impossible for us to conceive that the action of the railroad strikers, taking the worst view of either side of the case, justified the calling out of the military.

Time should have been allowed for a respectful parley between parties; time for the railroad company to properly consider the grievances complained of in the respectful petition of the strikers, and time for the railroad employés to act in response. There is tyranny in this country worse than anything ever known in Russia, and it is time we should get at the gist of it.

Strikes are common occurrences, but it appears that it is only when the "great monopoly," the hated company, which discriminates against the interests of Pittsburgh and western Pennsylvania, is subjected to one of these strikes, that the military are ordered out, and that, too, without a moment's consideration, as though the Pennsylvania railroad was more important than the peace and order and the lives of half the citizens of this State.

There is no use disguising the matter. The people of this city sympathize with the strikers. They are incensed beyond measure, with the cold, corrupt legislation which has fostered the colder and more corrupt organization known as the Pennsylvania Railroad Company. But we cannot disguise the legal technicalities which appear to brace up that company as against the people. All that we say and care to know is, that a fearful blunder was made by the constituted authorities, who from the Governor down to General Pearson and Sheriff Fife, appeared to be only the willing tools of the giant oppressor. . . .

The laboring class cannot, will not stand this longer. The war cry has been raised, and has gone far and wide. It will not confine itself to the narrow, nor even long stretch of the railroads. Labor will assert itself. It must have its equality, and that it will, sooner or later, amicably, it is desirable, forcibly, if necessary. Certainly rebellion against lawful authority is never lawful, but the principle that freed our nation from tyranny will free labor from domestic aggression.

Source: "Military Blunder—Uncalled for Bloodshed," *Pittsburgh Critic*, July 22, 1877, in Pennsylvania, *Report of Committee*, pp. 817–19.

3.4.   "Rampant Hoodlums," *San Francisco Chronicle*, July 24, 1877

This excerpt from a San Francisco Chronicle *article described how a workers' meeting called to support the strike disintegrated into an anti-Chinese riot on July 23, 1877.*

Last night was a scene of wild excitement through a considerable portion of the city, growing out of the demonstration instituted by the workingmen, ostensibly as an expression of sympathy for the railroad strikers at the East, and acts of violence were perpetrated that were calculated to create a general apprehension of impending rapine and slaughter. How far the workingmen were responsible for the outrages of the night, opinions may vary, but it is fair to state at the outset that the mob that started on its career of riot was instigated by an independent speaker, and was comprised of a class quite distinct from that of the workingmen's meeting proper. The meeting was called by an advertisement which appeared in all the morning papers yesterday, simply intimating that the design was "to express their sympathy and take other action in regard to their fellow-workmen in Pittsburgh and Baltimore." . . .

THE CROWD

Was composed in the main of sober and orderly persons of the laboring class, with a good proportion of citizens attracted by mere curiosity. Its tone was decidedly pacific, and for a time no serious disturbance seemed likely to attend the demonstration. The speakers, who were generally workingmen, while proclaiming sympathy with the Eastern strikers, expressed their disapprobation of mob violence, and their counsels to their fellows to refrain from disorganized action and indiscriminate destruction of property were repeatedly cheered. The tenor of the addresses was in keeping with the spirit of the resolutions given below. Such was the aspect of the demonstration up to about 9 o'clock, when an anti-coolie club with a band of music and displaying a transparency at the head of the column, inscribed "Anti-Coolie Club—Self-Preservation is the First Law of Nature," arrived upon the scene, marching up Market street. . . .

[The meeting passed a series of resolutions that expressed sympathy for the working people who had been killed and for the railroad strikers' human rights. Resolutions blamed the depression on capitalism, blasted the grabbing of public lands by railroad corporations and the money system considered unfair to labor, condemned government corruption in the midst of immense ongoing unemployment, and stated that physical force was sometimes patriotic when other means to secure justice were exhausted. Orators continued to talk.] Some

THREATS

Were made against the railroad magnates, but no names were mentioned. The peaceable character of the speeches made by some of the orators was not suited to part of the crowd, and the speakers were often interrupted by cries of "Tell us how to drive out the Chinamen;" "What do we care for ballots? It's the Chinamen we're after." [Gangs went off from the meeting in search of Chinese people and businesses to attack.]

Source: "Rampant Hoodlums," *San Francisco Chronicle*, July 24, 1877.

3.5.   "Communism Denounced," Henry Ward Beecher's Sermon, *New York Times*, July 30, 1877

The New York Times *covered Henry Ward Beecher's controversial sermons on the railroad strikes. In this excerpt from a sermon delivered at the Plymouth Church in Brooklyn, New York, in late July 1877, the noted preacher blasted unions as un-American and communistic. His Social Darwinist views are often considered representative of those of many wealthy and middle-class Americans at the time.*

We look upon the importation of the communistic and like European notions as abominations. Their notions and theories that the Government should be paternal and take care of the welfare of its subjects and provide them with labor, is un-American. It is the form in which oppression has had its most disastrous scope in the world. The American doctrine is that it is the duty of the Government merely to protect the people while they are taking care of themselves—nothing more than that. "Hands off," we say to the Government, "see to it that we are protected in our rights and our individuality. No more than that." The theories of Europe in regard to the community of property we reject because they are against natural law and will never be practicable. God has intended the great to be great, and the little to be little. No equalization process can ever take place until men are made equal as productive forces. It is a wild vision, not a practicable theory. The European theories of combinations between workmen and trades-unions and communes destroy the individuality of the person, and there is no possible way of preserving the liberty of the people except by the maintenance of individual liberty, intact from Government and intact from individual meddling. Persons have the right to work when or where they please, as long as they please, and for what they please, and any attempt to infringe on this right, and to put good workmen on a level with poor workmen—any such attempt to regiment labor is preposterous.

Source: "Communism Denounced," *New York Times*, July 30, 1877, p. 8.

3.6.   "The Late Riots," *The Nation*, August 2, 1877

The Nation, a popular contemporary journal, bitterly opposed the strikes. In this excerpt from an editorial shortly after the event, it openly expressed the fear that the United States was no

longer unique but producing a new and dangerous permanent
class of wage laborers—a proletariat.

It is impossible to deny that the events of the last fortnight constitute
a great national disgrace, and have created a profound sensation throughout the civilized world. They are likely to impress the foreign imagination far more than the outbreak of the Civil War, because the probability
that the slavery controversy would end in civil war or the disruption of
the Union had been long present to people's minds both at home and
abroad. Slavery, too, was well known to be an accident, and by no means
a natural product of American institutions, and its horrors and inconsis-
tencies did not seriously shake the general confidence in the soundness
and solidity of American polity, strong and numerous as were the attempts made for that purpose. There has for fifty years been throughout
Christendom a growing faith that outside the area of slave-soil the United
States had—of course with the help of great natural resources—solved
the problem of enabling labor and capital to live together in political harmony, and that this was the one country in which there was no proletariat
and no dangerous class, and in which the manners as well as legislation
effectually prevented the formation of one. That the occurrences of the
last fortnight will do, and have done, much to shake or destroy this faith,
and that whatever weakens it weakens also the fondly-cherished hopes
of many millions about the future of the race, there is unhappily little
question. We have had what appears a widespread rising, not against political oppression or unpopular government, but against society itself.
What is most curious about it is that it has probably taken people here
nearly as much by surprise as people in Europe.

Source: "The Late Riots," *The Nation*, August 2, 1877, p. 68.

3.7.   **"The Era of Common Sense,"** *National Labor*
          Tribune, **August 11, 1877**

In this optimistic editorial, the moderate National Labor Tribune, *based in Pittsburgh, expressed its opinion that the recent
strike had served as a wake-up call for capitalists, writers, and others. Working people and the Republic would be the beneficiaries
if a new "era of common sense" in labor relations prevailed.*

The strike appears to have brought about an Era of Common Sense.
The relations of capital and labor are now engaging the attention of the
leading journals of the country, and for the first time in years the *status*

of the workmen, the position of corporate and individual capital toward him, is being discussed with not only fairness, but with what seems to be an honest effort to get to the bottom of the differences, and the application of remedies that shall be found efficient. This is certainly a point gained which fully compensates for all losses by the strike. It tends toward a recognition of the rights of labor, and consequently to the endurance of our republican form of government; for no republic can hope to survive the classification of its inhabitants into labor and a monied aristocracy. Heretofore there has been too glaring injustice antagonizing capital and labor, and this culminated in desperation and general striking throughout the country. It is admitted by the better class of writers on the subject, who have been led to investigate by the sad events referred to, that labor has been wronged to a much greater extent than has capital. This is a confession that might have been looked for in vain a month ago. The strike set these political economists thinking; it was of such a character as was calculated to excite attention, and the causes underlying could not be ignored—hence we anticipate much lasting good from this dawn of the Era of Common Sense. An excellent feature of it is that these gentlemen seem to be more practical in their views than the ordinary run of writers who have been on the side of capital. They acknowledge there have been great wrongs perpetrated on labor, that the situation is so serious that these wrongs must be hunted out and the remedies applied without unnecessary delay, and that so far as they have examined, the working classes are not such unreasonable folk as they had been led to believe.

Source: "The Era of Common Sense," National Labor Tribune, August 11, 1877, p. 1.

3.8.   Final Report of the Committee of the Pennsylvania State Legislature that Investigated the Railroad Strikes and Riots in Pennsylvania, 1878

A committee of the Pennsylvania State Legislature investigated the Pennsylvania strikes. As this excerpt from the conclusion of its contradictory report indicates, it took special care to refute the notion that the strikes were an insurrection, blamed the riots on tramps and vagrants instead of the railroad workers or the unemployed, and sought to reassure a shocked public that such massive strikes and violence were an aberration in the United States.

The causes which led to the riots are, in the opinion of your committee, as follows, to wit: The riots grew out of the strike of the railroad men, and the strikers themselves were the protest of the laborer against the system by which his wages were arbitrarily fixed and lowered by his employer without consultation with him, and without his consent. There are many other causes that combined to bring about the strikes, but the cause mentioned underlies the whole question, and it is the foundation of all the trouble.

Instead of capital and labor working together in harmony, as their community of interests would dictate, a conflict has been growing up between them, which, if not averted or discontinued, will lead to more serious troubles than any that have yet occurred. . . .

. . . The railroad riots of 1877, have by some been called an insurrection, for the reason that strikes occurred at nearly the same time on several of the main trunk lines of the country, that several Governors of States issued proclamations warning the rioters to disperse, &c., some of them calling on the President of the United States for troops to assist the civil authorities in dispersing the mobs and enforcing the law, and the large number of men engaged in these troubles in the different parts of the county [sic country]. Insurrection is defined to be "a rising against civil or political authority; the open and active opposition of a number of persons to the execution of law in a city or State; a rebellion; a revolt."

The railroad riots in Pennsylvania were not a rising against civil or political authority; in their origin were not intended by their movers as an open and active opposition to the execution of the law. Most of the riots were the result of the strikes by a portion of the railroad men, the strikes being intended to bring the railroad officers to a compromise with the strikers, of the differences between them. In some places the men merely proposed to quit work, and not interfere with the running of trains by any men the railroad authorities could get; in other places they would not allow other men to work in their places, nor railroad officials to send out freight trains, if in their power to prevent. It was in no case an uprising against the law as such, but a combination of men to assert an illegal right as between them and the railroad company. There was no organized movement throughout the country, no pre-arranged plan of the trainmen to prevent the running of freight trains by violence or combination, understanding or agreement between the men on any one railroad and the men on another. Each strike was independent of those on other roads, each having a local cause particularly its own. As before stated, there was a sort of an epidemic of strikes running through the laboring classes of the country, more particularly those in the employ of large corporations, caused by the great depression of business, which followed the panic of 1873, by means whereof many men were thrown out of work, and the wages of those who could get work were reduced to correspond with the reduction in the prices of all commodities and the reduced amount of business to be done. Each strike, except at Reading, although commenced originally by men then at work for a railroad or some other corporation, to carry out their own purposes, was soon joined by all the idlers and vagabonds in the vicinity, and these being by far the largest in number, soon took the movement out of the hands of the originators and carried it clear beyond anything they ever anticipated. The vagabonds having no object but plunder, and having no particular interest in anything else, were ready to resort to violent measures to accomplish their object.

Source: Pennsylvania, *Report of the Committee*, pp. 37, 46.

SELECTED ANNOTATED BIBLIOGRAPHY

Books

Brecher, Jeremy. *Strike!* Rev. ed. Cambridge, MA: South End Press, 1997. An important work on U.S. strikes that situates the 1877 railroad strikes and other labor conflicts in broad perspective.

Bruce, Robert V. *1877: Year of Violence.* Indianapolis: Bobbs-Merrill Company, 1959. An essential, pioneering, well-researched historical work that stands out today for its interesting, comprehensive narratives of the strikes.

Burbank, David Thayer. *Reign of the Rabble: The St. Louis General Strike of 1977.* New York: Augustus M. Kelley, 1966. A standard book-length treatment of events in St. Louis.

Chandler, Alfred D., Jr., ed. *The Railroads: The Nation's First Big Business; Sources and Readings.* New York: Harcourt, Brace & World, 1965. Contains excellent documents pertaining to the many issues surrounding railroad development in the United States.

Commons, John R. et al. *History of Labour in the United States.* Introduction by Henry W. Farnam. 4 vols. New York: Macmillan Company, 1918–1935. See volume 2, pp. 185–91, for a classic treatment of the strikes by an important labor economist and historian.

Cross, Ira B. *A History of the Labor Movement in California.* Berkeley: University of California Press, 1935. Contains valuable information on strike events in San Francisco and on labor's role in the anti-Chinese movement in California.

Dacus, J[oseph] A. *Annals of the Great Strikes in the United States.* c. 1877. Reprint, New York: Burt Franklin, 1969. A detailed contemporary narrative of the strikes by a St. Louis journalist.

Eggert, Gerald G. *Railroad Labor Disputes: The Beginnings of Federal Strike Policy.* Ann Arbor: University of Michigan Press, 1967. An important work that focuses on the role of the federal government in the railroad strikes from 1877 to 1894, and on the formulation of a federal strike policy.

Filippelli, Ronald L., ed. *Labor Conflict in the United States: An Encyclopedia.* New York: Garland Publishing, 1990. See especially Gerald G. Eggert's excellent brief overview, "Railroad Strikes of 1877," pp. 441–46.

Foner, Philip S. *The Great Labor Uprising of 1877.* New York: Monad Press, 1977. An important supplement to Bruce, with additional information and insights, especially on the role of the Workingmen's Party of the United States.

Gutman, Herbert G. *Work, Culture, and Society in Industrializing America: Essays in American Working-Class and Social History*. New York: Vintage Books, 1976. This valuable collection of essays by a noted labor historian includes a pathbreaking article, "Trouble on the Railroads in 1873–74: Prelude to the 1877 Crisis?" pp. 295–320.

Licht, Walter. *Industrializing America: The Nineteenth Century*. Baltimore, MD: Johns Hopkins University Press, 1995. A broad synthesis of American industrial development in the nineteenth century.

———. *Working for the Railroad: The Organization of Work in the Nineteenth Century*. Princeton, NJ: Princeton University Press, 1983. An analysis of how and why the organization of railroad work, corporate bureaucracy, and unionization changed from 1830 to 1877.

Martin, Edward Winslow [James Dabney McCabe]. *The History of the Great Riots*. Philadelphia: National Publishing Company, 1877. Another contemporary account by a prolific southern writer.

Pennsylvania. Adjutant-General's Office. *Annual Report of the Adjutant General of Pennsylvania, Transmitted to the Governor in Pursuance of Law, for the Year 1877*. Harrisburg: Lane S. Hart, 1878. Contains important primary documents related to the Pennsylvania strikes.

Pennsylvania. General Assembly. Committee Appointed to Investigate the Railroad Riots in July, 1877. *Report of the Committee Appointed to Investigate the Railroad Riots in July, 1877*. Harrisburg: Lane S. Hart, 1878. Essential source, with the committee's findings and the testimonies of government officials, railroad officers, and others, but readers should note that these state documents typically exclude the testimonies and perspectives of the strikers and rioters.

Pinkerton, Allan. *Strikers, Communists, Tramps, and Detectives*. 1878. New York: G. W. Carleton & Co. Reprint, New York: Arno Press and The New York Times, 1969. Contemporary account of the strikes, with scathing critiques of unions, strikers, communists, and the Paris Commune, by the founder of a famous private detective agency noted for its strikebreaking and industrial espionage activities.

Richardson, James D. *A Compilation of the Messages and Papers of the Presidents 1789–1897*. 10 vols. Washington, DC: GPO, 1898, 7:447–49. Collection contains President Hayes's strike-related proclamations.

Saxton, Alexander. *The Indispensable Enemy: Labor and the Anti-Chinese Movement in California*. Berkeley: University of California Press, 1971. A readable and useful contribution to the literature on the history of the San Francisco strike and the anti-Chinese movement in California.

Stowell, David O. *Streets, Railroads, and the Great Strike of 1877*. Chicago: University of Chicago Press, 1999. A recent work that examines the strikes in Albany, Buffalo, and Syracuse from the standpoints of urban middle-class residents and the community.

Stromquist, Shelton. *A Generation of Boomers: The Pattern of Railroad Labor Conflict in Nineteenth-Century America*. Urbana: University of Illinois Press, 1987. Brief treatment of the 1877 strikes in this innovative analytical study of labor radicalism and labor relations in the railroad industry from the 1870s to 1894.

Ware, Norman J. *The Labor Movement in the United States 1860–1895: A Study in De-mocracy.* New York: D. Appleton and Company, 1929, pp. 45–50. This study of labor after the Civil War contains a brief but classic account of the strikes.

Yellen, Samuel. *American Labor Struggles.* New York: Harcourt, Brace and Company, 1936. Reprint, New York: Arno and The New York Times, 1969, pp. 3–38. Contains a dated but substantial chapter on the 1877 railroad strikes.

Web Sites

Teachers and researchers will find valuable sources on the B&O strike on the Internet at the Maryland State Archives' Web site—http://www.mdarchives.state.md.us. The Archives' series, *Documents for the Classroom,* offers suggested readings, important primary sources, and classroom exercises on "The Baltimore Railroad Strike & Riot of 1877" at http://www.mdarchives.state.md.us/msa/educ/html/sc2221.html.

Two unions have sites with descriptions of the strikes. For an overview of the broad event, see "The Great Strike of 1877: Remembering a Worker Rebellion" at the United Electrical Workers' site at http://www.ranknfile-ue.org/uen_1877.html. The Pittsburgh strike is the subject of Paul LeBlanc's "The Railroad Strike of 1877," located at the Pittsburgh AFL-CIO's site at http://www.pittsburghaflcio.org/railroad.html.

Video

The American Social History Project's dramatic, well-researched, award-winning documentary, *1877: Grand Army of Starvation* (New York: American Social History Productions, Inc., 1987) is perhaps the best introduction of all to the general subject. Narrated by James Earl Jones, this video is ideal for classroom use because of its 30-minute length. It also comes with a viewer's guide.

4

The Pullman Strike and Boycott of 1894

The Pullman strike of 1894 was a watershed event in the history of U.S. labor relations, primarily because it marked a turning point in the federal government's active involvement in ending strikes that transcended state lines and that it deemed harmful to the public's interest. Although the federal government had taken action and sent troops into previous labor conflicts such as the railroad strikes of 1877, it had done so on limited legal and constitutional grounds, and only at the formal request of the top officials of the states affected. Its actions in 1894 exceeded those limits, established important precedents, and inaugurated a new era in industrial and labor relations. Thereafter, American unions contemplating national strikes could expect to confront the power of the government in new hostile forms, including intervening federal courts, sweeping injunctions, and the use against it of the Sherman Antitrust Act or other reform measures originally enacted to protect organized labor and the public from abusive concentrations of businesses. Trade unions drew many lessons from this important strike, but after it, none could afford to ignore the power of the state and the new role it had undertaken.

It is significant that the Pullman strike took place during a decade that is often considered a critical turning point in the making of modern American society. In many ways, the consolidation of industrial and corporate capitalism in the United States was achieved during this period, but not without protest. By the 1890s, large numbers of Americans realized that permanent social classes and class conflict existed in the United States and that a small portion of the population had accumulated a disproportionate amount of wealth and power. Despite major reforms such as the Interstate Commerce Act in 1887 and the Sherman Antitrust Act in 1890, which declared combinations and trusts that restrained trade or commerce to be illegal, railroads and other giant anti-union business consolidations continued to emerge and to engage in abusive practices. Meanwhile, a conservative U.S. Supreme Court granted corporations protection by extending their rights and redefining them as "persons" instead of inanimate human creations. The critical decade itself was marked by a severe depression that lasted from 1893 to 1898; massive strikes such as those at Homestead and Pullman; a failed Populist political challenge; a nativist upsurge; reactionary Supreme Court decisions such as *Plessy v. Ferguson*, that legalized racial segregation; and U.S. imperial expansion abroad. Social Darwinism was the preeminent ideology of the day. The Pullman strike was a signal event during this important era.

What was often called the Chicago strike began as a local conflict involving the Pullman Palace Car Company, one of the nation's richest and most successful railroad car-building enterprises, and its diverse workers in the company town of Pullman, Illinois, just outside of Chicago. The industrialist George M. Pullman had founded the corporation in 1867 and built the company town in 1880. He had two primary, interrelated goals in mind when he constructed what he considered a model community for workers. The first was to create a profitable business venture; the second was to avert and solve the growing problem of labor unrest. Consequently, the company retained ownership of all the property in the town, and all civic and other authority stemmed paternalistically from the company. To attract skilled mechanics and other workers to the site of the company's main car-building operations and to ensure a happy and contented work force, Pullman provided good-quality housing, attractive streets, beautiful parks, and other facilities. To ward off what he considered unhealthy outside influences, he prohibited unions, taverns, and brothels in the town, and instituted a spying system. Before the strike, the Pullman "experiment" was widely hailed in many quarters as a solution to the nation's "labor problem," and by 1894, Pullman employees were constructing and repairing general railroad cars in addition to making the luxurious Pullman sleeping and dining cars that were then running on three-quarters of the country's railroads.

The Pullman Palace Car Company was one of the great capitalist success stories of the age, and it was in an excellent financial condition to withstand the 1893 depression. Its stock had grown in value from an initial $1 million in 1867 to $36 million in 1894. It had accumulated an additional surplus of $25 million in profits, and, throughout its history, it paid its stockholders annual dividends of at least 8 percent, a rate it continued to pay during the depression years of 1893 and 1894. Moreover, until 1894, the press and the general public often uncritically accepted Pullman's notions of paternalism and the assessment of his company town as a model town.

This presumed capitalist workers' paradise exploded on May 11, 1894, when the diverse Pullman Palace Car Company workers in Pullman, Illinois, went out on strike. The immediate cause was the arbitrary discharge, on the alleged grounds of slack business, of two members of a grievance committee that had met with George Pullman, the company's president, and Thomas Wickes, the company's second vice president, on May 9. According to the workers, Pullman and Wickes had reneged on an explicit promise not to retaliate against committee members.

The strikers were also protesting broader issues, including the company's latest wage reduction, high noncompetitive rents in the company town, and autocratic working and living conditions. During the 1893 depression, the company had laid off one-third of its 5,500 employees and reduced wages five times in a grossly uneven manner, totaling an average loss of 25 percent. At the same time, it made no corresponding reduction in its rents or prices at company stores, which became a major issue of the strike. From the outset, Pullman's well-built town residences and stores were designed to be profit-making enterprises, and they were. For legal and tax advantages, a separate company, the Pullman Land Association, managed these affairs, but the stockholders in the land company were the same as those in the car company.

The United States Strike Commission, a federal investigating committee appointed by President Grover Cleveland to investigate the strike after it was over, found that it cost workers 20 to 25 percent more to live in Pullman company housing than it did for them to live in similar accommodations in nearby Chicago neighborhoods. It also criticized company leases because of a clause that made tenants legally responsible for any and all repairs. The company's claim that Pullman workers were free to live anywhere also proved to be fallacious. Workers felt pressured to live in company housing, whenever it was available, because the corporation routinely hired or retained those who did over those who did not. Only a minority of highly skilled workers—those who were irreplaceable—could afford to live elsewhere.

"We are born in a Pullman house, fed from the Pullman shop, taught in the Pullman school, catechized in a Pullman church, and when we die we shall be buried in the Pullman cemetery and go to the Pullman hell,"[1] complained a striker. In fact, the Pullman corporation did own and control everything in the company town, where unions, free speech, and alcohol were prohibited. It had successfully suppressed all past strikes and labor initiatives. But, before the 1894 strike, in March and April, disgruntled Pullman workers defied their bosses and secretly joined the American Railway Union (ARU), a fledgling industrial railroad union that had just won an unprecedented victory in a major strike against the Great

Northern Railroad. Railroad workers had founded the ARU in 1893 to transcend the limits of the four existing internecine-warring, conservative railroad brotherhoods that represented skilled craftsmen in the industry. By joining the more inclusive ARU, the Pullman workers were looking for help and signifying their rejection of dependence, company paternalism, and capitalist notions of supply and demand. By striking and voicing a desire for greater control over their lives, they were asserting their rights to independent American citizenship.

About 90 percent of the company's workers went out on strike on May 11, but Pullman and his officials refused to negotiate with them. In testimony before the U.S. Strike Commission after the strike was over, George Pullman and Thomas Wickes explained their reasoning by offering a classic defense of laissez-faire capitalism. Both men justified the company's last wage cut before the strike—and all previous ones—as necessary to cut costs so that it would be in a better position to compete for car contracts. For them, the number of existing jobs, and the level of wage rates, were a simple matter of the law of supply and demand, a law that working people had to accept as given. In their view, the development of gigantic corporate concentrations did not change such laws or suggest that the company change its policy of dealing only with individuals, not unions. Thus, despite the depression, the company owed its workers—even its long-term ones—nothing, not even a reduction in its rents. Moreover, because property and property rights were sacred and shareholders owned the company, workers had no legitimate claims to a share of its wealth. Both men were adamant that, as a matter of principle, it was unthinkable to consider arbitration by any third party because only they had the right to manage their business. Significantly, Pullman added, he and his officials were the only proper people—not labor, government, or any third parties—to speak for the general interest, the public's interest.

The local conflict expanded into a national one only after desperate Pullman strikers, members of the American Railway Union, formally appealed to the young labor union for support. On June 12, the ARU opened its first annual convention in Chicago, and on June 15, the Pullman strikers eloquently presented their case to the delegates. The ARU's dilemma was grave. Eugene Debs, the union's president, and ARU members felt a deep moral commitment to the Pullman workers, but how could the conscience-stricken union help these workers without engaging in another battle against a powerful corporation, a battle that would jeopardize the ARU's precarious existence? At the time, the promising industrial union had only 150,000 members across the country, and it lacked the money and other resources necessary to support a major strike.

It was a dilemma that ultimately proved unresolvable. In response to the strikers' appeal, the ARU quickly endorsed a relief measure, and members began to consider a sympathetic boycott, which Debs opposed.

Instead, he sought and won the convention's approval to appoint a committee to visit Pullman and propose arbitration, the settling of the dispute, based on the facts and the merits of the case, by a neutral third party. But after the industrialist rejected arbitration, the ARU body voted, unanimously, for a national boycott of Pullman cars, to begin on June 26, unless the strike was resolved by then. Arbitration efforts again failed, and the die was cast. The ARU did launch an effective boycott on June 26. Debs, who fully appreciated the dangers his organization faced, strongly cautioned the union's members to avoid violence and to allow railroad cars other than Pullman cars to move. As the boycott spread to other states and railroads, press reports were often hysterical and highly inaccurate.

In the meantime, Pullman met with the General Managers' Association, a wealthy anti-union conglomerate of twenty-four railroad corporations centered in Chicago. The General Managers then took charge of a larger corporate movement to crush the strike and boycott. It quickly hired 2,500 strikebreakers, organized press relations, and made plans to involve the federal government on its side. On June 30, it wired Richard B. Olney, Attorney General of the United States and a noted railroad corporation attorney, to ask him to appoint Edwin Walker as a special federal lawyer to take charge of a legal effort to end the boycott. Olney did so while stressing that it was essential to use overwhelming force, especially in Chicago, the ARU's center, and to bypass leading Chicago and State of Illinois officials because they were considered sympathetic to organized labor.

On July 2, Walker went into Federal District Court in Chicago and got a historic sweeping injunction against the union from a sympathetic judge on the grounds that the boycott was impeding interstate commerce and the passage of the U.S. mails. To make that charge more creditable, the Association had ordered its railroads to attach mail cars to Pullman cars. It also ordered the firing of all workers who refused to handle Pullman cars. The request for the injunction was loosely based on the Sherman Antitrust Act (1890), which had prohibited "combinations or conspiracies" in restraint of trade but had never been applied to corporations. Then, on July 3, Walker and a federal judge wired Olney to urge President Cleveland to send federal troops. Despite the vigorous protest of John P. Altgeld, the bypassed governor of Illinois, who maintained that the boycott had been peaceful until then, federal troops were placed on strike duty in Chicago on July 4. As the exchanges between Altgeld and Cleveland indicated, this was an unprecedented federal action that raised serious constitutional, political, and moral issues about the respective rights and powers of federal versus state authorities. Upon the arrival of the troops, violence ensued.

In his testimony before the U.S. Strike Commission in August, Debs held the federal courts—not the troops or anyone else—responsible for the boycott's failure, and he blasted the sweeping injunction of July 2 that sealed its fate. Indeed, it had presented the ARU with a cruel dilemma. If the union leaders obeyed it, they could not do anything whatsoever to manage the strike anywhere in the country. And if they disobeyed it, they would face the full thrust of a hostile federal government. In all conscience, they could not obey it, and on July 10, Debs and three ARU officers were arrested, and jailed briefly, for conspiracy to obstruct the mails. Labor leaders began to denounce "government by injunction."

It was in this context that talk in labor circles turned to the notion of a general strike, talk that forced Samuel Gompers, president of the American Federation of Labor (AFL), to come to Chicago for a meeting with the organization's executive committee on July 12. The four railroad brotherhoods, members of the AFL, had denounced the ARU, but there were other AFL members who supported it. It was clear that the strike would collapse without additional support. After some discussion, the AFL committee, which sympathized with the strikers but did not want to oppose the federal government, formally rejected the proposal to take part in a sympathetic general strike. It ordered its members to refrain from striking, or to return to work, if they were already out on strike.

On July 17, Debs and the other officers were again arrested for violating the original injunction. With them incarcerated, on July 18, the Pullman company posted signs announcing it was hiring and reopening its operations. The strike was over. Henceforth, as a condition of employment, Pullman workers had to sign a pledge promising they would not join any unions. Governor Altgeld led a public relief effort for a thousand destitute former Pullman employees.

To set an example, prosecutors then brought Debs and three ARU officers to trial on conspiracy charges in January 1895, but when the case against the ARU men did not go well and a juror pleaded illness, the judge discharged the jury, and the case was not taken up again. Debs subsequently served a six-month jail sentence for contempt, for having violated the July 2 injunction. This famous case went all the way to the U.S. Supreme Court, which virtually ignored the Sherman Antitrust Act. In *In re Debs*, it ruled that the equity powers held by federal courts gave the courts the right to issue sweeping injunctions against labor—not against business—during strikes to prevent interference with interstate commerce or the U.S. mails. This ruling, partial to the railroad corporations, would thwart organized labor for decades, despite labor's success in 1914 in getting congressional passage of the Clayton Antitrust Act to limit the use of the injunction against labor under the Sherman Antitrust Act. In a series of legal cases during and after World War I, the U.S. Supreme Court upheld loopholes in the Clayton Antitrust Act that allowed the courts to return to issuing massive numbers of injunctions against labor throughout the 1920s.

The Pullman boycott resulted in the demise of the ARU, but, ironically, also in the demise of Pullman as a company town. In 1898 the Illinois Supreme Court ruled that the company had violated its original charter and that company towns were not good public policy or compatible with democratic American institutions. In an era when coal and steel corporations were founding hundreds of similar autocratic company towns in Pennsylvania and West Virginia, the Illinois court ordered the company to sell off all its nonmanufacturing properties and enterprises.

The Pullman strike and boycott crystallized a number of labor relations issues that had come into being during the Gilded Age. Throughout, the U.S. government had acted as an ally of the railroad corporations. It had made no effort whatsoever to induce Pullman to settle the strike. Federal intervention in railroad or other national strikes, the use of federal injunctions against labor, and the application of antitrust laws to labor unions emerged as important lasting legal measures from this event. But the strike also brought company towns, paternalistic capitalism, industrial unionism, and conflicts between the state and federal governments to the public's attention. Afterwards, the U.S. Strike Commission recommended a permanent U.S. Strike Commission to resolve railroad disputes, arbitration, greater legal rights for labor, and more public control over corporations. Some middle-class and progressive reformers agreed. Nevertheless, the Pullman strike and the ARU's demise dealt a severe long-term blow to the rights of labor and industrial unionism. Despite a few exceptions, a general movement toward industrial unionism was aborted and not revived until the 1930s. No national railroad strike occurred again until 1922.

The strike and boycott had two other important, somewhat contradictory, results for labor. First, the workers' loss—and the marginalization or demise of alternative labor organizations such as the Knights of Labor and reform movements that challenged class relations, capitalism, and the state in the 1890s—paved the way for the craft-based, more conservative American Federation of Labor (AFL) to emerge as the nation's leading labor organization. The AFL, the first prominent American labor body to accept capitalism and wage-labor status openly, concentrated, almost exclusively, on winning specific gains for its skilled and segregated members. The second related result of the strike was equally significant. The Pullman experience led to the radicalization of Eugene Debs, once a conservative craft unionist. While serving his sentence for contempt in a Woodstock, Illinois, jail, the future founder and preeminent leader of the Socialist Party of America read radical literature for the first time.

NOTE

1. Quoted in Ray Ginger, *Eugene V. Debs: The Making of an American Radical* (c. 1949; reprint, New York: Collier Books, 1962), p. 125.

DOCUMENTS

4.1. Appeal of the Pullman Strikers to the American Railway Union Convention, June 15, 1894

> *On June 15, 1894, the ARU convention, assembled in Chicago, heard the eloquent plea of despairing Pullman strikers, who were without hope and seeking help. This excerpt from their statement outlines the immediate and longer-term grievances that led to the strike in May.*

Mr. President and Brothers of the American Railway Union: We struck at Pullman because we were without hope. We joined the American Railway Union because it gave us a glimmer of hope. Twenty thousand souls, men, women, and little ones, have their eyes turned toward this convention today, straining eagerly through dark despondency for a glimmer of the heaven-sent message you alone can give us on this earth.

In stating to this body our grievances it is hard to tell where to begin. You all must know that the proximate cause of our strike was the discharge of two members of our grievance committee the day after, George M. Pullman, himself, and Thomas H. Wickes, his second vice-president, had guaranteed them absolute immunity. The more remote causes are still imminent. Five reductions in wages, in work, and in conditions of employment swept through the shops at Pullman between May and December, 1893. The last was the most severe, amounting to nearly 30 per cent, and our rents had not fallen. We owed Pullman $70,000 when we struck May 11. We owe him twice as much today. He does not evict us for two reasons: One, the force of popular sentiment and public opinion; the other because he hopes to starve us out, to break through in the back of the American Railway Union, and to deduct from our miserable wages when we are forced to return to him the last dollar we owe him for the occupancy of his houses.

Rents all over the city in every quarter of its vast extent have fallen, in some cases to one-half. Residences, compared with which ours are hovels, can be had a few miles away at the prices we have been contributing to make a millionaire a billionaire. What we pay $15 for in Pullman is leased for $8 in Roseland; and remember that just as no man or woman of our 4,000 toilers has ever felt the friendly pressure of George M. Pullman's hand, so no man or woman of us all has ever owned or can ever hope to own one inch of George M. Pullman's land. Why, even the very streets are his. His ground has never been platted of record, and today he may debar any man who has acquiring rights as his tenant from walking in his highways. And those streets; do you know what he has named them? He says after the four great inventors in methods of transportation. And do you know what their names are? Why, Fulton, Stephenson, Watt, and Pullman.

Water which Pullman buys from the city at 8 cents a thousand gallons he retails to us at 500 per cent advance and claims he is losing $400 a month on it. Gas which sells at 75 cents per thousand feet in Hyde Park, just north of us, he sells for $2.25. When we went to tell him our grievances he said we were all his "children."

Pullman, both the man and the town, is an ulcer on the body politic. He owns the houses, the schoolhouses, and churches of God in the town he gave his once humble name. The revenue he derives from these, the wages he pays out with one hand—the Pullman Palace Car Company, he takes back with the other—the Pullman Land Association. He is able by this to bid under any contract car shop in this country. His competitors in business, to meet this, must reduce the wages of their men. This gives him the excuse to reduce ours to conform to the market. His business rivals must in turn scale down; so must he. And thus the merry war—the dance of skeletons bathed in human tears—goes on, and it will go on, brothers, forever, unless you, the American Railway Union, stop it; end it; crush it out.

Source: U.S. Strike Commission, *Report on the Chicago Strike of June–July 1894* (Washington, DC: GPO, 1895), pp. 87–88.

4.2.   On Rents, The U.S. Strike Commission, *Report on the Chicago Strike of June–July 1894*, 1895

The Pullman strikers considered rents to be a major issue as well as wages. The company's refusal to reduce its noncompetitively high rents even though it had repeatedly cut wages during the depression seemed particularly unjust. In this excerpt from its investigation, the U.S. Strike Commission confirmed most of the workers' claims about the company's policy on rents. This excerpt does not include the commission's footnotes that appear in the original.

If we exclude the aesthetic and sanitary features at Pullman, the rents there are from 20 to 25 per cent higher than rents in Chicago or surrounding towns for similar accommodations. The aesthetic features are admired by visitors, but have little money value to employees, especially when they lack bread. The company aims to secure 6 per cent upon the cost of its tenements, which cost includes a proportionate share for paving, sewerage, water, parks, etc. It claims now to receive less than 4 per cent. It has some brickmakers' cottages upon which, at $8 per month, it must obtain at least 40 per cent return upon their value. These are, however, exceptional. The company makes all repairs, and heretofore has not compelled tenants to pay for them. Under the printed leases, however, which tenants must sign, they agree to pay for *all repairs* which are either necessary (ordinary wear and damages by the elements *not* excepted) or which the company *chooses* to make.

The company's claim that the workmen need not hire its tenements and can live elsewhere if they choose is not entirely tenable. The fear of losing work keeps them in Pullman as long as there are tenements unoccupied, because the company is supposed, as a matter of business, to give a preference to its tenants when work is slack. The employees, believing that a tenant at Pullman has this advantage, naturally feel some compulsion to rent at Pullman, and thus to stand well with the management. Exceptional and necessary expert workmen do not share this feeling to the same extent and are more free to hire or own homes elsewhere. While reducing wages the company made no reduction in rents. Its position is that the two matters are distinct, and that none of the reasons urged as justifying wage reduction by it as an employer can be considered by the company as a landlord.

The company claims that it is simply legitimate business to use its position and resources to hire in the labor market as cheaply as possible and at the same time to keep rents up regardless of what wages are paid to its tenants or what similar tenements rent for elsewhere; to avail itself to the full extent of business depression and competition in reducing wages, and to disregard these same conditions as to rents. No valid reason is assigned for this position except simply that the company had the power and the legal right to do it.

Prior to the so-called "truck" law in Illinois, rent was deducted from the wages. Since then a check is given for the amount of the rent and another for the balance due for wages. There is nothing to prevent the payee of the check from cashing it outside of the bank, but as the bank is rent collector it presses for the rent and is aided in collecting it by knowledge on the part of the tenant that by arrears he may lose his job. At the time of the strike about $70,000 of unpaid rents had accumulated. It is fair to say that this accumulation of unpaid rent was due to leniency on the part of the company toward those who could not pay the rent and support their families. Neither have any actual evictions taken place. The company has held these matters in abeyance pending wage reductions and strike difficulties.

Source: U.S. Strike Commission, *Report on the Chicago Strike of June–July 1894* (Washington, DC: GPO, 1895), pp. xxxv–xxxvi.

4.3. Testimony of Thomas H. Wickes before the U.S. Strike Commission, August 27, 1894

> *During his testimony before the U.S. Strike Commission in August 1894, Thomas H. Wickes, the second vice president of the Pullman Palace Car Company, defended classic laissez-faire capitalism. In this response to questions posed by Commissioner John D. Kernan, he described the company's intransigent hostility toward labor unions despite the depression and corporate consolidations.*

222 (Commissioner KERNAN). Has the company had any policy with reference to labor unions among its help?—Ans[wer]. No; we have never objected to unions except in one instance. I presume that there are quite a number of unions in our shops now.

223 (Commissioner KERNAN). What are they?—Ans. I couldn't tell you, but I have heard of some of them. I suppose the cabinetmakers have a union, and I suppose the car builders have a union, and the carvers and the painters and other classes of men. We do not inquire into that at all.

224 (Commissioner KERNAN). That is, unions among themselves in the works?—Ans. Members of the craft, belonging to other unions; that is, the cabinet union might have its headquarters in Chicago and our men would be members of it; but we did not object to anything of that kind.

225 (Commissioner KERNAN). The only objection you ever made was to the American Railway Union, wasn't it?—Ans. Yes, sir.

226 (Commissioner KERNAN). What is the basis of your objection to that union?—Ans. Our objection to that was that we would not treat with our men as members of the American Railway Union, and we would not treat with them as members of any union. We treat with them as individuals and as men.

227 (Commissioner KERNAN). That is, each man as an individual, do you mean that?—Ans. Yes, sir.

228 (Commissioner KERNAN). Don't you think, Mr. Wickes, that would give the corporation a very great advantage over those men if it could take them up one at a time and discuss the question with him. With the ability that you have got, for instance, where do you think the man would stand in such a discussion?—Ans. The man has got probably more ability than I have.

229 (Commissioner KERNAN). You think that it would be fair to your men for each one of them to come before you and take up the question of his grievances and attempt to maintain his end of the discussion, do you?—Ans. I think so; yes. If he is not able to do that that is his misfortune.

230 (Commissioner KERNAN). Don't you think that the fact that you represent a vast concentration of capital, and are selected for that because of your ability to represent it, entitles him if he pleases to unite with all of the men of his craft and select the ablest one they have got to represent the cause?—Ans. As a union?

231 (Commissioner KERNAN). As a union.—Ans. They have the right; yes, sir. We have the right to say whether we will receive them or not.

232 (Commissioner KERNAN). Do you think you have any right to refuse to recognize that right in treating with the men?—Ans. Yes, sir; if we chose to.

233 (Commissioner KERNAN). If you chose to. Is it your policy to do that?—Ans. Yes, sir.

Source: U.S. Strike Commission, *Report on the Chicago Strike of June–July 1894* (Washington, DC: GPO, 1895), pp. 621–22.

4.4.   Testimony of George M. Pullman before the U.S. Strike Commission, August 27, 1894

In this excerpt from his testimony before the U.S. Strike Commission, George M. Pullman was questioned extensively about his views on arbitration and wages. The industrialist's responses—on who should share and not share in the company's wealth, on labor's inevitable subjugation to the capitalist law of supply and demand, and on how business alone had the right to speak for the public's interest—were opinions widely shared by his class.

199 (Commissioner [Nicholas E.] WORTHINGTON). Did you, as president of the company, ever express to any parties your willingness or unwillingness to submit these matters to arbitration?—Ans[wer]. I expressed my unwillingness to submit these matters to arbitration. . . .

210 (Commissioner WORTHINGTON). I wanted to know what you had in mind at the time you made this statement that "it was very clear that no prudent man could submit to arbitration in this matter" when you were referring to your daily losses as a reason why any prudent man could not submit to arbitration?—Ans. The amount of the losses would

not cut any figure; it was the principle involved, not the amount that would affect my views as to arbitration.

. . . It was the principle that that should not be submitted to a third party. That was a matter that the company should decide for itself.

212 (Commissioner WORTHINGTON). You did not have in view the amount of the losses that the company had already sustained, but you did have in view the principle that if it continued at the wages of 1893 it would lose money?—Ans. Yes, sir; and that we must be the parties to decide whether we were willing to continue the manufacturing business at a loss, instead of being told by some third party. . . .

223 (Commissioner WORTHINGTON). Did the Pullman company during its years of prosperity ever voluntarily increase the wages of any class or of all classes of its employes?—Ans. Not specially on account of prosperous business. It has always paid its employees liberal wages. . . .

224 (Commissioner WORTHINGTON). But it has never increased the wages of its employees voluntarily?—Ans. Certainly it has not increased them any other way.

225 (Commissioner WORTHINGTON). It has never divided any of its profits with them in any shape or form?—Ans. The Pullman company divides its profits with the people who own the property. It would not have a right to take the profits belonging to the people who own that property. . . .

. . . [When Worthington returns to the subject of arbitration, Pullman replies]. Of course there are matters which are proper subjects of arbitration—matters of opinion.

239 (Commissioner WORTHINGTON). What are those matters that are proper subjects for arbitration?—Ans. A matter of opinion would be a proper subject of arbitration, as, for instance, a question of title, or a disagreement on a matter of opinion; what settlement shall be made of a transaction which has come to an end, may be made the subject of arbitration and be put at rest by it; but as to whether a fact that I know to be true is true or not, I could not agree to submit to arbitration. Take the case in hand, the question as to whether the shops at Pullman shall be continuously operated at a loss or not, is one which it was impossible for the company, as a matter of principle, to submit to the opinion of any third party, and as to whether they were running at a loss on contract work in general, as explained to the committee of the men in my interview with them—that was a simple fact that I knew to be true, and which could not be made otherwise by the opinion of any third party.

240 (Commissioner WORTHINGTON). You use the expression, "Impossible to be submitted." Why is it impossible?—Ans. Because it would violate a principle.

241 (Commissioner WORTHINGTON). What principle?—Ans. The principle that a man should have the right to manage his own property.

242 (Commissioner WORTHINGTON). The decision of arbitrators would not be compulsory, would it?—Ans. I still think, having managed the property of the Pullman company for twenty-seven years, that, I am perhaps as well calculated to manage it for the interests of its stockholders and for the interests of the public—for the general interest—as some man who is not interested, who comes in to arbitrate certain points. . . .

244 (Commissioner WORTHINGTON). . . . it would be impossible to submit the question, whether you ought to pay any more wages or not?—Ans. Yes, sir; of course. Suppose an arbitrator had said, "Yes, you are able. Go on and pay these additional wages;" it would only be a question of time, of course, when any concern would be bankrupt under that condition of things, and therefore the principle would be violated in that.

245 (Commissioner WORTHINGTON). Suppose a board of arbitration had examined into the matter and had said: "Yes, we accept your statement that you are losing money on these jobs and that the times are hard, and you are not receiving as much money on car mileage as heretofore; but with a body of workmen who had been with you some time—and a person would imagine it would be a good thing to do that under all the circumstances—you ought to divide with them a little, give them at least enough to make a good living"—wouldn't that have been a fair matter to be considered?—Ans. I think not. How long a time should a man be with a company before he would be entitled to a gift of money? For that is what this would mean. The wage question is settled by the law of supply and demand. We were obliged to reduce wages in order to get these cars—to compete with other people in the same business, that were doing the same thing. . . .

358 (Commissioner [John D.] KERNAN). When this reduction of wages was made was your salary reduced and that of the other officers?—Ans. No, sir.

359 (Commissioner KERNAN). Were the salaries of the superintendents and foremen reduced?—Ans. No, sir.

Source: U.S. Strike Commission, *Report on the Chicago Strike of June–July 1894* (Washington, DC: GPO, 1895), pp. 552–54, 556–57, 567.

4.5.   On The General Managers' Association, The U.S. Strike Commission, *Report on the Chicago Strike of June–July 1894*, 1895

In this excerpt from its report, the U.S. Strike Commission described the important role played by the General Managers' Association in crushing the strike and boycott. A footnote that appeared in the original text has been eliminated.

On June 22 an officer of the Pullman company met the general managers by invitation, and the general managers, among other things, resolved:

That we hereby declare it to be the lawful right and duty of said railway companies to protest against said proposed boycott; to resist the same in the interest of their existing contracts, and for the benefit of the traveling public, and that we will act unitedly to that end.

From June 22 until the practical end of the strike, the General Managers' Association directed and controlled the contest on the part of the railroads, using the combined resources of all the roads to support the contentions and insure the protection of each. On June 26 we find in the proceedings of the association the following statement:

A general discussion of the situation followed. It was suggested that some common plan of action ought to be adopted in case employees refused to do switching of passenger trains with Pullman cars, but were willing to continue all of their other work, and it was the general expression that in case any man refused to do his duty he would be discharged.

Headquarters were established; agencies for hiring men opened; as the men arrived they were cared for and assigned to duty upon the different lines; a bureau was started to furnish information to the press; the lawyers of the different roads were called into conference and combination in legal and criminal proceedings; the general managers met daily to hear reports and to direct proceedings; constant communication was kept up with the civil and military authorities as to the movements and assignments of police, marshals, and troops. Each road did what it could with its operating forces, but all the leadership, direction, and concentration of power, resources, and influence on the part of the railroads were centered in the General Managers' Association. That association stood for each and all of its 24 combined members, and all that they could command, in fighting and crushing the strike.

Source: U.S. Strike Commission, *Report on the Chicago Strike of June–July 1894* (Washington, DC: GPO, 1895), pp. xlii–xliii.

4.6.   Testimony of Eugene V. Debs before the U.S. Strike Commission, August 20, 1894

In this excerpt from his testimony before the U.S. Strike Commission, Eugene V. Debs vividly described the devastating impact of the courts and the injunction on the ARU's boycott.

. . . On the 2d day of July I was served with a very sweeping injunction that restrained me, as president of the union, from sending out any telegram or any letter or issuing any order that would have the effect of inducing or persuading men to withdraw from the service of the company, or that would in any manner whatsoever, according to the language of the injunction, interfere with the operation.

. . . That injunction was served simultaneously, or practically so, by all of the courts embracing or having jurisdiction in the territory in which the trouble existed. From Michigan to California there seemed to be concerted action on the part of the courts in restraining us from exercising any of the functions of our offices. That resulted practically in the demoralization of our ranks. Not only this, but we were organized in a way that this was the center, of course, of operations. It is understood that a strike is war; not necessarily a war of blood and bullets, but a war in the sense that it is a conflict between two contending interests or classes of interests. There is more or less strategy resorted to in war, and this was the center in our operations. Orders were issued from here, questions were answered, and our men were kept in line from here.

At the time I was served with this injunction all of the officers at all of the points at the headquarters or terminals of all of these roads were served with a similar injunction restraining them all from sending any telegrams or from discharging the functions attached to their several offices. Following the issuance of that injunction a few days, I have forgotten the exact date, a special grand jury was convened for the purpose of examining into my conduct as president of the American Railway Union in connection with this trouble. The grand jury was in session very briefly, but found a bill upon an information that was filed, and I was ordered to be arrested. A warrant was issued and placed in the hands of a United States marshal for that purpose. On the 7th day of July, if I am not mistaken, I was arrested and brought before the court, and my bond was fixed, with my three official associates, Mr. Howard, vice-president; Mr. Rodgers, auditor of the Times, and Mr. Keliher, our secretary, we were simultaneously arrested and we were placed under a joint bond of $10,000. Very shortly after this there was an attachment issued for an alleged contempt of court, upon information that I had, as president, violated the injunction issued by Judges Wood and Grosscup.

78 (Commissioner [Carroll D.] WRIGHT). That is, the injunction served on you on the 2d day of July?—Ans[wer]. Yes. As soon as the employees found that we were arrested and taken from the scene of action, they became demoralized, and that ended the strike. It was not the soldiers that ended the strike; it was not the old brotherhoods that ended the strike; it was simply the United States courts that ended the strike. Our men were in a position that never would have been shaken under any circumstances if we had been permitted to remain upon the field, remain among them; but once that we were taken from the scene of action and restrained from sending telegrams or issuing the orders necessary, or answering ques-

tions; when the minions of the corporations would be put to work at such a place, for instance, as Nickerson, Kans., where they would go and say to the men that the men at Newton had gone back to work, and Nickerson would wire me to ask if that were true; no answer would come to the message, because I was under arrest, and we were all under arrest. The headquarters were demoralized and abandoned, and we could not answer any telegrams or questions that would come in. Our headquarters were temporarily demoralized and abandoned, and we could not answer any messages. The men went back to work, and the ranks were broken, and the strike was broken up by the Federal courts of the United States, and not by the Army, and not by any other power, but simply and solely by the action of the United States courts in restraining us from discharging our duties as officers and representatives of the employees.

Source: U.S. Strike Commission, *Report on the Chicago Strike of June–July 1894* (Washington, DC: GPO, 1895), pp. 142–44.

4.7.   Grover Cleveland's Reply to John P. Altgeld, July 5, 1894

On July 5, 1894, after federal troops were placed on duty in Chicago, Governor John Altgeld sent a telegram of protest to President Grover Cleveland and asked him to remove the troops. In this brief reply, Cleveland stated his reasons for the unprecedented federal intervention that bypassed state and local authorities.

Executive Mansion, Washington, July 5, 1894

Hon. John P. Altgeld, Governor of Illinois, Springfield, Ill.:

Sir:—Federal Troops were sent to Chicago in strict accordance with the Constitution and laws of the United States, upon the demand of the postoffice department that obstruction of the mails should be removed, and upon the representations of the judicial officers of the United States that the process of the Federal courts could not be executed through the ordinary means, and upon competent proof that conspiracies existed against commerce between the States. To meet these conditions, which are clearly within the province of Federal authority, the presence of Federal troops in the city of Chicago was deemed not only proper, but necessary, and there has been no intention of thereby interfering with the plain duty of the local authorities to preserve the peace of the city.

GROVER CLEVELAND

Source: John P. Altgeld, "Speech at Cooper Union, New York, October 17, 1896, on the Chicago Riots.—Government by Injunction.—Federal Interference," in *Live Questions: Comprising His Papers, Speeches and Interviews; Also His Messages to the Legislature of Illinois, and a Statement of the Facts Which Influenced His Course as Governor on Several Famous Occasions* (Chicago: Geo. S. Bowen, 1899), p. 670.

4.8.   The AFL Executive Committee's Statement on a General Strike, July 13, 1894

The AFL committee sealed the strike's fate when it rejected the idea of solidarity—of participating in a general strike to help the ARU and the boycott. Although this excerpt from its statement expresses some concern for the strikers, it also reveals the craft organization's self-interested conservative tendencies.

The great industrial upheaval now agitating the country has been carefully, calmly and fully considered. . . . In the light of all the evidence obtainable, and in view of the peculiar complications now enveloping the situation, we are forced to the conclusion that the best interests of the unions affiliated with the American Federation of Labor demand that they refrain from participating in any general or local strike which may be proposed in connection with the present railroad troubles.

In making this declaration, we do not wish it understood that we are in any way antagonistic to labor organizations now struggling for right or justice, but rather to the fact that the present contest has become surrounded and beset with complications so grave in their nature that we cannot consistently advise a course which would but add to the general confusion.

The public press ever alive to the interests of corporate wealth, have with few exceptions, so maliciously misrepresented matters that in the public mind the working classes are now arrayed in open hostility to federal authority. This is a position we do not wish to be placed in, nor will we occupy without a protest.

We claim to be patriotic and law abiding as any other class of citizens, a claim substantiated by our actions in times of public need and public peril. . . .

While we may not have the power to order a strike of the working people of our country, we are fully aware that a recommendation from this conference to them to lay down their tools of labor would largely influence the members of our affiliated organizations; and appreciating the responsibility resting upon us and the duty we owe to all, we declare it to be the sense of this conference that a general strike at this time is in-expedient, unwise and contrary to the best interests of the working people. We further recommend that all connected with the American Federation of Labor now out on sympathetic strike should return to work and those who contemplate going out on sympathetic strike are advised to remain at their usual vocations.

In this strike of the American Railway Union we recognize an impulsive vigorous protest against the gathering, growing forces of plutocratic power and corporation rule. In the sympathetic movement of that order to help the Pullman employees, they have demonstrated the hollow shams of Pullman's pharasaical [sic] paradise. Mr. Pullman in his persistent repulses of arbitration and in his heartless autocratic treatment of his employees has proven himself a public enemy. . . .

By this railway strike the people are once more reminded of the immense forces held at the call of corporate capital for the subjugation of labor. For years the railroad interests have shown the lawless example of defiance to injunctions and have set aside laws to control them. They have displayed the utmost contempt for the Inter-State Commerce Law, have avoided its penalties and sneered at its impotency to prevent pooling discriminations and other impositions on the public. In this disregard of law these corporations have given the greatest impetus to Anarchy and lawlessness. Still they did not hesitate, when confronted by outraged labor, to invoke the powers of the State. The Federal Government, backed by United States marshals, injunctions of courts, proclamations by the President and sustained by the bayonets of soldiers and all the civil and military machinery of the law, have rallied on the summons of the corporations.

Against this array of armed force and brutal moneyed aristocracy, would it not be worse than folly to call men out on a general or local strike in these days of stagnant trade and commercial depression? No, better let us organize more generally, combine more closely, unite our forces, educate and prepare ourselves to protect our interests, and that we may go to the ballot box and cast our votes as American freemen united and determined to redeem this country from its present political and industrial misrule, to take it from the hands of the plutocratic wreckers and place it in the hands of the common people.

Source: Quoted in "The Strike and Its Lessons," *American Federationist*, August 1894, p. 125.

SELECTED ANNOTATED BIBLIOGRAPHY

Books

Addams, Jane. *Twenty Years at Hull-House with Autobiographical Notes*. New York: The Macmillan Company, 1910. For the social worker's views on the strike, see pp. 213–18. See also her article, "A Modern Lear," in *Survey* 29 (November 2, 1912), pp. 131–37.

Adelman, William. *Touring Pullman: A Study in Company Paternalism; A Walking Guide to the Pullman Community in Chicago, Illinois.* 3rd ed. Chicago: Illinois Labor History Society, 1993. A useful guide and description of strike events.

Altgeld, John P. *Live Questions: Comprising His Papers, Speeches and Interviews; Also His Messages to the Legislature of Illinois, and a Statement of the Facts Which Influenced His Course as Governor on Several Famous Occasions.* Chicago: Geo. S. Bowen & Son, 1899. Contains important documents related to the strike.

Barnard, Harry. *"Eagle Forgotten": The Life of John Peter Altgeld.* Indianapolis: Bobbs-Merrill, 1938. Standard biography of Altgeld.

Belknap, Michal K., ed. *American Political Trials.* Westport, CT: Greenwood Press, 1981. Contains Daniel Novak's important essay, "The Pullman Strike Cases: Debs, Darrow, and the Labor Injunction," pp. 129–51.

Carwardine, William H. *The Pullman Strike.* 1894. Centennial Ed. Chicago: Charles Kerr, 1994. Classic account of events by the strike supporter who was the pastor of the Methodist Church in Pullman before and during the strike.

Cleveland, Grover. *The Government in the Chicago Strike of 1894.* Princeton, NJ: Princeton University Press, 1913. A 1904 lecture by Cleveland defending his actions in the strike.

Cobb, Stephen G. *Reverend William Carwardine and the Pullman Strike of 1894: The Christian Gospel and Social Justice.* Lewiston, NY: The Edwin Mellen Press, 1992. Exploration of the minister's ideas and role in the strike.

Debs, Eugene V. *Writings and Speeches of Eugene V. Debs.* Introduction by Arthur M. Schlesinger, Jr. New York: Hermitage Press, 1948. Contains strike-related documents such as "Liberty" and "The Federal Government and the Chicago Strike."

Eggert, Gerald G. *Railroad Labor Disputes: The Beginnings of Federal Strike Policy.* Ann Arbor: University of Michigan Press, 1967. Author considers Pullman the climax of an evolving federal policy.

———. *Richard Olney: Evolution of a Statesman.* University Park: The Pennsylvania State University Press, 1974. Revisionist biography argues Olney changed his views on labor and government in the years following the strike.

Ginger, Ray. *Altgeld's America: The Lincoln Ideal versus Changing Realities.* c. 1958. Reprint, Chicago: Quadrangle Books, 1965. Very readable history covers the Pullman strike and the people, ideas, and events of the 1890s.

———. *The Bending Cross: A Biography of Eugene Victor Debs.* New Brunswick, NJ: Rutgers University Press, 1949. Very readable sympathetic biography of Debs.

Hirsch, Susan E. *After the Strike: A Century of Labor Struggles at Pullman.* Urbana: University of Illinois Press, 2003. Provides long-term perspective and insights.

James, Henry. *Richard Olney and His Public Service.* Boston: Houghton Mifflin, 1923. The famous novelist's defense of Olney, with Pullman-related documents.

Lindsey, Almont. *The Pullman Strike: The Story of a Unique Experiment and of a Great Labor Upheaval.* Chicago: University of Chicago Press, 1942. Remains the best secondary account of strike events.

Salvatore, Nick. *Eugene V. Debs: Citizen and Socialist.* Urbana: University of Illinois Press, 1982. Important award-winning social biography of Debs.

Schneirov, Richard, Shelton Stromquist, and Nick Salvatore, eds. *The Pullman Strike and the Crisis of the 1890s: Essays on Labor and Politics.* Urbana: University of Illinois Press, 1999. Collection of eight valuable essays, originally presented at a centennial conference devoted to the strike, and an epilogue by David Montgomery.

Smith, Carl. *Urban Disorder and the Shape of Belief: The Great Chicago Fire, the Haymarket Bomb, and the Model Town of Pullman.* Chicago: University of Chicago Press, 1995. A cultural study of middle-class responses to events in the industrial city.

Stead, W[illiam] T[homas]. *Chicago To-day: Or, The Labour War in America.* London: "Review of Reviews" Office, 1894. Reprint, New York: Arno Press and The New York Times, 1969. A noted British journalist and social reformer's account of events.

Swinton, John, Samuel Gompers, Eugene V. Debs, and John William Hayes. *Striking for Life: Labor's Side of the Labor Question: The Right of the Workingman to a Fair Living.* [n.p.]: American Manufacturing and Publishing Co., 1894. Reprint, Westport, CT: Greenwood Press, 1970. Contains important contemporary articles on the strike.

U.S. Strike Commission. *Report on the Chicago Strike of June–July 1894.* Washington, DC: GPO, 1895. Indispensable primary source includes testimonies and the Commission's conclusions.

Web Sites

Teachers and students will find important strike-related documents online at three sites. Visit the Illinois Labor History Society's site at http://www.kentlaw.edu/ilhs/pullman.htm, George Mason University's History Matters site at http://historymatters.gmu.edu/, and the Illinois State Museum's On-line Exhibits at http://www.museum.state.il.us/.

The text of the historic 1895 Supreme Court decision, *In re Debs*, 158 U.S. 564, is easily accessible at http://supct.law.cornell.edu/supct/cases/name.htm. Historic Supreme Court decisions are available at this Cornell University, Legal Information Institute, Supreme Court Collection site. The case is also at FindLaw's http://laws.findlaw.com/us/158/564.html.

Videos

The Pullman Strike, written by Joyce Goldenstein, produced by Multi-Media Productions and Zenger Video in Culver City, California, 1985. This 20-minute video is a useful introduction to the strike and designed for classroom use. A teacher's guide is also available.

Eugene Debs and the American Movement, produced in Cambridge, Massachusetts, by Cambridge Documentary Films, 1977. This 44-minute VHS documentary, a biography of Debs, uses his own words as it covers the major events of his life, including the Pullman strike.

5

The Lawrence Strike of 1912

A new chapter in American labor relations was written during the nationally famous, ten-week-long Lawrence strike of 1912. This spontaneous strike, popularly known as the "Bread and Roses" strike, successfully brought together Polish women, Italian men, Syrian children, and an ethnically diverse work force of twenty-five nationalities in a common cause. What strike leaders, prominent journalists, and others subsequently hailed as one of the most significant strikes in U.S. history had pitted about 25,000 polyglot unskilled and semi-skilled Lawrence textile workers against the country's leading woolen and worsted employers. Despite the great obstacles confronting them, the strikers creatively waged their struggle, built and maintained an uncommon solidarity, and ultimately won the strike. The remarkable strike, and the workers' unprecedented victory that brought them immediate practical gains, had major implications for labor on the local, regional, and national levels. How the strikers won—and the broader meaning of their protest—immediately prompted vigorous debate.

The strike itself brought into the national limelight a whole host of older labor-related issues such as wages, working conditions, violence, constitutional rights, and child labor, along with a multitude of newer labor-related issues such as industrial unionism, immigrant labor, the nature of capitalist exploitation, and the revolutionary goals of the Industrial Workers of the World. For many workers, reformers, and radicals, Lawrence represented a symbol of hope, a catalyst for reform, an inspiration for long-term radical change. For many corporations, business classes, and others, it meant a warning, a dangerous revolt, a potential social revolution.

The immediate cause of the strike was the refusal of Lawrence's textile employers to adjust wage rates so that their employees did not lose any money when a new state law came into effect on January 1, 1912. The Massachusetts legislature had reduced the number of maximum weekly working hours for female and child operatives from 56 to 54 hours but had said nothing about wage rates. Once the spontaneous strike began, but not before, the companies adamantly claimed they would not and could not afford any raise. The issue was not trivial. The mass of the mill workers, who lived on the margin at best, calculated the loss of two hours' pay—30 or 40 or 50 cents—in terms of the number of loaves of bread their families would not have that week.

In 1912, Lawrence was a one-industry city that was extremely dependent upon the textile corporations that had concentrated there since the Civil War. One-half of the city's 85,000 residents over the age of fourteen worked in one of these textile conglomerates. Lawrence's single biggest firm, which employed almost half of all city mill workers, was the American Woolen Company, the largest textile corporation in the United States and one of the wealthiest. The other half of the Lawrence mill workers worked in one of the other prominent textile concerns, such as the Pacific Mills, the Arlington Mills, or the Everett Mills. In this one-industry setting, the city and its nonmill population were, directly or indirectly, as dependent upon the mills as the workers were.

Lawrence was representative of other American industrial centers at the time in that so much of its population was either foreign-born or of foreign parentage, but with 86 percent of the population, the foreign-born and the children of the foreign-born made up one of the largest such concentrations in the United States. Mill workers were accordingly divided by nationality, language, skill, and religion. In the 1890s and 1900s, Italians, Russian Jews, Syrians, Poles, and other southern and eastern European immigrants had joined the Irish, French-Canadians, Franco-Belgians, and Americans who were already working there. By 1912 the majority of mill workers were women, and immigrant children, prompted by family need, often left school to work in the mills at the age of fourteen, legally, or at an earlier age, illegally.

Lawrence mill workers lived in poverty and misery long before the strike. A U.S. Bureau of Labor report in 1912 found congested tenements and boarding houses and an extremely high infant mortality rate. It also found wages so low that a typical family of five had to send three of its members into the mill in order to have the bare necessities of life. Malnourished mill children survived on a penny's lunch of bread and molasses. And during the strike, a shocked public learned that they often wore no underwear because their families could not afford it. The mill workers who made the nation's woolen goods could not afford what they themselves made.

Mill owners considered a strike unlikely. After all, the vast majority of its divided workers belonged to no union. Skilled workers had several independent unions, but the American Federation of Labor (AFL), the nation's leading labor organization of craft workers, had only one small local there. More significant was the presence of several nationality-based branches of the Industrial Workers of the World (IWW), a radical syndicalist organization that welcomed women, immigrants, and unskilled workers. But, at the time of the strike, there were only about 300 paid-up IWW members in Lawrence. Most skilled American trade unionists affiliated with the AFL considered the very diversity and social composition of the Lawrence work force—largely foreign-born, unskilled, and female—as poor union material and ignored such workers. At most, the mill owners, who abhorred all unions, had to deal only with the members of one trade in one plant.

The Lawrence strike began on January 11 and 12, when mill workers received their first paychecks under the new state law. Until then, considerable anxiety and uncertainty prevailed. Mill owners had said nothing about changing wage rates, and when workers' delegations visited mill offices on January 3 for a clarification of company positions, mill managers arbitrarily dismissed them. From then on, the IWW held meetings to discuss the situation; the Poles and Italians voted to strike, if wages were actually cut. For the Polish women weavers at the Everett Mills, uncertainty about company policy ended when they received their pay on January 11, 1912, one day earlier than the mass of mill workers. Shouting "Short pay," they immediately stopped work. That evening, Angelo Rocco of the IWW Italian Local 20 wired the international union and asked for Joseph Ettor, a second-generation Italian organizer, to come to Lawrence.

It was uncertain what other workers would do on January 12, but when the Italians and others in the Everett Mills also received "short pay," they abruptly stopped work, shut down their machines, persuaded other workers to join them, and dismantled the machines of those who didn't. They left the building, traveled the mill district, and got other workers to join them. In so doing, they smashed some factory windows and damaged some machines. By nightfall, 10,000 or more operatives had joined the strike. City officials used this initial violence as a reason to hire special policemen and to call out the first of twelve companies of militiamen who would eventually come to Lawrence. On January 13, Ettor arrived and began to hold meetings.

The Lawrence strike thus began under incongruous circumstances. A workers' spontaneous protest, fueled by a modest and moderate demand, came to be supported by a syndicalist organization that did not believe in contracts or collective bargaining, one that stressed that "the working class and the employing class have nothing in common." Unlike the AFL, which accepted capitalism, the wage system, and "a fair day's wage for a fair day's work," the IWW sought the demise of capitalism and the "abolition of the wage system." It popularized notions and tactics such as direct action, sabotage, the general strike, "one big union," and the ability of workers to run their own industries democratically for their and society's benefit. The IWW's entrance into the strike brought it to prominence in the eastern United States for the first time.

Despite the IWW's radical goals and rhetoric, Joseph Ettor and other IWW leaders worked pragmatically with all the strikers to win the strike. Together, they pioneered in important new methods designed to bring about genuine solidarity among the vastly diverse workers. On January 13, they met and organized on a new industrial basis that included all workers. They formed a strike committee of fifty-six members with elected representatives from each of the different nationalities. From the outset, their meetings were long, democratically conducted in multiple languages, and open to the public. Moreover, from the outset, Ettor emphatically urged the strikers to refrain from violence. Violence would only help the mill owners.

On January 14, the strikers met again and formulated four specific demands, including (1) a 15 percent increase in wages on the 54-hour basis; (2) double time for overtime; (3) the abolition of the premium bonus system; and (4) no discrimination against the strikers after the strike. The strikers did not return to work on the critical day of January 15, and mill owners rejected their demands.

As many as 25,000 workers subsequently took part in the strike, which lasted from January 11 to March 14, and during which sporadic outside efforts to resolve it all failed. For example, when Massachusetts Governor Eugene Foss, a mill owner himself, made a proposal on January 29 that the strikers return to work for thirty days while he tried to find a solution, both the strike committee and the mill owners rejected it. It was a tense stalemate.

To maintain solidarity, the strikers had to overcome many enemies. Priests and ministers often sided with the mill owners. And the labor leader, John Golden, president of the Textile Workers Union of America, an AFL affiliate, denounced the strike for its radical connections. Of all workers, skilled workers were least likely to join or remain on strike, although some skilled workers, led by Annie Welzenbach, the highest paid piece worker in the mills, proudly took part.

Almost immediately, violence, the role of the police and militia, and constitutional rights emerged as key issues. Mill owners and the members of the Lawrence Citizens' Association quickly hailed the militia for bringing law and order to a city supposedly racked with violence linked to ignorant foreigners and a lawless IWW, while strikers viewed the police and militia as strikebreakers in the outright service of the mill owners. Indeed, the militia did rigorously control the streets, arbitrarily stop and query pedestrians, prohibit any three people from gathering, and make minor and questionable arrests. It allowed no one to stand still on the streets and hampered the strikers' efforts to talk to strikebreakers.

In response, the strikers devised new and effective strategies. To support the strike, women, whom the IWW leader Big Bill Haywood later said won the strike, used neighborhood groups to discipline strikebreakers, while ethnic people used their respective cultures and organizations. They set up soup kitchens and relief stations and publicized their cause. The strikers also acted creatively to overcome restrictions on picketing. Each day, at opening and closing times, hundreds or thousands of strikers formed a moving picket line which roved from mill gate to mill gate, in an effort to dissuade others from returning to work. By singing the "Internationale" and other songs in their respective languages, they also reinforced their common solidarity. Lawrence became known as a "singing strike" famous for its novel roving picket line.

The strikers had many good reasons to question the impartiality of law enforcement and the legal system. Among them were the courts' harsh sentences for minor offenses, the failure of authorities to investigate the death of an unarmed Syrian youth who had been bayoneted in the back, and the arbitrary arrest of strikers in a notorious case of dynamite plantings that later turned out to be a frame-up, with William Wood, president of the American Woolen Mills, as the probable person behind the scheme. But the greatest injustice of all was the arrest, on January 30, of two prominent strike leaders, Joseph Ettor and Arturo Giovannitti, an Italian editor and poet, as accessories to murder. The night before, during a fracas between the police and strikers, a stray bullet had killed Anna Lo Pizza, an Italian striker. Lawrence authorities quickly seized upon her murder as a pretext for arresting the two IWW men, even though they were known to have been far away from the scene at the time. Viewing the arrests as an obvious attempt to break the strike, the strikers asked the IWW for more help. In response, Big Bill Haywood, Elizabeth Gurley Flynn, and Carlo Tresca came to Lawrence. The demand for the release of Ettor and Giovannitti became a national and international cause célèbre that outlasted the strike's duration.

The turning point of the strike occurred as a result of violent events that took place on February 24. Earlier that month, the Italian Socialist Federation had proposed a plan that would simultaneously aid the strike and give the strikers' children better food and living conditions. The idea was to send large numbers of the children to other cities where socialists and responsible working families provided for their well-being for the strike's duration. On February 10, the first contingent of 119 children left for New

York City; other groups soon followed and went to other places. The tactic garnered considerable national publicity, much of which was favorable to the strikers, with the result that, on February 17, the commander of the militia announced that he would no longer tolerate the transport of any more strikers' children from Lawrence.

Meanwhile, a delegation of four Philadelphia socialists and IWW members, who had arranged to take as many as 300 children to Philadelphia, arrived in Lawrence on February 23. On the next morning, when parents brought about forty children to the train station for the trip, the police intervened, clubbing the women and forcefully throwing the children into a police wagon. They also made thirty arrests, sent some of the children to a poor farm, and brought protesting parents before a judge for being "unfit parents." Newspaper reports of police brutality, the clear violation of constitutional liberties, and the denial of parental rights made Lawrence infamous overnight. Prominent national politicians called for a congressional investigation.

Bowing to popular demand, Congress did launch an inquiry into the strike. The House Committee on Rules scheduled hearings for early March, and Margaret Sanger, a nurse and socialist, brought sixteen child laborers, all strikers, from Lawrence to Washington to testify. President William Howard Taft's wife attended the hearings on the day when fourteen-year-old Camella Teoli told how her hair had gotten caught in a machine and she had been "scalped" on the job. As other children testified, the nation learned about speed-ups, harsh working conditions, and the mill workers' difficult, impoverished lives. After the strike, such testimony, and the Lawrence strike itself, were critical events in mobilizing support for the successful creation of a U.S. Industrial Relations Commission to investigate national working conditions and labor relations.

It was in this context of unfavorable publicity that the mill owners decided to negotiate. On March 12, the final settlement was reached, and Lawrence strikers accepted it in a vote on the Lawrence Commons on March 14. The terms were in keeping with the spirit of unselfishness and solidarity that had won the strike. The wage increase ranged from 5 to 20 percent. Every worker was ensured a 5 percent increase, but, at the unselfish suggestion of the skilled strikers, those paid the lowest rate in the mills received the greatest increase, while those paid the highest rate received the least increase. Workers also won time and one-quarter for overtime, the promise of no discrimination against the strikers, and a modification of the premium or bonus system in their favor.

Long before the founding of the Congress of Industrial Organizations in 1937, the Lawrence strike brought industrial unionism into the national limelight in significant new ways. It showed immigrant workers and the nation that disparate workers could, under certain circumstances, overcome national and linguistic differences, organize their labor power, and win concessions from powerful employers. Industrial unionism was an issue skilled workers and the AFL would increasingly have to face. As a direct or indirect result of the strike, approximately 438,000 U.S. textile workers gained better wages and working conditions. In some mills, employers quickly raised wages; in others, workers went on strike to win gains.

The decision of Lawrence authorities to pursue the capital case against Ettor and Giovannitti cast a pall on the workers' victory, however. Trial was set to begin on September 30, a day Lawrence mill workers protested with a one-day general strike, which, in turn, prompted a massive "For God and Country" counterprotest. The men's case drew significant national and international support because of the belief that, like the Haymarket victims of 1886, they were on trial merely because of their radical political beliefs. In November, a jury acquitted them.

The workers' spectacular victory was short-lived. Lawrence mill owners remained hostile to unions and workers' rights, and they soon discharged strike leaders. A combination of repression and the recession of 1913 virtually wiped out the IWW. Meanwhile, on the national level, a conservative backlash evident in corporate policies, a broad anti-IWW, anti-radical movement, and a reinvigorated immigration restriction drive emerged. In the long run, the employers had greater economic and political power than did the workers, whose struggles would be ongoing.

Perhaps the most enduring legacy of the Lawrence strike of 1912 was that, more than almost any other strike in U.S. history, it embodied the solidarity, unselfishness, and ideals of the American labor movement. It symbolically became known, and is commemorated today, as the "Bread and Roses" strike because Lawrence workers believed they deserved more than the means of a mere existence. They deserved beauty, better working conditions, and the means for higher pursuits. Above all, they deserved dignity and respect—they deserved both bread and roses.

DOCUMENTS

5.1.   Fred Beal, "The Lawrence Strike," *Proletarian Journey*, 1937

> *Fred Beal was a fifteen-year-old Yankee doffer at the Pacific Mills when the Lawrence strike began. He joined the strike and subsequently devoted his life to the labor movement. This excerpt from his autobiography,* Proletarian Journey, *conveys the astonishing impact the IWW had on the young worker, the militancy of the Italians, and the atmosphere in his workplace on the eve of the strike.*

I suddenly discovered that I did not want to be a textile worker. I was fifteen. . . . Mill work was dreary. . . .

Then one day, at noon-time, another kind of lecturer addressed the crowd in front of our mill gate. . . . This strange lecturer urged us to organize into a union, to join the Industrial Workers of the World, and to demand from the bosses more wages and shorter hours. He declared with emphasis that we, the textile workers, were *wage slaves* and that all the mill owners were slave drivers, as bad and as brutal as Simon Legree of *Uncle Tom's Cabin*.

This was news to me. I had always thought that only colored people could be slaves and that they had been freed long ago by us Yankees who fought in the Civil War. Yet there was something convincing about his talk although I could not quite understand just who were the bosses who, according to the speaker, were enjoying the Florida sunshine while we slaved in the mills for their profit. All the subordinate bosses I had ever known were working in the mill, like "Slim Jim the Burglar" and Paddy Parker.

The Irish workers did not like the speaker; the Italians did. The Irish cupped their hands to their mouths, made strange noises every time the Italians applauded, and yelled: "Ef ye don't loike this countr-r-ry, go back where ye coime fr-r-rom!"

The speaker ignored these remarks and continued: "The working class and the employing class have nothing in common. Between these two classes a struggle must go on until the workers of the world organize as a class, take possession of the earth and the machinery of production, and abolish the wage system."

Then, rudely, as if by prearrangement, the ten-minutes-to-one bells, high up in the mill's belfry, began tolling their dismal warning to us workers that it was time for us to get back to work. *"The slave bells are calling*!"

yelled the I.W.W. speaker. "The master wants you back at the bench and machine. Go, slaves! But remember, these very bells will some day toll the death-knell of the slave-drivers!"

The bells tolled on defiantly. . . .

That afternoon, during the rest period, we doffers talked about the I.W.W. speaker and the union he was organizing. We had good reason to talk. Things were about to happen. The State Legislature had just passed a law reducing the hours of labor from 56 to 54 per week, and there was rumor that our pay would be reduced accordingly. Our next pay day was Friday, January 12th, and the grown-up workers were talking about going on strike if wages were cut. . . .

While the discussion was on, two Italian spinners came to me with a long white paper. They wanted me to be among the first to sign a petition against the threatened wage cut because, they said, I was American. The idea was to present Paddy Parker with a long list of those opposed to any reduction. I read the words at the top of the paper:
THE FOLLOWING PEOPLE WORKING IN THE SPINNING ROOM WILL GO ON STRIKE FRIDAY, JANUARY 12TH, IF WAGES ARE CUT—

Queenie read it over my shoulder. "Don't sign it, Lobster," she cautioned. "These Wops'll get you in trouble. You'll be put on the blacklist if you sign that paper!"

But I signed it. So did "Gyp" and "Lefty Louie."

And January 12th was only two days away.

Source: Fred E. Beal, "The Lawrence Strike," in *Proletarian Journey: New England, Gastonia, Moscow* (New York: Hillman-Curl, 1937), pp. 35–38.

5.2.   Letter of William Wood to American Woolen Co. Employees, January 19, 1912

A week after the strike began, William Wood, president of the American Woolen Co., finally clarified his position on wage rates in this letter to his employees. In a paternalistic manner, he vigorously asserted that his company could not afford any raise and even cited the new law as one reason why.

AMERICAN WOOLEN Co.,
Lawrence, Mass., January 19, 1912.

To our employees:

Last Friday many of you left our mills and have since remained away. This action was wholly a surprise to me. You sent no notice of what you were intending to do and you stated no grievance and made no demand.

I learn from the newspapers that the reason for your staying away is that the company paid you for only 54 hours' work; but you know your wages are paid by the hour or by the piece, and as you work only 54 hours you could be paid only for 54 hours' work. . . .

I am an employee of the company as you are. As its president I am bound, on the one hand, to take proper care of the interests of 13,000 stockholders. Quite a number of them are employees, and most of them are not rich. Many of them necessarily depend on their dividends for their living just as you depend on your wages for yours. On the other hand I am bound to look out for the interests of some 25,000 employees. It is my duty to see that each side has a square deal, and I try my best to perform that duty fairly and honestly.

I want every man and woman working for the American Woolen Co. to get the best wages that the company can afford. You work best for the interests of the company when you are contented, but you must realize that I must also care reasonably for the stockholders' interests and see that the business is properly managed. You know we have very sharp competition, and if we do not do our work economically our competitors will drive us out.

The last two years have been very discouraging years for us and for all manufacturers in our line. The present year being a presidential year is also bad for business. You realize, too, that the hours of labor are shorter here than in other States. If we should pay as much for 54 hours' labor as our competitors in other States pay for 56, or even 60, we should soon have to quit. I am not criticising [sic] our Massachusetts law, but for the present, you see, it puts us under a handicap. . . .

. . . Trade conditions do not justify an increase.

I ask you to have confidence in this statement and to return to your work. . . .

You are being advised (so I am informed) by men who are not and never have been employees of the company, and who do not live in this State and are strangers to you. . . . Your advisers have nothing to lose in the disasters of an unfortunate strike or lockout. You and I have everything to lose.

I therefore as head of this organization of which we are all members, appeal to you to return to your work and faithfully discharge your duties. I will try conscientiously to discharge mine, and together we will try and create a prosperity for the company which will help us all.

We shall thus end a situation perilous to your interests, perilous to the interests of the company, perilous to the interests of the city—a situation from which nothing but ill feeling and disaster can result.

Very sincerely,

(Signed) WILLIAM M. WOOD, *President.*

Source: U.S. Bureau of Labor, *Report on Strike of Textile Workers in Lawrence, Mass., in 1912* (Washington, DC: GPO, 1912), pp. 39–41.

5.3.   **Appeal, "To All the Working Men and Women of Massachusetts and Elsewhere," Lawrence, January 1912**

In this widely circulated appeal, the Lawrence strikers asked their fellow workers for support and documented their reasons for the strike. It clearly shows how important the wage cut was to them but that wages per se were only one issue in a broad range of "unbearable conditions" that included the speed-up, child labor, and the deterioration of family life.

FELLOW WORKERS: We, textile workers of Lawrence, are on strike. We are striking against unbearable conditions.

It is not sufficient that our wages are low, but the masters, taking advantage of the 54-hour law that was passed to reduce the admittedly too long working hours of women and children, have cut our pay to an average of 50 cents a week, which to us means 10 loaves of bread. . . .

It is considered and admitted that this is the busy season, and if $6 a week is the average wage in the busy season, then, fellow workers, consider what must be our miserable lot in the slack periods.

For years past it was not sufficient that the employers had forced conditions upon us that gradually but surely broke up our homes and what was left was but an excuse; they have forced our wives to the mills to work alongside of us, not that their wages be leveled up to the men, but that the men's be reduced and they be forced to compete with women.

They have taken away our wives from the home, our children have been driven from the playground, stolen out of the schools and driven into the mills, where they were strapped to the machines, not only to force the fathers to compete but that their young lives may be coined into dollars for a parasite class, that their very nerves, their laughter and joy denied, may be woven into cloth.

For all these past years the operators have gradually reduced our wages, and at the same time have speeded up the machines so that we turn out in some cases three times the amount of work and receive about one-third of the old rate. . . .

Taking advantage of the 54-hour law, they have, it is true, cut the wages, and are now making it their war cry: "Fifty-four hours' pay for fifty-four hours' work;" but we submit to a candid world the fact that the hours have only been reduced "officially," and in order to comply with the law, but some of the mills are stealing sufficient time around the hours of starting and quitting each day in the week to make up the two hours "reduced." . . .

Because we dared to rebel, militiamen have been sent to drive us back to work, and already the bayonets of hired Hessians have wetted in the blood of our fellow workers.

Fellow workers! Men and women! Take heed! We are waging a battle that means much to us, but we are equally fighting the battle of the wage-workers throughout this State who have been affected as we have. If we can, by our devotion and your support, win, it will mean a victory for all the workers of this State and all the workers in the wool and cotton industry. If lack of support on your part drives us back into the mills, then not only we but you may prepare yourselves for the lash that the masters will lay on with that much more force. . . .

So we appeal to all the workers. . . .

To the aid of your fellow workers who are battling against worse misery than the past. An injury to one is an injury to all. It is we who are in need today; who knows, it may be your turn to ask us after our victory.

Sincerely, yours, for the cause of 25,000 men, women, and children,

STRIKE COMMITTEE.

JOSEPH BEDARD, *Secretary.*

P.S.—Our demands on the operators: Fifteen per cent increase in wages and prices on the 54-hour basis. Abolition of the premium system. Double time and pay for all overtime. All strikers must be taken back to their positions occupied before the strike.

Source: U.S. Bureau of Labor, *Report on Strike of Textile Workers in Lawrence, Mass., in 1912* (Washington, DC: GPO, 1912), pp. 497–98.

5.4.   Statement of Jane Bock to the U.S. House Committee on Rules, March 1912

Jane Bock, a young Russian Jewish immigrant, was one of four delegates who came to Lawrence to transport a group of strikers' children to Philadelphia on February 24. In this excerpt of her testimony before the U.S. House Committee on Rules in March, she described the arrangements made for the children and the violent behavior of the police on that critical day.

The CHAIRMAN. You were at the station this Saturday morning of which we have been speaking?

Miss BOCK. Yes, sir.

The CHAIRMAN. Now, tell the committee in your own way, why you were there, what you were doing, and what occurred?

Miss BOCK. I was elected as a member of the committee of four to go to Lawrence and bring the children to Philadelphia. Previous to that we organized a joint committee of the Socialist Party and the Industrial Workers of the World. This joint committee had arranged to have these children given into homes. The applications for the children were entirely voluntary. The people came and asked us to take these children and find them homes. The committee had many applications—about 200 in number—and the homes were very carefully picked out for these children. In order that the homes should be carefully selected, it was decided that the women of the committee were the more competent judges about the fitness of the homes, and in accordance with this decision, the women of the committee inspected these homes. The women of the committee inquired very carefully about the conditions in the homes and examined the conditions of the house. If the house was simply clean, but if [a] woman did not seem intelligent enough to take care of other children than her own, the application was turned down. Because of that we had 175 applications that we turned down, and unless the conditions in the home were satisfactory the children were not taken there. If the application came from a furnished-room house the application was turned down. We had only private houses, where the children were not likely to meet with any danger.

After this work was finished by the committee, on Thursday evening at 8:55 we left Philadelphia to bring these children with us. We had no idea as to how many children we were to have. We applied for 200. They told us they would give us 100. On Friday afternoon we had a number of nationality mass meetings at Lawrence, and we were requested by the strike committee to visit these meetings and tell them the purpose of our visit. I personally addressed five of these meetings. I told them why we came and told them about the arrangements to put the children in the homes. I forgot to tell you we had arranged with 10 or 15 physicians to examine these children before they were taken into the homes to see that none of them had any contagious diseases. I told these things to those people, and they willingly signed the application form which the committee had arranged. That very evening a train was chartered—I did not take any part in these arrangements. The next morning our committee was at the station to take these children to Philadelphia. . . .

. . . About 7 o'clock Miss Carmitta and myself arranged the children in two lines, and we were taking the children through the door to the station where the car was awaiting us. Some of the parents of the children came out, and when the police formed in two lines on each side of the door, they closed in on us with their clubs, and I was pushed close against a train and kept there absolutely so that I could not move. The other woman was in the same position. Evidently the police and detectives singled us out as Philadelphians and tried to have as little to do with us as possible. They kept us against the wall. I had 40 tickets bought for the children, and I was standing there helpless. About five minutes later, when the police began clubbing and the children were screaming and thrown to the floor, they hastily grabbed them and carried them to a military truck that was standing a few paces from the platform and threw them in without regard for their screams or where they were throwing them. When I was released from against the wall—I do not remember just how they kept me there—I was running toward the truck, my intention being to take those children from them, because I felt the responsibility; every mother had trusted her child to me; but they simply drove me away from the military truck and the military truck with the children and the police on it, continuing their beating of the mothers and children, drove away to the station.

Mr. WILSON. What was the average age of the children?

Miss BOCK. I should say from about 5 to 12. . . .

Mr. HARDWICK. Did the people there with the children fight back, or resist in any way?

Miss BOCK. I hardly think they had a chance. They were thrown in such a way that there was not enough room to extend an arm. . . .

Mr. HARDWICK. Did these policemen beat the people and just take the children away?

Miss BOCK. Beat the people.

Mr. HARDWICK. Club them without any further excuse except that they were trying to take the children away?

Miss BOCK. Without any further provocation.

Mr. HARDWICK. You saw them do that pretty plainly?

Miss BOCK. Yes, sir. . . .

Mr. HARDWICK. . . . did the policemen actually strike them [the children]?

Miss BOCK. They did.

Mr. HARDWICK. With their hands or with their clubs?

Miss BOCK. I should say with clubs; that was the handiest thing.

Source: U.S. Congress, House, Committee on Rules, *The Strike at Lawrence, Mass.: Hearings Before the Committee on Rules of the House of Representatives on House Resolutions 409 and 433, March 2–7, 1912* (Washington, DC: GPO, 1912), pp. 189–94.

5.5.   [Lawrence] Citizens' Association, "A Reign of Terror in an American City," March 1912

After the strike ended, the city officials, business people, and English-speaking residents of Lawrence who had formed an active Citizens' Association to fight the strike, published "A Reign of Terror in an American City." The purpose of the tract was to defend Lawrence, the police, and the militia from outside criticism. This excerpt shows that the association took IWW ideology very seriously and feared social change, while it grossly exaggerated and distorted the violence committed by the strikers and placed all blame for turmoil on IWW outside agitators and ignorant foreigners.

Lawrence, Mass., March—The ease with which an American city of nearly one hundred thousand inhabitants may be taken possession of by a gang of outside agitators and terrorized for weeks is well illustrated in what actually happened in Lawrence during the past two months. . . .

It was like a city in the grip of a foreign enemy. . . .

The big strike that started on Jan. 12 began as a violent and destructive strike. It grew more violent and destructive every day of its existence until after it had been going more than two weeks, when a greatly enlarged force of militia, infantry and mounted men, brought the force of law and ordder [*sic*] into such prominence that it was able to overawe the force of disorder and lawlessness that was being used boldly, defiantly.

The leaders of this strike came from outside of Lawrence. They were not mill workers, and knew nothing of actual working conditions in the mill. They were and presumably are members of the Industrial Workers of the World. This society does not disguise its purposes or the methods it approves in bringing to pass the condition of affairs which it believes desirable. It preaches that force is justifiable in labor wars, and that such force may be carried to any extent to carry a strike to success.

It proclaims that it aims to abolish the wage system and inaugurate a regime, where the worker will take possession of the machinery of production and receive all the profits to be made out of the manufacture or sale of any article.

With such principles is plain that no agreements to be entered into by it with an employer could be for any length of time, for it does not believe in tolerating the employer for one instant longer than the time it takes to expropriate him. . . .

By means of representatives of each nationality they indoctrinated this heterogeneous means of strikers with all the radical doctrines their society stood for and made most of these nine thousand poor people [whom the association says joined the IWW] believe that all the property in the city belonged to them, including the mills, and that it was going to be divided among them just as soon as the I.W.W. won the strike.

It may easily be imagined what possibilities for destruction lay in the nine thousand strikers after they had been talked to for a time by the leaders of a movement which boldly inculcated the doctrine that violence and destruction of the most extreme type were justifiable when used as part of the tactics to win more wages or inaugurate a social revolution. . . .

The English speaking people of Lawrence, including their leaders, clerical and lay, wanted very much to have the strikers get more pay, but they wanted more to uphold American law and order. So when the serious rioting began they set themselves solidly against the anarchistic socialists, and demanded that the city and state authorities uphold law and order at any cost. . . .

If it were not for the soldiers and police there would have been an exceedingly long list of assassinations and assaults to record before the Lawrence strike was brought to an end. For the nine thousand non-English speaking strikers, urged, not led, by the cunning leaders from outside Lawrence were convinced that the one way to win their rights was to prevent the fifteen thousand English speaking operatives from remaining at work. . . .

The Lawrence police made no attempt to prevent the first detachment of children being taken to New York for exploitation. But when all the humanitarians in and out of the State denounced as inhuman the taking of children out of Lawrence to be exhibited like cattle and demanded that no more be allowed to leave the State, the Lawrence authorities simply tried to live up to the ideas of these humanitarians. And the testimony of all impartial witnesses is that the police used not unnecessary force in preventing the children from leaving Lawrence, and that no women were clubbed then or any other time during the strike.

CITIZENS' ASSOCIATION,
LAWRENCE, MASS.

Source: [Lawrence] Citizens' Association, *A Reign of Terror in an American City: Some of the Ways in Which Lawrence Was Held in Subjection by a Gang of Out of Town Agitators* (Lawrence, MA: Citizens' Association, 1912), pp. [1–4].

5.6.   Mary K. O'Sullivan, "The Labor War at Lawrence," *Survey*, April 6, 1912

> *Mary K. O'Sullivan, the first woman organizer for the AFL and a founder of the Women's Trade Union League, was one of the old-line labor leaders who were deeply impressed by the Lawrence strike and thought it had much to teach trade unionists. In this excerpt from an article she wrote soon after the strike, she criticized the AFL but suggested the possibility of a new hopeful era in which skilled and unskilled workers might work together.*

Up to the present time, the Textile Workers of the American Federation of Labor have failed to organize the unskilled and underpaid workers. Blocked by the mill interests, they have been defeated in their larger efforts for the skilled workers, and they have neglected the interests of the unskilled. They have ignored their capacity for strength and failed to win them to their cause or to better their condition.

In the past foreigners have been the element through which strikes in the textile industry have been lost. This is the first time in the history of our labor struggles that the foreigners have stood to the man to better their conditions as underpaid workers. . . .

In the long run, from the organizer's standpoint this new insurgent movement may be the best possible thing that could happen to the labor unions of America. On the one hand the success of this struggle is a warning to employers who are on the job that they can no longer afford to beat down and block conservative organizations that stand for contracts and trade agreements which give the management a guarantee and surety in making estimates in business. On the other hand, the trade union with a vision will also profit by this note of warning.

Source: Mary K. O'Sullivan, "The Labor War at Lawrence," *Survey* 28 (April 6, 1912): 72–73.

5.7.   Address of Joseph Ettor to the Jury, Salem, Massachusetts, November 23, 1912

> *Joseph Ettor and Arturo Giovannitti each made eloquent closing statements at their trial in Salem, Massachusetts, in November 1912. In this excerpt from his speech, Ettor argued that the*

IWW leaders were on trial as accessories to murder not for any of their actions but for their radical political beliefs. Ideas, he stressed, could not be either tried or silenced.

MR. FOREMAN AND GENTLEMEN OF THE JURY:

. . . I have not been tried on my acts. I have been tried here because of my social ideals. Gentlemen, I make no threats. But history does, and history records things, with little variation here and there, but nothing can efface the fact that because of my political and social views I am brought here to the bar. I am impelled to speak because of that fact, and nothing else. . . .

. . . My social views are that the working class produces everything that there is. In order to produce wealth, machinery nowadays and the implements of production are not used by one individual. They are used by a class. They are not owned by that class but they are owned by a class that is unable to operate them, but has workers to operate them on a wage basis. . . .

. . . Because I hold the views that all wealth is the product of labor and therefore should belong to labor, it follows, according to his [the district attorney's] argument, that I am in favor of destroying property. I stated on the stand that I believe all property is social property.

I haven't in mind, gentlemen of the jury, a tooth brush or pipes or anything of that kind. I have in mind machines. I have in mind railroads. I have in mind the things that are necessary to the world and what the world of labor produces and uses should belong to the world of labor.

I stated on the stand that if the working class with a policy of violence destroys any of those machines or any of that property, when it comes into possession of its own it will have that much less. . . .

. . . I do believe—I may be wrong, but, gentlemen, only history can pass judgment upon them [ideas]. All wealth is the product of labor, and all wealth being the product of labor belongs to labor and to no one else. . . .

I want to state further, gentlemen, that whatever my social views are, as I stated before, they are what they are. They cannot be tried in this courtroom. . . .

If the idea can live it lives, because history adjudges it right. And what has been considered an idea constituting a social crime in one age, has in the next age become the very religion of humanity. The social criminals of one age have become the saints of the next. . . .

My ideas are what they are, gentlemen. They might be indicted and you might believe, as the District Attorney has suggested, that you can pass judgment and that you can choke them; but you can't. Ideas can't be choked.

Source: Joseph J. Ettor and Arturo Giovannitti, *Ettor and Giovannitti Before the Jury at Salem, Massachusetts, November 23, 1912* (Chicago: The Industrial Workers of the World, 1912), pp. 20–22, 35–39.

5.8.   James Oppenheim, "Bread and Roses," 1911

James Oppenheim (1882–1932) wrote this poem, "Bread and Roses," shortly before the Lawrence strike, with which it is closely identified. The phrase apparently struck a chord with the female strikers who carried a sign, "We want bread and roses too," during a street parade in Lawrence in 1912. Caroline Kohlsaat later set Oppenheim's poem to music, and it has since become a classic labor song, used by women's organizations throughout the world.

As we come marching, marching, in the beauty of the day,
A million darkened kitchens, a thousand mill-lofts gray
Are touched with all the radiance that a sudden sun discloses,
For the people hear us singing, "Bread and Roses, Bread and Roses."

As we come marching, marching, we battle, too, for men—
For they are women's children, and we mother them again.
Our lives shall not be sweated from birth until life closes—
Hearts starve as well as bodies: Give us Bread, but give us Roses.

As we come marching, marching, unnumbered women dead
Go crying through our singing their ancient song of Bread;
Small art and love and beauty their drudging spirits knew—
Yes, it is Bread we fight for—but we fight for Roses, too.

As we come marching, marching, we bring the Greater Days—
The rising of the women means the rising of the race—
No more the drudge and idler—ten that toil where one reposes—
But a share of life's glories: Bread and Roses, Bread and Roses.

Source: James Oppenheim, "Bread and Roses," *The American Magazine* 73 (December 1911): 214.

SELECTED ANNOTATED BIBLIOGRAPHY

Books

Beal, Fred. *Proletarian Journey: New England, Gastonia, Moscow*. New York: Da Capo Press, 1971. Reprint of Beal's engaging 1937 autobiography in which he describes his experiences as a young textile striker in Lawrence in 1912.

Cahn, William. *Lawrence 1912: The Bread and Roses Strike*. New York: Pilgrim Press, 1980. A valuable photographic essay and introduction to the subject.

Cameron, Ardis. *Radicals of the Worst Sort: Laboring Women in Lawrence, Massachusetts, 1860–1912*. Urbana: University of Illinois Press, 1993. Important contribution documents the key role women and female neighborhood networks played in the strike.

Dubofsky, Melvyn. *We Shall Be All: A History of the Industrial Workers of the World*. Chicago: Quadrangle Books, 1969. For a classic account of the strike, see chapter 10, "Satan's Dark Mills: Lawrence, 1912," pp. 227–62.

Fenton, Edwin. *Immigrants and Unions, A Case Study: Italians and American Labor, 1870–1920*. New York: Arno Press, 1975. See pp. 313–76 for detailed information on Italians and the strike.

Flynn, Elizabeth Gurley. *The Rebel Girl: An Autobiography, My First Life (1906–1926)*. Rev. ed. New York: International Publishers, 1973. For an important IWW female strike leader's reminiscences of the strike, see pp. 127–51.

Foner, Philip S. *History of the Labor Movement in the United States*. Vol. 4: *The Industrial Workers of the World, 1905–1917*. New York: International Publishers, 1965. See pp. 306–50 for useful account of the strike and its significance.

Haywood, William D. *Bill Haywood's Book: The Autobiography of William D. Haywood*. New York: International Publishers, 1929. For the colorful IWW leader's comments on the strike, see pp. 239–57.

Kornbluh, Joyce L., ed. *Rebel Voices: An IWW Anthology*. Ann Arbor: University of Michigan Press, 1964. See pp. 158–96 for more valuable documents on the strike.

Massachusetts, Office of the Secretary of State; the Massachusetts AFL-CIO; and the Commonwealth Museum. *The Massachusetts Labor Movement: Collective Voices: The Textile Strike of 1912: A Joint Educational Project*. Excellent secondary social studies curriculum guide is useful for teachers on various educational levels.

U.S. Bureau of Labor. *Report on Strike of Textile Workers in Lawrence, Mass., in 1912*. Washington, DC: GPO, 1912. Essential primary source with data, tables, documents, analysis, and results of the department's investigation into the strike.

U.S. Congress. House. Committee on Rules. *The Strike at Lawrence, Mass.: Hearings Before the Committee on Rules of the House of Representatives on House Resolutions 409 and 433, March 2–7, 1912*. Washington, DC: GPO, 1912. Critical primary source contains transcripts of the testimony of strikers and other witnesses before the committee.

Vorse, Mary Heaton. *A Footnote to Folly: Reminiscences of Mary Heaton Vorse*. New York: Farrar & Rinehart, 1935. See pp. 1–21 for a journalist's description of the strike and the profound impact it had on her life.

Web Sites

Rare documents on the strike are available online. Visit the State University of New York's Binghamton site at http://www.womhist.binghamton.edu/. The "Women and Social Movements" database, co-sponsored by the Alexander Street Press and the Center for the Historical Study of Women and Gender at SUNY,

Binghamton, is superb for those institutions that subscribe to it. Its "Women and the Lawrence Textile Strike, 1912, Document List" contains 28 primary documents, including rare Italian ones, explanatory information, and an essay on the controversial origins of "bread and roses."

See the "Lawrence Textile Strike" at the Ohio State University's History Department Web site—http://1912.history.ohio-state.edu/labor/lawrence.htm—for images and brief text.

The testimony of Camella Teoli, a "scalped" fourteen-year old millworker, before the U.S. Congressional hearing in March 1912, is in the documents collection at George Mason University's site—http://historymatters.gmu.edu/.

Video

Labor History in Massachusetts: Collective Voices: The Textile Strike, 1912, produced and directed by Capital Services, Inc., 1990, is an excellent 22-minute video that can serve as an introductory overview of the strike in secondary school and college classes. Sponsored by the Massachusetts Office of the Secretary of State, it can be used independently or in conjunction with a curriculum guide and audiocassette that were part of a broad state project.

6

The Miners' Program, 1919–1923

"The year 1919 was like none other in American history,"[1] remarked the historian Melvyn Dubofsky. Indeed, 1919 arguably stands out as the single most significant year of labor unrest in the country's history. It was a year in which the Great Steel Strike, the Seattle General Strike, the Boston Police Strike, and over 3,300 strikes involving 4 million American workers took place. It was a year in which workers actively expanded upon Woodrow Wilson's wartime ideology of pursuing the war "to make the world safe for democracy" by publicizing postwar labor versions of "industrial democracy" and by acting to form an independent labor or farmer-labor party. It was an unprecedented year in which workers in many industries not only sought higher wages but also an increase in "workers' control."

The year that was like no other in U.S. history was also a year in which the world seemed to have turned upside down. The Bolsheviks were in power in Russia, English miners were demanding government ownership of the nation's mines, and workers in many countries were striving toward the goal of building more equitable societies out of the ruins of their demolished countries. Intellectuals, labor organizations, and governments throughout the world, including the United States, were debating, and sometimes implementing, radical programs and ideas, including the nationalization or socialization of railroads, coal mines, and other industries.

One of the prominent characteristics of this remarkable year was that a rare window of opportunity seemed to open for substantial social change in the United States and, with it, a change in the nation's labor relations. That moment passed, and such changes did not occur. Yet the aspirations and actions of ordinary working people and the labor movement during this momentous time were important. In this context, the Miners' Program remains a classic example of the class-conscious labor radicalism that characterized the post–World War 1 era. That it came into being at all in the United States is a significant indication that American workers have not always been as conservative as they are often portrayed. Moreover, even though the controversial program was never fully developed nor implemented, it did succeed in attracting the attention not only of miners and coal operators, but also of concerned government officials, consumers, intellectuals, and the general public during the early 1920s. This chapter examines an alternative course for the American labor movement and the U.S. government, a choice that held broad implications for the nation's future.

What was this "Miners' Program" that the United Mine Workers of America (UMWA) adopted at the union's heady international convention in Cleveland in September 1919? At the core of the program were two fundamental provisions: (1) nationalization of the coal mines and railroads, with democratic management; and (2) a six-hour day and five-day work week for miners. Closely associated with the core proposals were several other measures, including: (1) the founding of a labor party; (2) campaigns to organize the unorganized; and (3) workers' education. On October 1, 1919, the *United Mine Workers Journal*, the official organ of the United Mine Workers of America, enthusiastically proclaimed: "No previous convention ever was confronted by as large a number of problems and questions of vital importance, not only to the coal miners of the country, but to labor in general. Out of the convention came a program of the most progressive policies and principles that any trades union has ever adopted."[2]

A few facts should be emphasized. First, the core program was one that was unanimously approved by the vote of more than 2,000 delegates representing over 400,000 organized rank-and-file miners in the United States; it was not the proposal of a few marginal leaders or intellectuals. For years, UMWA locals had brought nationalization resolutions to the national convention, but this was the first time that the national union itself promoted the idea. Second, the UMWA was a mainstream industrial union, the largest affiliate of the American Federation of Labor (AFL), and not the radical Industrial Workers of the World. As historian David Montgomery has argued, even the conservative AFL was a "house of many mansions" at that time, and socialists, radicals, and class-conscious workers were important members of mainstream labor organizations during the Progressive Era. Third, the program was a serious, pragmatic proposal and not the expression of a mere utopian ideal. No one believed it could or should be adopted overnight; nor was outright confiscation of the mines by the government considered an option. Instead, the miners' resolution authorized the union to formulate a specific congressional bill that empowered the federal government to purchase title to the nation's mining properties on the basis of the government's actual evaluation of their worth.

A mixture of contradictory events, originating in the wartime era, and conditions peculiar to the coal industry brought the Miners' Program to the fore in 1919. One important result of the country's entry into the world conflict in April 1917 was that the federal government assumed vastly increased powers. Passage of the Lever Act in August 1917 gave the president power to regulate food and fuel supplies and prices. Harry A. Garfield was placed in charge of the new Fuel Administration responsible for overseeing the production, pricing, and distribution of coal, the valuable energy source that heated American homes and kept American industry and ships running. And when privately owned railroads failed to transport coal efficiently and otherwise meet the nation's needs, in December 1917, Woodrow Wilson established the Railroad Administration, and the government took over control of that industry. Most notably, as far as labor relations were concerned, the government established the National War Labor Board (NWLB) to avert labor unrest and mediate labor disputes so that production would be uninterrupted. The NWLB's activities reflected both the rising importance of the labor movement and the limitations of its influence. On the one hand, the agency set a precedent for the New Deal by recognizing the right of labor to organize and bargain collectively. On the other hand, it had no authority to force recalcitrant employers to recognize unions or to bargain. Winning the war was a tripartite effort involving the cooperation of government, business, and labor.

The federal government's assumption of new powers during the conflict created a climate in which the nationalization of major industries could receive serious public attention after the war. The concept was not new. From 1892 on, the Populist Party had urged the federal government to assume ownership of the railroads, and, throughout the Progressive Era, the Socialist Party had publicly campaigned for the nationalization and democratic management of the nation's major industries.

Long before the war, the soft coal industry had been considered a "sick" industry, plagued by chronic instability, overproduction, and labor unrest. Once the war ended, the huge demand for coal created by the war disappeared. Miners again faced underemployment and unemployment, along with rampant inflation, a high cost of living, and the return of dreaded old conditions. Journalists and government officials routinely proclaimed that there were "too many mines, too many miners." In fact, by 1921, there were at least 200,000 more coal miners than were necessary to sustain the nation's needs. As it was, the 660,000 miners who mined the coal had only enough work for 149 days a year, and the social distress in the coal regions was pitiful. Moreover, consumers faced high prices and periodic coal shortages. In this context, the Miners' Program represented a genuine popular hope for "workers' control" and stabilization of a badly managed, "sick" industry, but stabilization in a manner that offered working people and the nation a genuine alternative to private enterprise and existing capitalist relations.

As the war ended in November 1918, Americans continued to debate how, or if, the postwar American economy should be reconstructed. But the Wilson administration quickly removed the wartime controls, and former railroad owners vigorously demanded the return of the roads to them, especially after the railroad brotherhoods endorsed the Plumb Plan, a proposal to nationalize the railroads. Meanwhile, coal operators and the UMWA positioned themselves for battle. The operators who wanted to thwart growing labor demands and return to prewar wages and conditions insisted that the Washington Agreement remain in effect. The Washington Agreement was a soft coal contract that had been negotiated under the government's auspices in 1917, a contract that was binding for the duration of the war. To the miners, any prolongation of the agreement after the armistice had been signed seemed blatantly unfair. Besides, the 1917 contract fixed their wage rates but not coal operators' profits. It also contained a detested clause invoking automatic penalties for strikes.

It was in a context of massive unrest in the coalfields that Frank J. Hayes, international UMWA president, convened a meeting of the union's National Policy Committee in March 1919, and recommended a large wage increase, along with the essential terms of the Miners' Program— nationalization of the mines, with democratic management, and a six-hour day and five-day work week. Hayes's proposal subsequently became the popular program adopted by the international UMWA convention in Cleveland in September 1919. The miners had talked about nationalization for years, but it took domestic root in 1919.

During the summer of 1919, however, important changes occurred at the helm of the UMWA that would ultimately shape the fate of the Miners' Program. Frank J. Hayes resigned the union presidency for health reasons, and John L. Lewis, the union's appointed vice president, assumed the office as acting president. Biographers report that Lewis had risen to positions of power within the AFL and the UMWA, in large part, by currying favor with important labor personalities such as Samuel Gompers, president of the AFL, and, according to critics, by making questionable dealings with shady coal operators. Nothing in his past suggested that he would seriously support a militant labor movement or a Miners' Program that challenged capitalism and fundamentally altered the structure of the coal industry. In time, it would become clear that Lewis was not in agree-

ment with those UMWA leaders and the mass of miners who supported
the radical Miners' Program. According to biographers Melvyn Dubofsky
and Warren Van Tine, Lewis was masterful at employing class-conscious
rhetoric while practicing class-collaboration.

The nation's reaction to the Miners' Plan of 1919 was not particularly
dramatic. The steel strike and so much else was going on. Coal operators
typically greeted the nationalization proposal with ridicule, when they
discussed it at all. In what may have been an allusion to Lewis, *Coal Age*,
the operators' leading journal, even suggested that conservative union
leaders dared not openly oppose it at the convention because of the rank
and file's decided interest in the plan. But certain journals and newspapers reacted otherwise. *The New Republic* reported the program fairly,
while noting the extraordinary tenor of the times. Most of the media
focused attention on the UMWA convention's demand for a 60 percent
wage increase and the threat of a national coal strike, if the Washington
Agreement remained in force. The miners did strike on November 1, and,
on November 8, the government imposed a far-ranging injunction that
the miners disobeyed. In a controversial decision, Lewis ordered the miners to return to work but managed to maintain some face by accepting
Woodrow Wilson's offer of an immediate 14 percent increase, with a pres-
identially appointed bituminous commission to make further readjust-
ments in 1920. Lewis skillfully consolidated his power and formally won
the union's presidency in a democratic election held in December 1920.

From 1919 on, the fate of the Miners' Program was linked to many factors, including the continued vitality of a class-conscious labor movement, effective leadership, public support, the role of the government,
and the economic power of the coal operators. Warren G. Harding's victory in the presidential election of 1920 doomed any hope of maintaining
wartime working relationships, as many in Washington returned to old
notions of a very limited role for government, except to promote business
stability and growth through cooperation, and a disdain for unions of any
sort. The fortified government–business alliance also encouraged employers to launch the Open Shop and American Plan to destroy unions. Yet the
coal industry remained chaotic, and progressives who were concerned
about the public interest spoke increasingly of government regulation, if
not ownership. As the *Christian Science Monitor* reported on November 9,
1920: "Nationalization of the coal industry in the United States may be
recommended to Congress by the Senate committee on reconstruction
and production unless coal prices are reduced before the convening of the
new Congress."[3]

After the 1919 convention, John Brophy, president of UMWA District 2,
an important coal-producing region in central Pennsylvania, actively
championed the Miners' Program. He brought the program to life in a
major speech at a District 2 convention held in DuBois, Pennsylvania, in

February 1921. Then, later that year, John L. Lewis decided to run against Samuel Gompers for presidency of the AFL. To court the votes of Brophy and radicals in the labor movement, he tactically supported nationalization, which Gompers opposed. Brophy did support Lewis, who subsequently lost the AFL election. Shortly afterwards, when the UMWA's national convention enthusiastically reiterated its support for nationalization, Lewis appointed a Nationalization Research Committee to study the issue. He named Brophy head, with William Mitch, of Indianapolis, and Chris Golden, president of UMWA District 9, as the other members. At the time, Lewis promised cooperation and, in written instructions, gave the committee a wide latitude to develop and publicize a practical plan.

The Nationalization Research Committee (NRC) consulted widely, with interested intellectuals, activists, and progressive organizations such as the Bureau of Industrial Research, an independent liberal research organization, and the League for Industrial Democracy, a socialist labor and educational service that produced pamphlets on public ownership and industrial democracy. In 1922 the NRC produced a number of pamphlets advocating research and the importance of a permanent fact-finding agency to study the industry as a preliminary to nationalization. It hoped to win broad political support and avoid problems associated with either "state socialism" or syndicalism. Its most important publication, *How to Run Coal: Suggestions for a Plan of Public Ownership, Public Control, and Democratic Management in the Coal Industry,* spelled out a detailed plan as the basis for further discussion. Its specific proposals included the appointment of a Secretary of Mines to the cabinet; the formation of a budgetary and policy-making Federal Commission of Mines; the representation of miners, technicians, and consumers on an administrative national mining council; the protection of collective bargaining; and structural guarantees to protect the interests of the public, the consumer, and organized labor.

Meanwhile, the postwar agreement between the bituminous coal operators and miners expired on March 31, 1922, and a national coal strike was imminent. In response, on April 1, Senator William E. Borah, a Republican from Idaho and chair of the Senate Labor Committee, publicly decried the chaotic wastefulness of the industry and declared: "If the coal industry is not recognized [reorganized] in the interests of the public . . . then it will be up to the public to try the experiment of public ownership. I do not underestimate the task which the public will assume when it undertakes this. . . . There is no possible explanation nor justification for the price of coal at the present time other than that of waste and bad management and unconscionable profits."[4]

The UMWA launched the national strike on April 1, 1922, just as the House Labor Committee began to hold hearings on H.R. 11022, a bill "to establish a commission to inquire into labor conditions in the coal industry." On April 3, UMWA President John L. Lewis testified before the committee. After presenting a formal statement about the industry's woes in which he said that the miners wanted the industry nationalized, he undercut support for it under the questioning that followed. He claimed nationalization was "impractical" and handed opponents and operators a valuable weapon to use in subsequent efforts to discredit the Miners' Program.

The strike, which ended in August after Lewis concluded a controversial national strike settlement that did not cover the strikers who had worked in nonunion mines before the strike, strengthened the call for a coal commission. On September 7, the Senate held a heated debate over whether or not the proposed commission should study the feasibility of nationalizing the industry. For some, the thought of studying nationalization was a danger to be avoided at any cost. For others, investigation of the possibility was a public responsibility. On September 8, by a vote of 30 to 19, the Senate approved inclusion of the study of nationalization in the bill, which Congress passed on September 22, 1922. Henceforth, the country awaited the U.S. Bituminous Coal Commission's findings and what it would have to say about the industry and nationalization.

Nationalization was never a popular notion for mine owners and business interests, but it received occasional, if surprising, support in unexpected quarters in 1922. Senator David Walsh of Massachusetts noted that manufacturing associations, whose members were hard-pressed by coal costs and shortages, wanted relief and were petitioning him for nationalization. Also, a prominent committee of New York City's financial officials and others who studied the labor conditions in the Berwind-White Coal Mining Company's mines in Windber, Pennsylvania, that year found the miners' conditions there "worse than the condition of slaves" and recommended nationalization of the coal mines as a solution. On January 2, 1923, the committee's notable conclusions were featured on the front page of the *New York Times* and other newspapers.

By then, Lewis's strike policy and the Miners' Program were emerging as major issues in an intra-union ideological power struggle. At stake were two competing versions of the role of the union, the direction of the labor movement, and the overall nature of U.S. labor relations. One version, frequently termed "business unionism," meant labor's acceptance of laissez-faire capitalism, albeit with a provision for decent wages and working conditions. It also entailed a limited role for unions as bargaining agents for members and as disciplinarians of labor. In sharp contrast, the alternative version associated with the Miners' Program challenged capitalist social relations and redefined the purposes of the miners' union in the direction of greater democracy and rank-and-file militancy. It specifically meant "workers' control" through nationalization, with democratic management, of the coal and railroad industries; the founding of a labor party; and commitments to organize the unorganized and institute programs of workers' education.

Ellis Searles, a Lewis loyalist and editor of the *United Mine Workers Journal*, launched the initial blow in what subsequently became an all-out internal union assault on the Miners' Program and its supporters. On January 28, 1923, Searles issued a press release to denounce Greenwich village "reds," a label he applied to all the intellectuals and groups who had contributed to the Miners' Program. Lewis himself personally attacked Chris Golden for making what he deemed an "unauthorized" public speech to a group in Chicago in December. One by one, the members of the Nationalization Research Committee resigned in disgust. In an article in *The Outlook* in March, Golden responded to Lewis's attack by citing the interest that the media and the general public were beginning to take in the Miners' Program. Dissident radicals and rank-and-file miners subsequently went on to form the Progressive International Committee of the UMWA and, then, the "Save the Union" committee in a futile effort to oust Lewis and reform the union from within. From February 1923 on, it was clear that Lewis and the international union would not support the Miners' Program, despite its popularity with a class-conscious rank-and-file movement. Henceforth, the program and its adherents would be marginalized.

The U.S. Bituminous Coal Commission placed its seal on the fate of nationalization, too. President Warren Harding appointed seven men whose political worldviews quickly led them to dismiss any possibility of nationalization. The government and public immediately perceived the commission as weak and ineffective, and its modest suggestions were subsequently ignored. In the end, it reached a dismal conclusion: "The commission realizes that the largest opportunity and the largest responsibility for putting the coal industry in order lies with the industry itself."[5]

The Miners' Program, a significant event in U.S. history that had originated in the heady labor atmosphere of 1919, continued to enjoy substantial support and public consideration afterwards. Ultimately it met defeat during labor's "lean years" because of the hostility of the operators, government officials, business interests, and conservative unionists. Some would say that the greatest tragedy of its demise was that a mainstream union lost a rare historic golden opportunity to lead the U.S. labor movement and the country in a qualitatively different direction.

NOTES

1. Melvyn Dubofsky, *The State and Labor in Modern America* (Chapel Hill: University of North Carolina Press, 1994), p. 76.

2. "Cleveland Convention Adjourns, Adopting Most Progressive Policy Ever Enunciated by the United Mine Workers in the History of the Organization," *United Mine Workers Journal*, October 1, 1919, p. 3.

3. "Coal Industry May Be Nationalized," *Christian Science Monitor*, November 9, 1920, p. 1.

4. "Government Control and Operation of Coal Mines Is Proposed by Mr. Borah," *Christian Science Monitor*, April 1, 1922, p. 1.

5. U.S. Coal Commission, *Report of the United States Coal Commission*, 5 vols. (Washington, DC: GPO, 1925), 1:273.

DOCUMENTS

6.1. Address of President Frank J. Hayes at the Policy Meeting of the United Mine Workers of America, March 18, 1919

UMWA President Frank J. Hayes recommended the Miners' Program to the National Policy Committee meeting he convened on March 18, 1919. In this excerpt from his speech, he accurately conveyed a militant postwar labor movement's aroused hopes for a democratic reconstruction of society.

I have called this meeting of our policy committee, representative as it is of all our districts, for the purpose of formulating and adopting some definite program to meet the needs of our people when peace is officially declared. As you know, our present wage agreements terminate when peace is promulgated. No one can predict with any degree of certainty when the Peace Congress will conclude its labors and give to the world the official terms of peace. It may be a month, it may be two months or it may be longer. However, I am sure we are all agreed that it is time we took stock of ourselves and planned for the future of our people. We want to be prepared with a definite program and an established policy when we meet the coal operators. [With great pride, Hayes then described the contributions the miners made to winning the war].

Now that . . . the Prussian idea has been forever destroyed, it is time to think and plan for a realization of the ideals and principles of a democratic people. Out of the shambles of Europe there comes the dawn of a brighter day. The old social order can no longer exist. The day of master and slave can be no more. Labor must now come into its own, must take its rightful place in all the civilized nations of the world. Too long have we been ruled by the privileged few; by those born to the purple and splendor of high estate; by those who through inheritance or excessive exploitation of the poor have been able to shape the destinies of men to direct governmental policies which affect the lives and happiness of all human beings. However, we must not become intoxicated with power nor be unfair in our administration of same. We must not tear down or destroy the superstructure of civilization. We must build upon the present foundation in an orderly, sensible way a society in which labor shall share fully in the reward which is its due. We must build sanely and constructively, not for today alone but for all the days that are to come. The forces of evolution intelligently guided by the power of labor will do no man wrong and will create a social order in which every right thinking man can find his place and do his part in making the world a better and brighter place for all mankind. There is no organization of labor in America which should play a more prominent part in this reconstruction period than our own union, the largest trade organization affiliated with the American Federation of Labor. Therefore, in accord with the thoughts I have expressed, I take the liberty of submitting for the consideration of this policy committee meeting the following fundamental principles as a basis to guide us in our coming negotiations with the operators.

1st. I recommend the establishment of a six-hour workday, five days a week, as a remedial proposition to solve the peculiar situation existing in the mining industry today. I have long entertained the idea of a shorter workday, believing that it was the only sure means of promoting a condition in which all the mine workers of America could share in the markets of the nation. I need not say that thousands of our people are idle today; that a very large number of the coal miners of the country are working only half time; that if the necessary requirements of the market were apportioned among all the mines of the country a workday of six hours, five days a week, would more than supply the existing demands. We are engaged in a hazardous occupation, shut out from the light of day, working amid poisonous fumes and gases that too often shorten the lives of our people. If there is any calling in our industrial life that is entitled to a short workday as an economic measure as well as a measure to protect the health and life of the worker, then it is the calling in which we are engaged. . . .

2nd. I recommend a substantial increase on all existing tonnage, day work, yardage and dead work prices. In support of this claim I wish to refer to the high cost of living and to the lack of opportunity, due to the idleness of the mines, to make an average wage that will compare favorably with other classifications of skilled labor. . . .

3rd. I urge upon this conference to declare for nationalization of mines. I feel that we should use all the economic and political power of our great organization to attain this end. This recommendation is in accord with the past action of our International conventions. The nationalization of mines will substitute cooperation for competition and insure in a practical way the stability of the great basic industry in which we are engaged. As an indication of what governmental power in our industry can do in a stabilizing way we have but to refer to the progress achieved under the direction of the Federal Fuel Administration. To revert to the old days when competition ran wild would create industrial stagnation and hamper the rightful development of our great coal resources. Under the nationalization of mines we find a practical way to realize the reforms so necessary to the well-being of the mine worker. With the industry on a competitive basis, disorganized and demoralized, we can expect a recurrence of the economic evils which so vitally affected the coal industry a few years ago. Coal is the basis of all modern civilization, entering into every industrial process, and, in view of its utilitarian character, nationalization and control democratically administered will solve, in my judgment, one of the greatest industrial problems of our time. In emphasizing the need of the nationalization of mines we also want to emphasize the rights of our people in the premises.

First. The free and unrestricted right to organize.

Second. The right to maintain the function of our economic organization, to collectively bargain with the representatives of the government with fair and equal representation in such conferences as will determine the wages and conditions under which we must work.

Source: "Address of President Frank J. Hayes at the Policy Meeting of the United Mine Workers of America," *United Mine Workers Journal*, April 1, 1919, pp. 5, 7.

6.2.   Resolution on Nationalization, United Mine Workers Convention, 1919

This is the text of the nationalization resolution miners unanimously approved at the international UMWA convention in September 1919. Its far-reaching provisions included the federal government's purchase of the mines from private mine owners and a miners' alliance with the railroad workers.

Coal mining is a basic industry, indispensable to the economic life of the Nation, and to the well-being of the Nation's citizens.

The all-important coal resources of our country are owned and controlled by private interests. Under the prevailing system of private ownership coal is mined primarily for the purpose of creating profits for the coal owners. The production of coal under this system is characterized by an appalling economic waste.

The incomparable natural resources of America, and particularly those of timber and coal, are being despoiled under a system of production which wastes from 33 to 50 per cent of these resources in order that the maximum amount of dividends may accrue to those capitalists who have secured ownership of these indispensable commodities.

We hold that the coal supply of our Nation should be owned by the Commonwealth and operated in the interest of and for the use and comfort of all the people of the Commonwealth.

Countless generations of men and women will doubtless follow us, and the American people of this generation owe a solemn duty to them in protecting with jealous care and conserving with wise administration those great treasures that a bounteous nature has bestowed upon us in such generous measure.

Our coal resources are the birthright of the American people for all time to come, and we hold that it is the immediate duty of the American people to prevent the profligate waste that is taking place under private ownership of these resources by having the Government take such steps as may be necessary providing for the nationalization of the coal-mining industry of the United States.

Under private ownership, where production is conducted for private gain, the spirit of the times seems to be: "After us the Deluge."

This must be supplanted by a system where production will be for use and the common good, and economic waste will give way to conservation of the Nation's heritage in the interest of posterity.

We, the United Mine Workers of America, in international convention assembled, representing the workers who have their lives and the welfare of their dependents invested in the coal mines of our country, do therefore

Resolve, That we demand the immediate nationalization of the coal mining industry of the United States.

That we instruct our international officers and the international executive board to have a bill prepared for submission to Congress containing the following provisions:

1. That the Government, through Act of Congress, acquire title to all coal properties within the United States now owned by private interests; by purchasing said properties at a figure representing the actual valuation of said properties as determined upon investigation by accredited agents of the Federal Government.

2. That the coal-mining industry be operated by the Federal Government and that the mine workers be given equal representation upon such councils or commissions as may be delegated the authority to administer the affairs of the coal-mining industry, authority to act upon the question of wages, hours of labor, conditions of employment, or the adjudication of disputes and grievances within the industry.

3. Realizing as we do that the masses of the American people, while they have been dispossessed of their rights of ownership to the coal and other natural resources upon which their well-being depends, still own and control the Government of the United States whenever they care to exercise their power in the matter; and realizing that the success of our effort to secure nationalization of the coal mining industry depends upon our ability to convince a majority of the American people of the justice of this proposal, we herewith further instruct our international officers and international executive board to use their influence to bring our demand

for nationalization to the attention of the American people and to endeavor to secure the cooperation and support of every progressive force and every liberal, fair-minded individual, with a regard for our duty to posterity and a belief in the principle of common ownership of our natural resources, to the accomplishment of this end.

We further instruct our representatives to urge in the coming conference with the representatives of the railroad workers' unions, a working alliance for the purpose of securing the adoption of the Plumb Plan for nationalization of railroads, as the initial step in the fight for the principle of nationalization, with the understanding that such alliance will continue to press the issue with unabated vigor until the principle of nationalization has been extended to embrace the coal-mining industry of the Nation,

And be it further resolved, That our organization, for the reasons set forth above, carry its fight for nationalization of mines into the Dominion of Canada, and throw its influence wherever possible behind our members in Canada to the accomplishment of that end.

Source: Quoted in Ethelbert Stewart, "Trade-Union Attitude Toward Nationalization of Coal Mines," *Monthly Labor Review* 9 (November 1919): 68–70.

6.3.   "General Labor Review," *Coal Age*, October 2, 1919

On October 2, 1919, Coal Age, the nation's leading operators' journal, commented on the UMWA convention's adoption of the Miners' Program. In this excerpt, it poked fun at the demands and claimed that union leaders who opposed nationalization dared not do so because of a militant rank and file.

Labor developments of the current week have been many. It seems that the mania to strike is as contagious as the "flu," if not even more so; nor is the germ confined to any one trade or calling. The demands to be made by the United Mine Workers of America, assembled in convention at Cleveland, Ohio, have been formulated and are in many respects the most radical yet drawn up. They include demands for $8 per day for six hours' work and 60 per cent. increase on all tonnage, yardage and deadwork prices, a five-day week, time-and-one-half for overtime, the abolition of double shifts, elimination of the automatic penalty clause and the establishment of weekly paydays.

Even such demands as these have their humorous side. One of the delegates to the convention aptly stated conditions when he remarked that the committee had omitted just one important point, and that was that they had not demanded that the weekly pay be given in advance.

The miners say that unless these demands are granted in toto on or before Nov. 1 next, a strike will be inaugurated. The radical tendencies of the rank and file, and the unrest of manual workers everywhere, appear to have instilled in the breasts of the leaders a fear that unless the demands of the radicals are put to a test they (the leaders) will face political defeat and oblivion. . . .

It is said that conservative leaders of the mine workers do not favor nationalization of the mines, nor entertain the hope that the miners will succeed in nationalizing American industries. They dared not, however, or at least did not protest in the miners' convention when that body unanimously adopted a resolution calling for the nationalization of the coal industry.

Source: "General Labor Review," *Coal Age*, October 2, 1919, p. 583.

6.4.   [Comments on the UMWA convention], *The New Republic*, September 24, 1919

> *Throughout the UMWA's 1919 convention, journals such as* The New Republic *fairly reported the proceedings. This comment summarized the basic Miners' Plan and suggested that it was the product of extraordinary times.*

TWO decisions have been reached by the United Mine Workers, in convention at Cleveland, that will have a profound effect on the development of American trade union policy. The miners have proposed an alliance with the Railway Brotherhoods which, if consummated, will establish the strongest partnership in American industry. They have also determined to demand the nationalization of the mines in which they labor. Concrete proposals for nationalization may be submitted by the Committee on Resolutions. Apparently the right of way is first to be granted to the Railway Brotherhoods, in their campaign for the Plumb Plan, with nationalization of the mines to be demanded subsequently. The depth to which traditional American trade union policy has been shaken by recent events is most clearly shown when conservative unions like the Mine Workers and the Brotherhoods, with conservative leaders, go on beyond wages and hours and demand fundamental changes in the control of their industries.

Source: [Comments], *The New Republic*, September 24, 1919, p. 215.

6.5.   John L. Lewis, Testimony before the House of Representatives' Committee on Labor, April 3, 1922

Two days after the national strike of 1922 began, UMWA President John L. Lewis testified before a congressional committee considering H.R. 11022, a bill to create a coal commission. This excerpt contains the equivocal wording that handed operators a valuable weapon to use against the Miners' Program.

The United Mine Workers of America have demanded that the coal industry be nationalized. . . .

. . . I think that Government ownership is an impossibility under present circumstances. The people of the country are not in a position to acquire title to the mining deposits of the country or the developed mining properties. It would constitute a tremendous financial burden upon the country, and it would be extremely difficult to secure any appraisal of the valuation of the mining deposits and the developed properties of the country.

It would possibly take many years to determine that particular point. On the other hand, the question of the Government taking over and operating the mines after the manner in which the railroads were operated during the war period is repugnant to many; and as a feasible proposition it seems that the creation of some board of control, if a proper legal premise can be found, would be the most practical method of stabilizing the industry and bringing it into some degree of proper regulation.

Source: Statement of John L. Lewis, Congress, House of Representatives, Committee on Labor, *Investigation of Wages and Working Conditions in the Coal-Mining Industry: Hearings Before the Committee on Labor, House of Representatives, Sixty-Seventh Congress, Second Session, on H.R. 11022* (Washington, DC: GPO, 1922), pp. 220, 233.

6.6.   United Mine Workers of America, Nationalization Research Committee, *How to Run Coal*, 1922

In 1922 the Nationalization Research Committee produced How to Run Coal: Suggestions for a Plan of Public Ownership, Public Control, and Democratic Management in the Coal Industry, *in which it outlined a concrete plan as the basis for further discussion. In this excerpt, the committee explained the*

reasons for the plan, "workers' control," and "democratic man-
agement." Note that the authors used the term "American Plan"
to counter the use of that term by business interests to mean the
open shop.

I. THE AMERICAN PLAN

We shall first present our plan in summary form, and then tell why we believe each item is necessary. These are our proposals:

NATIONALIZATION OF COAL MINES

1. A Secretary of Mines in the Cabinet.
2. A Federal Commission of Mines, to control budget and policy on the basis of continuous fact-finding.
3. A national mining council, to administer policies, with miners, technicians and consumers represented.
4. The safe-guarding of collective bargaining through joint-conference.
5. Freeing production management from wage squabbles and sales problems, by making wages the first charge against the industry and therefore making wage measurement one of the functions of the Federal Commission under the principles of collective bargaining, which will be safeguarded by an independent joint wage scale committee.

WHY. . . .

The coal industry has been so disorganized and mismanaged that the situation in recent years has approached what big business men and stand-pat senators describe as a "catastrophe." Intelligent men, with the welfare of the industry at heart, agree that the "game is up"—the old game of speculative profits, over-production, shortages, sky-high prices, unemployment, gunmen, spies, the murder of miners, a sullen, desperate public. Unless unification and order enter the industry, there will be a blow-up somewhere, followed by drastic, angry and frenzied legislation. The American Kingdom of Coal is today in as chaotic and explosive condition as the states of Europe. No single constructive suggestion has come from the operators. No large leading idea has come from the public. The public is feeling intensely, but is not yet thinking wisely.

The operators have a fresh explanation for the annual crisis as often as it rolls around. One year it is car shortage, another year, high wages, then the war, then government interference. Of thought-out plan and remedy they have offered none.

The only large-scale proposal has come from the United Mine Workers of America in their demand for nationalization. It is the only proposal that grapples with slack work for the miners, high prices and irregular supply for the consumers. It is now the job of the miners to decide what kind of nationalization they want. There are only three plans possible for control and administration. All other plans are minor variations on those three. There are only three plans possible, because, after the owners are bought out, only three interests are concerned—the public, the miners and the technical and managerial group. The plans differ in the proportion of power they give to each of the three interests.

DEMOCRATIC MANAGEMENT

Any plan of unification to be acceptable to a free people must fulfill several demands. It must not only yield a good American life to the worker in the sense of wages, hours, safety, health, and all other living conditions; it must also satisfy his demand for a voice in management, for a share in the actual administration of the industry. The American worker has no use for the thing called state socialism. To have a group of politicians at Washington manage coal would be as distasteful to the miner as it would be to the long-suffering public.

Any plan of nationalization must give a larger area of control inside the industry to all workers. Against great odds and powerful opposition the workers have won a measure of control, certain negative functions of management. Their method has been collective bargaining, and their instrument has been the union. The workers have won at least a measure of control over the rate of pay; the length of working day; the details of daily life inside the mine and in leisure hours; the qualification of the worker to be hired; the manner and tone of the manager; the right to inspect the conditions of the mine and, through the check-weighman, to inspect the amount of work done. These are real gains in personal freedom and economic status. They have been largely won by the union. The proof is that these rights are not granted in a non-union field.

But these gains are not enough for a worker in a democratically managed industry. He wishes the right to make suggestions on technical improvements, on car-pushing, on slack work, on output, and the right to take part in carrying them out. There will be no complete cooperation until his suggestions are welcomed and weighed. His good will and intelligence should be encouraged. They must be incorporated in any successful scheme of administration. The working miner must have a real part in the government of coal. Democratic management is what the worker wants. By democratic management he means that coal shall be run by the people who mine it, who apply their scientific knowledge to its problems, who transport it, who sell it, who use it. If coal were run by a bureau at Washington, the miner would feel as far away from being represented in the industry as he feels today under private ownership.— Democratic management must be the blood and bones of a plan of nationalization for the mines.

Source: United Mine Workers of America, Nationalization Research Committee, *How to Run Coal: Suggestions for a Plan of Public Ownership, Public Control, and Democratic Management in the Coal Industry* [Altoona, PA: The Committee, 1922], pp. 7–11.

6.7.   U.S. Senate, Debate on Coal Commission Bill, September 7, 1922

The U.S. Senate heatedly debated Section (d) of the proposed coal commission bill, a provision that mandated the commission investigate the possibility of nationalization. As this excerpt from the debate on September 7, 1922, indicates, there were wide differences of opinion on the subject. Especially noteworthy are one opponent's comparisons of the nationalization of the mines to the nationalization of women, and the supporters' arguments about the public's interest. The Senate voted to retain Section (d) in the bill.

Mr. [Nathaniel—Au.] DIAL [of South Carolina—Au.]. Mr. President, in my opinion, subdivision (d) is merely an invitation to all of the disgruntled people of the country to appear before the proposed commission to complain and talk about nationalizing the coal industry. So far as I am concerned, I do not want to see any effort made to nationalize the railroads or the coal industry or anything else. I want the various industries of the country to remain in the hands of private individuals. I feel that the language which I seek to strike out will merely afford an invitation to people who have become dissatisfied to find fault and to complain with the conduct of business. I thought this administration were going to have less politics in business and more business in politics, or something of that sort, but it seems that they have in some way lost the text or, at any rate, they do not stick to it. . . .

Mr. [William—Au.] BORAH [of Idaho—Au.]. Mr. President, I may have a different view of this matter from my colleague on the committee, the Senator from South Carolina [Mr. DIAL], and I may not. This is simply an investigation of a subject which is up for discussion among a great many people in this country who are neither I.W.W.'s nor insane. It is a feature of the coal situation which has presented itself to men of very high intelligence who have given a great deal of study to it. They have felt, and I feel, that an investigation of it is a wise thing to have. If, as the Senator from South Dakota [Mr. STERLING] says, nationalization is impracticable and has proven impracticable in many instances and disastrous in others, that will be the thing which this commission will likely report to this body. If the evidence or the showing is to that effect, we will have it disposed of, as I assume that this commission is not going to be composed of the kind of men that Senators seems to fear. . . . But, Mr. President, I am not afraid of investigating any feature of the coal industry; and if there is anything at all in nationalization which it is worth while for this body to have when it comes to establish a national policy I want this body to have it. I do not want the ordinary commission, which goes out and gathers a lot of incoherent data and brings it back here and dumps it into the wastebasket of the Congress and leaves it there. I desire, so far as I have any ambition at all in regard to this matter, to see something of a crystallization of these facts into some policy which will enable the Congress to deal with the matter from a national standpoint and adopt a national policy in regard to the coal industry. It is altogether probable that the commission which will be appointed in this matter will be as desirous of arriving at a practical policy as anybody in the Senate; and it is not to be presumed, because they are investigating this matter, that it is foreordained that they are going to recommend nationalization.

I say, therefore, that it is wise to have a complete study, a thorough investigation, a comprehensive investigation of the entire subject. Let us know it in all its details and establish once for all, if we can, a national policy with reference to this great industry upon which the industrial life of our people so largely depends. . . .

Mr. [Augustus—Au.] STANLEY [of Kentucky—Au.]. . . . A man becomes a socialist not because he believes in any particular thing but because he is against many particular things. It is a cry of anger and resentment, a state of hysteria to a greater or less extent. It is fanned by agitation; it is fanned by discussion. Every disordered mind, every bug, every wheel that is loose in all the heads of all the cranks in the country will go fanning and buzzing the minute the Congress of the United States begins to discuss that sort of thing.

This is a country of happy homes; but there are people who believe in the destruction of the home and in the nationalization of women; they believe that the institution of marriage is an absurdity. Let us start an investigation touching the propriety of the proposition to nationalize women, to do away with marriage, and every unhappily married couple in the country, every bug that hates women, and every bugess that hates men will immediately be worked into a frenzy because the Federal Congress is considering the nationalization of women. All the cranks and all the criminals and all the fools in the country are stirred up by the waving of that sort of a red flag from the Dome of the Capitol. Leave these questions that act on bugs exactly like poking a hornets' nest acts on the hornets. It turns them all loose. Let the sleeping dog alone. Do not discuss the propriety of doing anything you know you are not going to do.

Do not talk about giving medicine to a patient that you know will either kill the patient or drive the patient crazy. . . .

Mr. [David—Au.] WALSH of Massachusetts. . . . I consider this bill a bill to stop nationalization of coal mines. Why? Because it is notice upon the part of the Congress of the United States to the coal industry that we are concerned about the successful and satisfactory conduct of this industry; that we consider it of such a peculiar relationship to the public that it must be conducted with an eye and a purpose of public service; that the public will not permit it to be so conducted that it paralyzes other industries and impairs health and life.

Mr. President, why do men form trusts? Why do men give up the private conduct of business and organize corporations? What is the spirit in which it is done? Let us be honest with each other. It is greed and selfishness. We can make more money by incorporating and enlarging our business than we can by doing it alone; and to assert that our Government can not check greed and selfishness when it recognizes no limits in an industry vital and essential to the prosperity and well being of the people, I say, is to confess the impotency and uselessness and absurdity of government itself.

I do not want my remarks misunderstood. I am not for the nationalization of coal mines or of other essential industries; but I do assert that when it is essential for public service to predominate in an industry and the industry collapses, then this Government should step in and regulate it, or, at least, indicate that unless it does keep in mind the public interest and service to the public, it proposes to regulate the industry rather than permit extortion or gross indifference to the general well-being.

Therefore, Mr. President, I am not afraid of the word "regulation." Neither am I afraid of the word "nationalization." I am, however, afraid of the growing sentiment in this country for nationalization. I am afraid when I see it indorsed and approved by conservative business men. I am afraid when I see manufacturers themselves pleading and asking for some relief and for some remedy, rather than financial ruin by being deprived of power, light, and heat. . . .

Mr. [Henry—Au.] MYERS [of Montana—Au.]. Nationalization of industry is the dream, the goal, of every socialist, every Bolshevist, every communist of this country. To investigate by action of Congress their visionary, confiscatory schemes would only encourage them and give a fresh impetus to their mischievous propaganda, already carried too far. If we start on nationalization of industries, where will it end? If we should nationalize the coal industry in the country, the next thing would be to nationalize the railroads of the country, and then the metalliferous mines of the country, and in turn the steel industry of the country, the clothing industry of the country, the boot and shoe industry of the country, and then to nationalize the farming industry of the country, agriculture.

Source: 67th Congress, 2nd sess., Senate, *Congressional Record* (September 7, 1922), vol. 62, pt. 12, pp. 12236–12237, 12241, 12242, 12244.

6.8. C. J. Golden, "Shall Our Coal Mines Be Nationalized?" *The Outlook*, March 28, 1923

C. J. Golden, President of UMWA District 9 and member of the UMWA's Nationalization Research Committee, wrote this article for The Outlook *shortly after Lewis attacked him for making a public speech on the Miners' Program. In this excerpt, Golden cited evidence that the media and public were not uniformly hostile, but often neutral, fair-minded, and interested in the plan.*

Our second report, "How to Run Coal," was a carefully planned, tentative scheme of administering a nationalized coal industry—tentative, so as to get the detailed criticisms of miners, engineers, consumers, Government officers, and everybody. Last autumn it was distributed among the miners. Afterwards, in order to make public that we had such a plan, I made a speech on it in New York and handed it to the press.

Was the public willing to discuss nationalization? . . .

The press of this country printed that plan fully, fairly, and emphatically. Why? Because alongside that news every paper was printing other coal stories about "anthracite shortage," "prices go higher," "fuel administrator helpless," and so forth. . . .

People soberly considered our figures—$1,500,000,000 to $2,000,000,000 for buying the mines, plus $2,500,000,000 for the coal reserves. People discussed our proposed Commission of Mines for the control of budget and policy and our National Mining Council, made up of miners, managers, and consumers, to get out coal. People saw that the plan took the same sort of union we have now and gave it greater power and bigger responsibility; and people didn't drop dead with horror.

Did all the editorial writers tear us to pieces? The operators say they did. . . .

. . . The fact is the editors did not do their usual job; overwhelming condemnation there was not. . . .

Most editors are non-committal; which is all we ask. For example, the "Ohio State Journal:" "The public may well ponder the subject with great care before deciding to do it." And the New York "World:" "Before anything like this is seriously considered the coal industry must have broken down altogether. On the other hand, it is hardly an exaggeration to say that it has broken down." . . .

The Baltimore "Sun" says the miners "think that the era of private control is drawing to a close because it has been found to be unworkable under post-war conditions. The public will suspend judgment until it hears what the Federal Coal Commission has to say on nationalization." . . .

The public was chewing on this plan, cutting its eye teeth and learning wisdom on the whole coal problem. A poor time, one would say, to try to muzzle the Nationalization Research Committee by ordering it to keep silence for a year and to throw the whole argument back into hot air by calling the plan "red." . . .

Time presses. The United States Coal Commission is ordered by law to examine plans for nationalization. There the operators will advocate any kind of poison substitute—trusts, for instance, with harmless "regulation." At the Chicago conference with the miners the operators in the lobbies talked nationalization a-plenty, but not for publication. Going to the recent New York conference, some big operators from the Middle West rode all the way with men whom they did not recognize as miners; the thing the operators talked most was "how far these damn miners are going with this nationalization business." All we ask of the coal owners is, "Talk out; let's have your nationalization kicks in the open. Meet our facts publicly." . . .

One plan exists—the miners'! Examine its facts, and criticize. Don't forget this set of facts: The miners' union has come of age. In its boyhood it was satisfied with a few cents an hour and with some recognition of its right to life. Grown-up unions nowadays are branching out into cooperatives and banking and insurance and education. "No forward step" would be poor advice to the unions. "Plan out your nationalization bills for Congress," sounds better among rank and file miners; among railroaders, too, I hear.

Source: C. J. Golden, "Shall Our Coal Mines Be Nationalized?" *The Outlook*, March 28, 1923, pp. 576–78.

SELECTED ANNOTATED BIBLIOGRAPHY

Books

Beik, Mildred Allen. *The Miners of Windber: The Struggles of New Immigrants for Unionization, 1890s–1930s*. University Park: Pennsylvania State University Press, 1996. A local study with valuable information on District 2, the war, and postwar eras.

Bernstein, Irving. *The Lean Years: A History of the American Worker, 1920–1933*. Boston: Houghton Mifflin, 1960. Excellent readable survey of U.S. labor during the 1920s.

Blankenhorn, Heber. *The Strike for Union*. New York: H. W. Wilson Company, 1924. Reprint, New York: Arno and The New York Times, 1969. Classic account of the sixteen-month long strike of Somerset County, Pennsylvania miners in UMWA District 2 in 1922–1923.

Brecher, Jeremy. *Strike!* Rev. ed. Cambridge, MA: South End Press, 1997. Chapter 4, "Nineteen Nineteen," covers the major strikes of that year.

Brophy, John. *A Miner's Life.* Edited by John O. P. Hall. Madison: University of Wisconsin Press, 1964. Brophy's autobiography and essential reading.

Dubofsky, Melvyn. *The State and Labor in Modern America.* Chapel Hill: University of North Carolina Press, 1994. Valuable contribution highlights the important role of the state.

Dubofsky, Melvyn and Warren Van Tine. *John L. Lewis: A Biography.* New York: Quadrangle/The New York Times Book Co., 1977. Classic biography of Lewis.

Everling, Arthur Clark. "Tactics over Strategy in the United Mine Workers of America: Internal Politics and the Question of the Nationalization of the Mines, 1908–1923." Ph.D. diss., Pennsylvania State University, 1977. Traces the union's internal political conflicts.

Goodrich, Carter. *The Miner's Freedom: A Study of the Working Life in a Changing Industry.* Boston: Marshall Jones Company, 1925. Best study of the impact of mechanization on the craft of mining and on the miner's traditional independence at the workplace.

Laslett, John H. M., ed. *The United Mine Workers of America: A Model of Industrial Solidarity?* University Park: Pennsylvania State University Press, 1996. Important collection of thematic essays on the union's history from 1890 to 1990.

Lewis, John L. *The Miners' Fight for American Standards.* Indianapolis: The Bell Publishing Co., 1925. Lewis's exposition of his conservative views in the 1920s.

McCartin, Joseph A. *Labor's Great War: The Struggle for Industrial Democracy and the Origins of Modern American Labor Relations, 1912–1921.* Chapel Hill: University of North Carolina Press, 1997. Important study of the war's impact on labor relations.

Montgomery, David. *The Fall of the House of Labor: The Workplace, the State, and American Labor Activism, 1865–1925.* Cambridge, Eng.: Cambridge University Press, 1987. See chapters entitled "Patriots or Paupers" and " 'This Great Struggle For Democracy.' "

———. *Workers' Control in America: Studies in the History of Work, Technology, and Labor Struggles.* Cambridge, Eng.: Cambridge University Press, 1979. See "The 'New Unionism' and the Transformation of Workers' Consciousness in America, 1909–22."

Ricketts, Elizabeth Cocke. " 'Our Battle For Industrial Freedom': Radical Politics in the Coal Fields of Central Pennsylvania, 1916–1926." Ph.D. diss., Emory University, 1996. Major recent study of District 2 and the Miners' Program.

Singer, Alan. "Which Side Are You On? Ideological Conflict in the United Mine Workers of America, 1919–1928." Ph.D. diss., Rutgers University, 1982. Key source documents the rise, fall, and broad importance of the Miners' Program.

United Mine Workers of America. District No. 2. *Why the Miners' Program?* Clearfield, PA: UMWA, District 2, 1921. Pioneering district document promoted the Miners' Program.

United Mine Workers of America. Nationalization Research Committee. *Compulsory Information in Coal: A Fact Finding Agency*. [Altoona, PA: The Committee], 1922. An important committee publication.

———. *How to Run Coal: Suggestions for a Plan of Public Ownership, Public Control, and Democratic Management in the Coal Industry*. [Altoona, PA: The Committee, 1922]. The committee's most noteworthy publication offers a detailed description of its plan.

Zieger, Robert H. *Republicans and Labor, 1919–1929*. Lexington: University Press of Kentucky, 1969. Valuable study of Republican labor policies in the decade after the war.

Web Site

John Brophy's Papers, located at The Catholic University of America, contain many documents on the Miners' Program. The "Finding Aid" for the collection is available at the university's Web site—http://libraries.cua.edu/brophy.html. The site contains a detailed description of the collection, plus historical notes and bibliographies of use to students and researchers.

Video

The Struggle for an American Way of Life: Coal Miners and Operators in Central Pennsylvania, 1919–1933, written and produced by Jim Dougherty, with David Lind and Connie Howard. Indiana, PA: Indiana University of Pennsylvania, Folklife Documentation Center, 1992. This excellent 56-minute video traces the region's turbulent labor relations from the UMWA's adoption of the Miners' Program to the rise of the New Deal. Teachers may show all, or half of it, during classes.

7

The General Textile Strike of 1934

The General Textile Strike of 1934 was the largest strike to take place in the United States during the turbulent year of 1934. It was a watershed year when American workers took part in several nationally significant general strikes and a total of 1,856 work stoppages, the greatest number of such happenings since 1919. The underlying impetus for this outbreak of strikes was the workers' desire to bring about a fundamental change in existing power relationships, that is, to get the federal government to shift its support to labor in important and concrete ways. Textile workers figured prominently in this general effort. In September, as many as 500,000 workers from various sections of the industry, including cotton goods, silk and rayon, woolen and worsted goods, took part in a massive strike that ranged from Maine to Alabama. The national scale of the strike was unprecedented. Strikers included previously unionized textile workers in the Northeast, a variety of mill operatives in the Middle Atlantic states, and large numbers of previously unorganized workers in the South.

The strike grew out of a combination of the workers' long-term grievances, worsening living and working conditions related to the ongoing depression afflicting textiles in the 1920s and 1930s, and the rising expectations produced by newly elected President Franklin Delano Roosevelt's promises of a "New Deal." Like workers in many other industries, the textile operatives felt heartened and emboldened by Section 7 (a) of the National Industrial Recovery Act (NIRA), passed in June 1933. This important provision granted workers the legal right to organize and engage in collective bargaining with their employers, through agents of their own choosing, free from interference by their employers. Although Section 7 (a) built upon a precedent established by the ephemeral National War Labor Board during World War I, working people accurately recognized that it represented a major, and possibly more durable, change in U.S. labor relations. The textile workers were among those who quickly realized that they had to mobilize to make Section 7 (a) a reality because the new law was enabling legislation that only sanctified workers' rights on paper. Once mobilized, employer and governmental attitudes would be critical.

Workers launched the General Textile Strike on Labor Day, September 3, 1934. Their primary goals were to secure union recognition and better working conditions. At the time, the strike was widely viewed as an important event and major test of the early New Deal, which was coming under increasing scrutiny and criticism from various quarters of the population. *The Nation* and much of the nation's media were focusing critical attention on the successes and shortcomings of the National Recovery Administration (NRA), the NIRA's administrative body, and the plethora of labor boards associated with it. In 1934 business interests were often unhappy because neither economic recovery nor industrial peace had been achieved. Working people were often unhappy because anti-union employers and an unresponsive NRA seemed to be thwarting fulfillment of the government's promises to them. Like many other aspects of the New Deal, the Roosevelt administration's policy on labor and industrial relations was a pragmatic and evolving matter, not simply pro-labor, as is often thought, nor the product of a preconceived and wholly consistent plan. Moreover, the U.S. Supreme Court had not yet ruled on the constitutionality of the NIRA, the cornerstone of early New Deal policy. In any case, in 1934, the viability and the enforcement of Section 7 (a) was seriously in question.

Thus, the textile workers' three-week-long strike took place in a highly politicized and uncertain context rife with labor conflict. It ended in a disastrous defeat for them on September 22, 1934, when their union, the United Textile Workers (UTW), called off the strike. That the strikers won none of their major demands, not national union recognition nor desired changes in their hours, wages, and work loads, was highly significant. In important ways, the strike had revealed the serious limitations and inherent deficiencies of the federal government's early New Deal labor policy. Thereafter, the textile employers successfully controlled and manipulated a plethora of new governmental boards, much as they had done from the beginning of the New Deal. The strike's defeat also helped shape a meaningful and lasting pattern of national industrial relations. In subsequent years, the industrial North became the core of the nation's unionized sector, and the South remained predominantly unorganized.

The textile strike had been preceded by an industrywide, long-term economic depression that hit the industry after World War I, continued on throughout the 1920s, and merged into the Great Depression. Throughout these years, textile manufacturers complained about chronic overproduction, declining prices, and fierce competition, while workers confronted unemployment, layoffs, and reduced wages. Meanwhile, an important regional shift with far-reaching implications occurred during the 1920s. For the first time, the number of spindles in southern mills outnumbered those in northeastern plants. This geographical shift in the locus of textile production undercut the existence of the United Textile Workers, the nation's leading textile union, because it was primarily northern-based. The numerous small and large textile mills of the South had won a competitive advantage, chiefly by their traditional practice of paying their nonunionized workers lower wages than those paid in the North. To maintain that edge, southern mills increasingly turned to technology and brought in machines that created "stretch-outs" and "speed-ups," that is, increased and intensified work loads for the operatives. Technological change was not new, but the number and speed of the new machines introduced in the 1920s were. For the employer, stretch-outs led to higher outputs that cut the cost of production per unit. For the overburdened worker, they often stimulated vigorous protests such as the strike in Gastonia, North Carolina, in 1929.

During the decade, the mill owners sought a remedy for their industry's woes through the formation of national trade associations, something many other industries were doing. Henceforth, cooperation was to replace ruthless competition and survival of the fittest. To promote common goals, northern and southern cotton trade associations thus merged to form the Cotton Textile Institute (CTI) in 1926. Its first priority was to seek a change in the nation's antitrust laws. The idea that an industry could regulate itself through its own efforts and through trade associations was popular with many businesses at the time. The major goal of the CTI, like that of other trade associations, was to achieve stability for the industry as a whole and to maintain that stability within a capitalistic framework.

The industry's ongoing economic problems provided the impetus for the CTI to embrace President Roosevelt's recovery program in the spring of 1933. Recovery, or putting the nation back to work during the Great Depression, was Roosevelt's top priority, and Congress quickly passed the National Industrial Recovery Act, in June. The inclusion of labor's rights in Section 7(a) of the NIRA, however, was an afterthought, a concession designed to win labor's support for the broader bill. The new law created the National Recovery Administration to administer the recovery program, and the gist of the program was to authorize businesses and trade associations to draw up industrywide codes of fair competition, codes then approved by the government. Their purpose was to end destructive competition by setting minimum wages, maximum hours, and standard working conditions. Industrial recovery was to be achieved by raising wages, increasing purchasing power, elevating prices, reducing the work week, creating jobs, and encouraging collective bargaining. To provide an incentive for business, the NIRA built on the precedent of the War Industries Board in World War I and made complying industries exempt from antitrust laws.

Roosevelt signed the cotton textile code on July 9, and it became effective on July 16, 1933. It was the first of hundreds of codes that were eventually adopted during the existence of the NRA from 1933 to 1935. Code No. 1 thus served as a model for other industries, including other segments of the diverse textile industry. Significantly, workers had no voice in its drafting; rather, industry representatives alone drew it up. At the time, the UTW was easy to ignore. It only had 15,000 paying members.

The government-approved code was a mixed blessing or curse for the workers. Some of its terms did benefit labor in the short term. With some notable exceptions, it established a minimum wage of $12 a week for southern employees and $13 a week for northern ones at a time when many operatives were earning only $5 or $6 a week. It also reduced the workers' typical 50–55-hour work week to a maximum of 40 hours, and limited production to two shifts. It prohibited the employment of people under the age of sixteen at a time when a diminishing number, about 3 percent of the textile work force, were children. The most important gain for the workers was the perfunctory inclusion, as required by the new law, of Section 7 (a) of the NIRA.

However, the Cotton Textile Institute had drawn up the code in accordance with the wishes of its members—all textile employers, and any benefits that accrued to the unrepresented workers were incidental to the general purpose of stabilizing and revitalizing the ailing industry. Thus, the code maintained regional wage differences, made the industry the administrator without granting any representation to the UTW, and ignored the stretch-out, one of the greatest grievances of the workers. It was left to South Carolina senator James Byrnes to criticize the omission of the stretch-out, and criticism subsequently led to an ineffective amendment that urged employers to refrain from increasing the machine work load beyond what it was on July 1.

Employer noncompliance and evasion of Section 7 (a) quickly became major issues, as did the NRA's enforcement of the code and the composition of the board that oversaw its enforcement. In August 1933, the NRA converted the committee that had drafted the code into the Cotton Textile National Industrial Relations Board (CTNIRB) and made it the Code Authority that had ultimate jurisdiction over the textile industry. The

CTNIRB's chairman, Robert Bruere, was an economist sympathetic to business; the spokesman for the industry was B. F. Geer, president of Furman University; and the nominal labor representative was an unqualified and ineffective printer, not a textile worker. The administration of the code had been placed into the hands of a governmental board that was, in theory, impartial, but in fact controlled by the employers.

The code also established a complex bureaucratic procedure for resolving industrial disputes, a procedure that favored the employers, most of whom were hostile to unions and Section 7 (a). In theory, each mill was supposed to set up an industrial relations committee with the employer and no more than three employees as representatives. If grievances could not be resolved at the local level, they were to be sent to the State Industrial Relations Board, and if still unsatisfied, passed on to the Cotton Textile National Industrial Relations Board. In fact, the CTNIRB resolved the grievances that reached it by passing them on to the Cotton Textile Institute; the CTI turned to the very employers the workers complained about; those employers then denied the charges or made superficial changes that satisfied the board.

Textile workers had responded to Section 7 (a) by taking the code at face value and organizing. By September 1933, the UTW had grown to 40,000 members, and membership increased thereafter. From August 1933 to August 1934, the workers brought 3,920 grievances about their employers' noncompliance with the code, the inhumanity of the stretch-out system, the firing of employees for joining a union, and other matters to the Bruere board, to no avail. The board's record in regard to labor's rights is considered notorious. It never did anything to uphold Section 7 (a). It never found a single employer guilty of discrimination against workers on account of their union membership or activities. It never called for a representative election for workers to choose union representatives in any plant in the country. While it often claimed to investigate stretch-out grievances, it merely consulted with the textile employer and found few charges justified. Workers were bewildered and shocked by the maze of such unresponsive or hostile governmental bureaucracy. Under these circumstances, their initial enthusiasm for the code soon turned to disappointment and anger.

A prelude to the general strike occurred in May 1934 when the NRA ordered a three-month reduction in machine hours with a corresponding cut in wages. The textile workers prepared for a general strike in June, but the federal government averted the walkout by making a few minor concessions to the UTW. Nonetheless, southern cotton workers remained particularly unhappy with their conditions and with the government's failure to enforce the code. On July 16, the new-formed Alabama State Council of Textile Workers declared an impressive statewide strike that continued throughout the summer and merged into the general strike in

September. Angry southern workers then pushed for a general strike at the convention the UTW held in New York City from August 13 to 18.

The UTW was a conservative, craft-based union that had been founded in 1901. It had occasionally supported past mass strikes, and although reluctant, its leadership felt compelled to do so again in 1934. The tenor of the turbulent times was evident in the resolutions the textile workers passed at the UTW convention. In addition to overwhelmingly endorsing a general strike, a 30-hour work week, higher pay, and abolition of the stretch-out, they supported the establishment of a national labor party, advocated concrete steps toward industrial unionism, and condemned fascism.

The UTW chose September 3, Labor Day, as the effective date for launching the general strike, and it placed Francis Gorman, the union's vice president, in charge. The U.S. government then made a number of futile efforts to avert the strike. First, the CTNIRB, in whom the UTW had no confidence, offered to arbitrate, and the union refused the offer. Then, the NRA's National Labor Relations Board proposed voluntary arbitration, which the union accepted but the employers refused. Meanwhile, the UTW publicized its five major demands: (1) recognition of the United Textile Workers as the industrywide bargaining agent for the nation's textile workers; (2) new machinery to arbitrate disputes and handle complaints about violations of Section 7 (a) and the code; (3) a 30-hour work week with maintenance of wages at the 40-hour level; (4) abolition of the stretch-out and establishment of a maximum work load; and (5) reinstatement of all workers fired for union activity. Textile owners began to portray the portending strike as an illegal strike against the government, a notion the union repudiated.

Contrary to predictions that few workers would strike, the textile workers did so, unevenly, but en masse. Cotton workers had precipitated the work stoppage, but the UTW also called out workers in other branches of the industry. Southern workers were the first to strike because few employers in the region celebrated the Labor Day holiday. As the strikers gradually expanded their ranks, they pioneered in new techniques. They formed "flying squadrons," that is, roaming convoys of pickets who traveled to working plants to call out the millhands and shut them down. Gorman was innovative in using the radio to deliver information to the strikers.

The effectiveness of the strike finally forced President Roosevelt to take action. On September 5, he issued an executive order and appointed a Board of Inquiry for the Cotton Textile Industry that he directed to investigate the strike, issue a report with recommendations no later than October 1, 1934, and serve as a "Board of Voluntary Arbitration." He named John Winant, a former governor of New Hampshire, head of the committee that became known as the Winant Board. The employers immediately rejected voluntary arbitration, and the Winant Board confined itself to the task of studying the situation and providing suggestions to Roosevelt.

Meanwhile, anti-union employers were busy publicizing their cause, hiring strikebreakers and deputies, and besieging state and federal authorities for troops. For the most part, the strikers were peaceful, but that was not the view of the mill owners. For them, peaceful picketing, either by individuals or by "flying squadrons," was an inherently violent act that intimidated workers and negated the individual's "right-to-work," an argument of great importance for the future. Real violence normally occurred after the mill owners' armed gunmen appeared on the scene. In one such incident, on September 6, seven members of a "flying squadron" were murdered at Honea Path, South Carolina. In all, thirteen people, including twelve strikers, were killed during the strike.

The southern states readily complied with the mill owners' requests for troops, and Governor Eugene Talmadge of Georgia gained special notoriety. Soon after winning a September 12 primary election in which he had promised not to send in troops against the strikers, he declared martial law and did just that. A shocked press reported that he ordered 128 members of a peaceful "flying squadron" that had been arrested at Newnan, Georgia, to be detained, without charge, in a "concentration camp" near Atlanta for the strike's duration. The state's mill owners were pleased with Talmadge and the troops, who effectively broke the strike there.

Throughout its duration, the media and much of the nation were divided on the strike. In a series of editorials, the *New York Times* condemned the strike, "flying squadrons," and what it termed "strikers' law." On the other hand, *The New Republic* supported the strike and distinguished it, with its moderate aims of union recognition and better working conditions, from more radical strikes and goals that posed a threat to the government. It had in mind the longshoremen's strike and the general strike that had just occurred in San Francisco. Indeed, the presence of radicals in the labor movement posed serious problems for the conservative leaders of the UTW and the AFL who disliked industrial unionism and radicalism and who linked their fates to that of the Roosevelt administration.

Rank-and-file textile strikers had good reason to be concerned about the steadfastness of their top union leaders and about the vacillating labor policy of the federal government. On September 15, they awoke to news that the NRA Administrator, General Hugh Johnson, had denounced the strike and organized labor in general in a well-publicized speech the night before at Carnegie Hall in New York City.

The climax of the strike occurred two days later, on September 17, when the Winant Board issued its report. After verifying the workers' charges about the Bruere Board, it made a number of modest suggestions that did not rectify any of the five grievances the workers cited for the strike. It merely recommended that an independent Textile Labor Relations Board be created to administer the textile codes, that the Department of Labor and the Federal Trade Commission investigate wage and occupational issues, and that a special committee be formed to study and regulate the stretch-out. In an effort to appear fair to both parties, it urged the strikers to call off the strike and then called upon the employers to reinstate them "without discrimination."

The conservative leadership of the UTW welcomed the findings of the Winant Board and called off the strike on September 22. Gorman and the union misleadingly hailed it as a "great victory" for labor. *Textile World*, one of the industry's leading journals, more accurately characterized the report as "an almost complete victory" for the mill owners because it did not even recognize the UTW as the representative for the nation's textile workers. *The New Republic* and most of the media agreed. The *Wall Street Journal* welcomed the strike's outcome but expressed concern for the rights of the individual worker, not unions or workers as a collective entity, and asked: "What is our labor policy?" It was a serious question, and the answer was not obvious to workers, business people, or the general public. The strike and other events had made the serious shortcomings, contradictions, and limitations of the New Deal's labor policy evident.

By November, shortly after the formation of the new Textile National Labor Relations Board, *Textile World* was assuring its readers that the NRA was in "friendly hands." An impartial board never materialized. Henceforth, as before, labor's rights and Section 7 (a) would not be enforced, and the stretch-out would continue. Above all, the unequal power relations that prevailed before the strike would remain essentially unchanged in the industry. Anti-union employers thus easily ignored government requests to reinstate the strikers and fired and blacklisted strikers and union employees en masse.

The U.S. Supreme Court declared the NIRA unconstitutional in 1935, and the New Deal necessarily entered a new phase. In that context, Senator Robert Wagner of New York set out to draft legislation that would meet court approval *and* grant labor the rights contained in Section 7 (a). The success of that new labor legislation, the National Labor Relations Act (1935), subsequently enabled many workers to organize and form effective unions, primarily in the North and in the mass-production industries such as coal, steel, automobiles, and rubber. Meanwhile, the legacy of the 1934 textile strike's defeat cast a long shadow over southern workers, and the consequences for the national labor movement were enormous. A successful textile strike in 1934 might have paved the way for broad-scale unionization in the South. As it was, organized labor reached the zenith of its power in the United States from 1933 to 1947, but the loss of this critically important strike had left the South a haven for the open shop and a long-term threat that undermined workers' rights and unions throughout the nation.

DOCUMENTS

7.1.   **Code of Fair Competition for the Cotton Textile Industry, approved July 9, 1933; effective July 17, 1933**

> *The National Recovery Administration's Code No. 1, the cotton textile code, was drafted by textile employers and the industry's representatives without the participation of textile workers or the UTW. Accordingly, its basic terms, contained in this excerpt, reflect the class interests of its drafters. Note especially the code's purpose, the differential wage rate, the omission of the stretch-out, and the perfunctory inclusion of Section 7 (a) of the NIRA, a legal requirement.*

To effectuate the policy of Title I of the National Industrial Recovery Act, during the period of the emergency, by reducing and relieving unemployment; improving the standards of labor; eliminating competitive practices destructive of the interests of the public, employees, and employers; relieving the disastrous effects of overcapacity, and otherwise rehabilitating the cotton textile industry; and by increasing the consumption of industrial and agricultural products by increasing purchasing power; and in other respects, the following provisions are established as a code of fair competition for the cotton textile industry:

I. *Definitions:*—The term "cotton textile industry" as used herein is defined to mean the manufacture of cotton yarn and/or cotton woven fabrics, whether as a final process or as a part of a larger or further process. The term "employees" as used herein shall include all persons employed in the conduct of such operations. The term "productive machinery" as used herein is defined to mean spinning spindles and/or looms. The term "effective date" as used herein is defined to be July 17, 1933, or if this code shall not have been approved by the President two weeks prior thereto, then the second Monday after such approval. The term "persons" shall include natural persons, partnerships, associations, and corporations.

II. On and after the effective date, the minimum wage that shall be paid by employers in the cotton textile industry to any of their employees—except learners during a six weeks' apprenticeship, cleaners, and outside employees—shall be at the rate of $12 per week when employed in the Southern section of the industry and at the rate of $13 per week when employed in the Northern section for 40 hours of labor.

III. On and after the effective date, employers in the cotton textile industry shall not operate on a schedule of hours of labor for their employees—except repair-shop crews, engineers, electricians, firemen, office and supervisory staff, shipping, watching and outside crews, and cleaners—in excess of 40 hours per week, and they shall not operate productive machinery in the cotton textile industry for more than 2 shifts of 40 hours each per week.

IV. On and after the effective date, employers in the cotton textile industry shall not employ any minor under the age of 16 years.

V. With a view to keeping the President informed as to the observance or nonobservance of this Code of Fair Competition, and as to whether the cotton textile industry is taking appropriate steps to effectuate the declared policy of the National Industrial Recovery Act, each person engaged in the cotton textile industry will furnish daily certified reports [pertaining to wages and hours of labor; machinery data; production, stocks, and orders]. . . .

VI. To further effectuate the policies of the Act, the Cotton Textile Industry Committee, the applicants herein, or such successor committee or committees as may hereafter be constituted by the action of the Cotton Textile Institute, the American Cotton Manufacturers Association, and the National Association of Cotton Manufacturers, is set up to cooperate with the Administrator as a planning and fair-practice agency for the cotton textile industry. Such agency may from time to time present to the Administrator recommendations based on conditions in the industry as they may develop from time to time which will tend to effectuate the operation of the provisions of this code and the policy of the National Industrial Recovery Act. . . .

VII. Where the costs of executing contracts entered into in the cotton textile industry prior to the presentation to Congress of the National Industrial Recovery Act are increased by the application of the provisions of that Act to the industry, it is equitable and promotive of the purposes of the Act that appropriate adjustments of such contracts to reflect such increased costs be arrived at by arbitral proceedings or otherwise, and the Cotton Textile Industry Committee, the applicant for this Code, is constituted an agency to assist in effecting such adjustments.

VIII. Employers in the Cotton Textile Industry shall comply with the requirements of the National Industrial Recovery Act as follows: "(1) That employees shall have the right to organize and bargain collectively through representatives of their own choosing, and shall be free from the interference, restraint, or coercion of employers of labor, or their agents, in the designation of such representatives or in self-organization or in other concerted activities for the purpose of collective bargaining or other mutual aid or protection; (2) that no employee and no one seeking employment shall be required as a condition of employment to join any company union or to refrain from joining, organizing, or assisting a labor organization of his own choosing; and (3) that employers shall comply with the maximum hours of labor, minimum rates of pay, and other conditions of employment, approved or prescribed by the President."

IX. This code and all the provisions thereof are expressly made subject to the right of the President, in accordance with the provision of Clause 10 (b) of the National Industrial Recovery Act, from time to time to cancel or modify any order, approval, license, rule, or regulation, issued under Title I of said Act, and specifically to the right of the President to cancel or modify his approval of this Code or any conditions imposed by him upon his approval thereof.

X. Such of the provisions of this code as are not required to be included therein by the National Industrial Recovery Act may, with the approval of the President, be modified or eliminated as changes in circumstances or experience may indicate. It is contemplated that from time to time supplementary provisions of this code or additional codes will be submitted for the approval of the President to prevent unfair competition in price and other unfair and destructive competitive practices and to effectuate the other purposes and policies of Title I of the National Industrial Recovery Act consistent with the provisions hereof.

Source: U.S. National Recovery Administration, *Codes of Fair Competition, Nos. 1–57, as Approved by President Roosevelt, June 16–October 11, 1933, with Supplemental Codes, Amendments, and Executive Orders Issued Between These Dates* (Washington, DC: GPO, 1933), 1:15–18.

7.2. Mrs. B. M. Miller, Charlotte, to General Hugh Johnson, Washington, July 23, 1933

Soon after the code's approval in July 1933, Mrs. B. M. Miller wrote this polite letter to General Hugh Johnson, the NRA administrator, to inform him about the stretch-out in her mill. She was one of the thousands of workers who welcomed the NIRA and hoped, in vain, for a redress of their grievances. The underlined phrases are as they appear now in the original document, but it is unclear whether Mrs. Miller or some government official underlined the phrases.

Dear Sir:

I just feel it my duty to notify you of the conditions of the <u>Hoskin Textile Plant</u> operating in <u>Charlotte N.C.</u> If I understand the Roosevelt administration it is for puting [*sic*] more people to work. <u>The Hoskin plant has layed</u> [*sic*] <u>off more than 100 people including them all</u> from different departments of the mill. Furthermore they have <u>stretched out the stretch out system</u>. Now please get what I mean. In "29" they had 4 hands on my job, "creeling warpers," paying us $14.85 per week. On July 6th 1933 they cut two people out and speeded up the machinery and are paying $12.00 per week. They have put more on the spooler hands than they can hardly do and tell them to do that or get out. Meaning about 25 people had to go out of the spooler room. As for spinners it's a shame. Please investigate this mill for I am sure you can have it straigtend [*sic*] out. I . . . will be glad to discuss with any of your representatives.

Mrs. B. M. Miller

Source: Mrs. B. M. Miller, Charlotte, to General Hugh Johnson, Washington, July 23, 1933, National Archives, Record Group 9, Entry 398, Box 9, Folder 131-C, Chadwick Hoskins Mill #1, Charlotte, NC.

7.3.   Mrs. B. M. Miller, Charlotte, to Miss Frances Perkins, Washington, December 13, 1933

On December 13, 1933, a disappointed and frustrated Mrs. B. M. Miller tried to enlist the government's help again. But this time she bypassed Johnson and wrote the following letter to Frances Perkins, Secretary of Labor. Her complaints about the bewildering maze of NRA bureaucracy, the mill owners' control of governmental boards, the stretch-out, and the ineffectiveness of the code in protecting the workers' right to organize were widely shared. The underlined words are as they appear now in the original document, but who underlined them is unclear.

Dear Madam:

I have been appointed by the Charlotte Central Labor Union, affilliated [*sic*] with the American Federation of Labor, to investigate and report on all violations of the Textile code.

I have several complaints including my own against the <u>Chadwick Hoskin Mill # 1 in Charlotte, N.C.</u>

Now there must be something wrong with the 'Boards' as we have tried to file these complaints with several different Boards and as yet have accomplished nothing. I am sending you a copy of these complaints which are most all signed and sworn to a notary Public.

I want you to read these complaints very carefully as they need attending to at once.

The President says and the code says we have a right to organize and bargain collectively. We are organizing and they are firing us for it every day. What are we to do? When we can't get a Board to function. You know this will cause serious trouble.

You take my case for an instance. I tried to put it before the State Board, but the industrial side would not try to arbitrate. As you know Mr. Dwelle is vice-President of this chain of mills, is there any wonder he would not arbitrate? I taken it then before the Local N.R.A. Compliance board, and I am sending you a copy of the sworn affidavit of what happened there. Is there any wonder that I protest John Small Jr. for the State N.R.A. head.[?] If he takes this post the Textile people will not have a showing. My complaint is before the District Compliance Board and I received a comunications [sic] from them today stating they were not the right board and were transfering [sic] my complaint to a board in Washington. Now if there is a right board I, as well as all the Laboring people of Charlotte would like to know where it is.

I want to tell you right now that Labor never did and never will get any thing through the Chamber of Commerces. There has got to be something done about it, we need people who will lend a helping hand, and that right away.

The Chadwick Hoskin Mill # 1 has overseers that are discriminating against the workers. Read these complaints. This mill so I am told is not even displaying the Blue Eagle [the NRA symbol]. These people here believe Mr. B. B. Gossett has bought over these boards. There is something wrong, but I don't know what it is.

Read the complaint where the mother has sworn against this company and its overseers. Read it carefully, do you think the citizens of Charlotte and Mecklenburg County will stand for this? Conditions like this which we are having to work under, not only this mill, but others as well, will cause serious trouble, if not attended to at once. I want to know where we can get help. I am a mother and also a textile worker, and I know the conditions of which we have to work are terrible.

The Laboring People here are trying to uphold our President and also the code. We believe in it.—We talk it—And we would so love to live it.

But the time has come when we need help. The reason why there is so many are out of work is because the mills have stretched the hands out, gave them more work to do and have layed off hundreds since the code became effective. Now you don't have to take my word for this. Read over their books. They tell the story.

The overseers boast they will run their mills to suit theirselves regardless of codes, Unoins [sic] or what ever happens. They rule us. They treat us as slaves. They must think we are heathens. But we are tired of it. We have just lots of good citizens in Textile Plants, but we cant come out of bondage alone. We must have help. We must have some one to breake [sic] the shackles. We need action now. If we don't get it, it will lead to strikes. WHO WILL BE TO BLAME? NOT THE LABORING PEOPLE. BUT THE PEOPLE WHO HAS POWER TO HELP US NOW. We want people to whom we can go to settle these complaints. We Must Have Help Now.

Please reply at once.

Sincerely,
Mrs. B. M. Miller

Source: Mrs. B. M. Miller, Charlotte, to Miss Francis [sic] Perkins, Washington, December 13, 1933, National Archives, Record Group 9, Entry 398, Box 9, Folder 131-C, Chadwick Hoskins Mill #1, Charlotte, NC.

7.4.   "Boards, Boards, Boards," *The Nation*, July 18, 1934

This editorial from The Nation, *a leading liberal national journal, conveys a critical review of the Roosevelt administration's commitment to Section 7 (a) and the ambivalent role the labor boards played in early New Deal labor policy. It questioned the comparison of the codes to collective bargaining agreements and asked an important question of the day: Was it really possible for the boards to enforce the codes' labor provisions, given the existence of two quite different types of employers, those who recognized unions and those who bitterly opposed them?*

IT began last summer [in 1933] with the establishment of the National Cotton Textiles Industrial Relations Board. Shortly thereafter, the Wagner board [the short-lived National Labor Board, the NLB] was created. Since then, labor boards have proliferated until today they fill the landscape of industrial relations. First, the National Labor Relations Board and its immediate affiliates, steel and longshoremen. Second, boards set up by the NRA [the National Recovery Administration] in connection with codes: cotton, silk, and wool textiles, bituminous-coal, newspaper-publishing, lumber, trucking, and so forth. Third, code boards independent of the NRA: petroleum (under the Petroleum Administration) and automobile, thanks to the March 25 settlement).

We see here emerging an elaborate system for governing industrial relations under Section 7-a. This system may be taken to express the Administration's labor policy. The government will not lend a direct hand to the job of bringing the employers and the trade unions to terms. Instead the government will assist in the creation of appropriate instrumentalities to perform this function.

It is doubtful, however, whether most of the boards now flowering in Washington pastures are fit instruments for their chief task: forcing our anti-union industrialists to bow to the clear provisions of the law requiring them to deal with trade unions. This might not be true if the Administration were inspired with a forthright will to put Section 7-a into effect. Unfortunately, the Administration manifests no such will. It projects its labor boards in vacuo. It projects them, not for the purpose of imposing New Deal labor policies upon Old Deal employers, but simply because it is expedient to maintain the industrial peace. The history of Senator Wagner's board [the NLB] is instructive. So long as the board contented itself with forestalling and checking strikes, things ran smoothly for it. In the course of time, the board advanced to a theory of industrial relations leading straight toward union recognition and collective agreements. This brought into play opposing forces which finally wrecked the board and ended its existence.

Virtually all of the new labor boards have been conceived in error. No doubt they have been modeled after devices for administering industrial relations which have proved more or less successful in a number of industries, for example, clothing and anthracite-coal. But clothing and anthracite-coal are organized industries wherein trade unionism has taken deep root. The employers recognize the trade union. What is more, the emloyers [sic] and the trade union are bound one to the other by a collective agreement. The board's job, accordingly, is the relatively simple one of interpreting and applying the specific provisions of an existing agreement. There are no psychological barriers to break down; no fixed habits to transform. The board is not called upon to waste its energies in battering away at a stubborn anti-union psychology. A totally different state of affairs confronts the boards created under Section 7-a. True, they have a document to administer, a code of fair competition, which on the surface resembles a collective agreement. In fact, however, only a handful of the NRA codes are the fruit of prior collective bargaining: the clothing codes, the soft-coal code, the legitimate-theater code, hardly any others. It is the least of the functions of these boards to interpret and apply the labor provisions of the code bearing on hours, wages, and other working conditions. Their chief problem arises when a trade union, fresh from an organizational campaign, seeks to press home recognition demands against employers determined not to grant them.

In their natural growth, labor boards have evolved as a device for regulating collective agreements—where there is already a mutual will to agree. In their hot-house forcing by the Roosevelt Administration, labor boards are applied to the composition of industrial disputes arising out of the unwillingness of employers to bargain collectively. Can the same mechanism be expected to perform successfully two utterly distinct if not positively opposed functions? This seems to us doubtful despite the care and conscience with which the President selected the personnel of the new National Labor Relations Board. Lloyd Garrison, Harry A. Millis, and Edwin S. Smith are not only experienced and intelligent; they will almost certainly attempt to induce employers to observe the intent and letter of Section 7-a. But they are confronted with an opposition that has wrecked the board that preceded them and has driven other men of similar liberal sympathies to the support of hopeless compromises such as the automobile settlement. And they take office at a moment of labor unrest unprecedented in the post-war years.

Source: "Boards, Boards, Boards," *The Nation*, July 18, 1934, p. 61. Reprinted with permission from the July 18, 1934 issue of *The Nation*. For subscription information, call 1-800-333-8536. Portions of each week's Nation magazine can be accessed at http://www.thenation.com.

7.5.   Hugh Johnson, Speech on Strike, New York City, September 14, 1934

The strike was still in progress when General Hugh Johnson, the NRA administrator, unexpectedly denounced the walkout in a speech at Carnegie Hall in New York City. In this excerpt, he criticized organized labor but placed the major blame for the strike on the socialists. His high praise of George A. Sloan, president of the Cotton Textile Institute, and his failure to mention enforcement of Section 7 (a) are particularly noteworthy. His comments angered the textile workers and brought the federal government's labor policy into further question.

Last June a strike was threatened in the textile industry. It was, as I remember, the fifth great strike of national importance with which I have had to deal. We reached an agreement and on that agreement the strike was called off. The present strike is an absolute violation of that understanding, and I must say here, with all the solemnity which should characterize such an announcement that if such agreements of organized labor are worth no more than this one, then that institution is not such a responsible instrumentality as can make contracts on which this country can rely. . . .

But I would not condemn these men cavalierly. I know young Gorman. I doubt if there is a more conscientious patriot and sincere man in the country than he.

The trouble is that when you unleash the forces of riot and rebellion you never know when you can control them. I know now how this strike was pulled in contravention of the solemn engagements of the federation.

Men circulated around the delegates [to the UTW convention in August] and told them that the government would feed the strikers. Norman Thomas [a leader of the Socialist party] appeared and urged the strike. He is a politico. Whatever there is of economic doctrines in the Socialist party, it is political first and economic afterward, and Norman Thomas—as much as I respect and admire him—had no business there. When a strike becomes political, it has no place in the lexicon of the NRA. . . .

The cotton textile industry is the very last place in this country where a strike should be ordered. It was the first industry to come forward with a code. The code increased employment by 140,000, or nearly 33 1-3 per cent. According to our studies, it increased hourly wage rates by 70 per cent.

When I think of George Sloan my heart weeps. I know what kind of opposition he went up against [in drafting a code the industry would approve]. He overcame it all and got these concessions for labor which were opposed by practically the whole industry. It is a pity that he now has to take the rap in the dissention [sic] between labor and management of the whole proposition. . . .

NRA has been attacked as obscure. As a matter of fact, it is very plain. It guarantees to labor the right to bargain, collectively, through representatives of their own choosing. To my mind that is a right which is absolutely essential in our modern industrial environment. Industry, under NRA, is given the right to organize to the ultimate. Labor should also have that right. . . .

It is a great pleasure to talk to members of the Code Authorities of New York. This is a new experience in economics. It is industrial self-government.

This act [the NIRA] means exactly what it says. For many years industry requested the right to act in unison. Under the anti-trust acts it was forbidden to do so. Under NRA it was at last given that right. The question is what use is going to be made of that right. Are you going to use it to exploit labor? Are you going to use it to exploit the public? Of course, if you wish it for either purpose it is going to be taken away from you and the President's great trust in you will be defeated.

Regardless of what we hear and read by a few critics, I know, and so does our Industrial Advisory Board, that all of industry, large and small, wants to see the recovery program carried out.

Source: "Speech of Gen. Johnson Denouncing Textile Strike," *New York Times*, September 15, 1934, p. 2.

7.6. Summary of Recommendations, The Winant Board of Inquiry's Report to the President on Ways to Settle the Textile Strike, September 17, 1934

Although the Winant Board's report confirmed a number of the workers' claims, its mild recommendations, quoted here, offered workers no genuine redress. Except for the call for an "impartial board," which never really emerged, it proposed little that was new. Most importantly, the board did not grant the strikers their foremost demand—recognition of the United Textile Workers as their collective bargaining agent for the nation's industry.

1. For the more adequate protection of labor's rights under the collective bargaining and other labor provisions of the code, there shall be created under Public Resolution No. 44 an impartial board of three to be known as the Textile Labor Relations Board which shall be provided with an adequate staff and other facilities. This Board shall have powers and duties in the textile field similar to those exercised by the National Labor Relations Board and the Steel Labor Relations Board in their respective fields, and shall have authority to administer, in addition to Section 7 (a), other labor provisions of the cotton, silk, and wool codes.

2. In order to obtain necessary data upon the ability of the cotton, silk, and wool textile industries to support an equal or a greater number of employees at higher wages, it is recommended that the President direct the Department of Labor and, in accordance with Section 6 (c) of the Recovery Act, the Federal Trade Commission, to investigate and report on these matters at the earliest possible time.

3. For the purpose of regulating the use of the stretch-out system in the cotton, wool and silk industries, it is recommended that the respective codes be amended to provide that a special committee be created under the Textile Labor Relations Board to supervise the use of the stretch-out; that until Feb. 1, 1935, no employer shall extend the work load of any em-

ployee, except in special circumstances with the approval of the stretch-out committee; that the stretch-out committee shall have power to investigate present work assignments and where it finds improper speeding up of work require reduction accordingly; that the stretch-out committee shall recommend to the President not later than January 1, 1935, a permanent plan for regulation of the stretch-out, under which employers shall be required to secure approval of an impartial agency prior to increasing the work load of the employees, which plan when approved by the President after such notice and public hearing as he may prescribe shall become effective as part of the code.

4. To aid in the enforcement of code provisions relating to wages above the minimum and to serve as an aid and guide in making collective agreements, it is recommended that the Department of Labor be directed to study definitions and classifications of occupations and existing wages for such occupations, and that the information thus collected be made available to labor and management of the industry.

CONCLUSION

The findings and recommendations here submitted to you are based on as comprehensive and careful a survey as the situation permitted. The Board is confident that these findings and recommendations are fair and reasonable, that they meet the basic sources of the difficulty and that they offer the possibility of a just and lasting settlement. We believe further that they provide a sound basis for that "united action of labor and management" contemplated by the Recovery Act and the recovery program.

We therefore earnestly hope that the United Textile Workers will call off the strike on the basis of these recommendations. At the same time we request the employers in the industry to take back the workers now on strike without discrimination.

Source: U.S. Board of Inquiry for the Cotton Textile Industry, *Report of the Board of Inquiry for the Cotton Textile Industry to the President* . . . [Washington, DC: GPO, 1935], pp. 15–16.

**7.7.   "The Textile Workers Lose," *The New Republic*,
          October 3, 1934**

The title of this New Republic *editorial accurately conveyed the outcome of the strike. In this excerpt from its comments on the workers' devastating loss, it commended the strikers' accomplishments and expressed major criticisms of the Winant Board and the New Deal labor policy that resulted in their defeat.*

THE NATIONWIDE strike of nearly 500,000 textile workers ended abruptly last week, bringing to a disheartening conclusion one of the most remarkable demonstrations of union solidarity in the history of American labor. Despite Gorman's optimistic statement, the strike failed in its major objectives: the strikers return to the mills under a settlement that grants them not one of the demands for which they struck. Indeed, they have not even the assurance that they can get their jobs back. Already there are reports of wholesale discrimination against militant strikers by manufacturers intent on demolishing the union. Viewed in this light, the settlement must be considered a disastrous defeat for the union. . . .

The [Winant] board's opinion on union recognition, which apparently has the approval of President Roosevelt, is a devastating blow to collective bargaining. The board, of course, could not grant the U.T.W. recognition; only the textile manufacturers can do that. But the board could have at least suggested that the U.T.W. should be recognized. Instead, it specifically declares that recognition of the U.T.W. by the industry as a whole is not "feasible," and recommends that collective dealing between workers and employers should be confined to an individual plant basis. Unfortunately, no explanation or defense of this extraordinary theory is offered. That the officials of the A.F. of L. should accept it without protest is difficult to explain—except on the basis of their antipathy toward industrial unionism—and perhaps a recognition of the fact that the strike was already, at least in the South, a disastrous failure. For industry-wide agreements, such as obtain in the garment and coal industries, are the essence of industrial unionism. And only in such agreements, supported by strong unions, is there assurance that provisions affecting hours, wages, and the like can be enforced in an industry. . . .

For Mr. Gorman and the U.T.W. officials to hail this "settlement" as an overwhelming victory is, of course, incomprehensible—unless one interprets their elation merely as face-saving. As The New Republic outlined editorially last week, the A.F. of L. has shown no indication that it was willing to fight the textile strike to a finish. As we stated then, the A.F. of L. leaders have repeatedly demonstrated that they wanted to "string along with Roosevelt and do their utmost to make the textile leaders string along with them." The Winant report gave them a perfect opportunity to carry out this policy and they seized it with alacrity. But that they will now continue to enjoy the united support and respect of the textile workers is highly dubious. Certainly the workers, as they return, disorganized and disillusioned, to the same conditions that precipitated the strike, will not be as jubilant as Mr. Gorman seems over the "victory."

Meanwhile, the textile workers have at least the satisfaction of knowing that the spirit of tenacity and determination with which they held their ranks during three weeks of virtual warfare was in itself a triumph to be remembered. At the height of the strike, it is estimated, nearly 40,000 militia and deputies were called to arms "to keep the mills open." Despite this, defections from the strikers' ranks were surprisingly small. If this triumph was turned into an empty victory, the fault, most observers will agree, was not the strikers'. It was the result of forces beyond their control. They might have won a decent compromise from the manufacturers alone. They could not beat the forces of industry and government combined.

Source: "The Textile Workers Lose," *The New Republic*, October 3, 1934, pp. 200–201. Used with permission of *The New Republic*.

SELECTED ANNOTATED BIBLIOGRAPHY

Books

Allen, John Earl. "The Governor and the Strike: Eugene Talmadge and the General Textile Strike, 1934." M.A. Thesis, Georgia State University, 1977. Standard account of the Georgia strike.

Bernstein, Irving. *The New Deal Collective Bargaining Policy*. Berkeley: University of California Press, 1950. Excellent introduction to the origins, enactment, and purpose of New Deal labor policy from 1933 to 1935.

———. *Turbulent Years: A History of the American Worker, 1933–1941*. Boston: Houghton Mifflin, 1969. Very readable survey of labor history in the 1930s includes a brief but excellent narrative of the strike.

Brooks, R. R. Robert. "The United Textile Workers of America." Ph.D. diss., Yale University, 1935. Authoritative account of the union's history, 1901–1935, includes the strike.

Fink, Gary M. and Merl E. Reed, eds. *Essays in Southern Labor History: Selected Papers, Southern Labor History Conference, 1976*. Westport, CT: Greenwood Press, 1977. See Dennis R. Nolan and Donald E. Jonas's "Textile Unionism in the Piedmont, 1901–1932," Bruce Raynor's "Unionism in the Southern Textile Industry: An Overview," and John E. Allen's "Eugene Talmadge and the Great Textile Strike in Georgia, September 1934."

Galloway, George B., ed. *Industrial Planning Under Codes*. New York: Harper & Brothers Publishers, 1935. For an industry perspective, see the essay, "The Cotton Textile Industry, Under the NRA," by George A. Sloan, Chairman of the Cotton Textile Code Authority, pp. 117–30.

Hall, Jacqueline et al. *Like a Family: The Making of a Southern Cotton Mill World*. Chapel Hill: University of North Carolina Press, 1987. Indispensable social history, based on oral histories of textile workers and workers' letters to the NRA, provides insights into the strike and the mill village world of white textile workers in the Carolina Piedmont from the 1880s to the 1930s.

Hodges, James A. *New Deal Labor Policy and the Southern Cotton Textile Industry, 1933–1941*. Knoxville: University of Tennessee Press, 1986. The textile strike is the key event in this important examination of the failure of New Deal labor policy in the South.

Irons, Janet. *Testing the New Deal: The General Textile Strike of 1934 in the American*

South. Urbana: University of Illinois Press, 2000. Weak on strike events, but a valuable case study that focuses on indigenous organizing, the weaknesses of the national union, the "schizophrenic" nature of the New Deal and its impact on southern workers.

Lynd, Staughton, ed. *"We Are All Leaders": The Alternative Unionism of the Early 1930s.* Urbana: University of Illinois Press, 1996. See Janet Irons's essay, "The Challenge of National Coordination: Southern Textile Workers and the General Strike of 1934," pp. 72–101.

McMahon, Thomas F. *United Textile Workers of America: Their History and Policies.* New York: Workers Education Bureau Press, 1926. For more on the UTW, see this book, written by the man who was the president of the union in 1926 and 1934.

Salmond, John A. *The General Strike of 1934: From Maine to Alabama.* Columbia: University of Missouri Press, 2002. Recent history is valuable for its treatment of the strike from a national and industrywide perspective.

Simon, Bryant. *A Fabric of Defeat: The Politics of South Carolina Millhands, 1910–1948.* Chapel Hill: University of North Carolina Press, 1998. Study of the political culture of the state's white male textile workers covers the strike, race relations, and the rise and fall of ephemeral class-based support for federal government action during the New Deal.

U.S. Bureau of Labor Statistics. "General Textile Strike, September 1934." January 15, 1935. A seven-page departmental unpublished overview of the strike is available through the U.S. Department of Labor.

Waldrep, George Calvin. *Southern Workers and the Search for Community: Spartanburg County, South Carolina.* Urbana: University of Illinois Press, 2000. The strike is a key event in this study of the rise and fall of "community unionism" in the county during the 1930s and 1940s.

Zieger, Robert H., ed. *Organized Labor in the Twentieth-Century South.* Knoxville: University of Tennessee Press, 1991. For a historiographical overview, see Zieger's "Introduction," pp. 3–9, and his essay, "Textile Workers and Historians," pp. 35–59.

Web Sites

Teachers and researchers will find valuable sources on the strike at the "Like a Family" Web site at http://www.sohp.org/laf/index.html. The site was developed by Dr. James Leloudis and Dr. Kathryn Walbert as an offshoot of the *Like a Family* project. It features oral history interviews, including some with 1934 textile strikers, and it contains important descriptive information about mill work and life.

A promising work in progress that includes lesson plans and resources on southern labor, textile history, and the 1934 strike is located at the Pullen Library, Special Collections, Georgia State University site: www.lib.gsu.edu/spcoll/labor/work_n_progress/index.htm. For some primary documents on the period after the strike, search for " 'Treated Like Slaves': Textile Workers Write to Washington in the 1930s and 1940s," located at George Mason University's History Matters, The U.S. Survey Course on the Web, Web site: http://historymatters.gmu.edu/d/125.

Video

The strike is the subject of a 90-minute award-winning documentary, *The Uprising of '34*, produced by George Stoney, Judith Helfand, and Susanne Rostock (Hard Times Productions, 1995, available from First Run Icarus Films, 32 Court St., 21st Flr., Brooklyn, NY 11202). The film, originally presented on PBS in 1995, explores the causes, critical events, and consequences of the strike while raising important issues about class, race, power, and memory.

8

The General Motors Sit-Down Strike of 1936–1937

If the textile strike of 1934 illustrates the failure of New Deal labor policy to ensure the rights of American workers to organize and bargain collectively, the General Motors (GM) Sit-Down Strike of 1936–1937 demonstrates a successful outcome for American workers. During the landmark six-week-long conflict, militant rank-and-file auto workers engaged in the dramatic tactic of the sit-down strike, a nontraditional protest in which workers did not walk out but remained at their workplaces and refused to work, thereby occupying and taking physical possession of their factories. After forty-four days, the strikers won a watershed victory by securing a contract and de facto recognition of their new industrial union, the United Auto Workers of America (UAW). Their victory at GM plants was a significant breach in the wall of the nonunion fortress that the Big Three auto manufacturers—GM, Chrysler, and Ford—had maintained, and it paved the way for the UAW to launch successful organizing campaigns, at Chrysler in 1937, and at Ford in 1941. After the GM strike, thousands of auto workers poured into the UAW and made it one of the nation's largest and most powerful new unions. Moreover, the strike itself catapulted labor leader John L. Lewis into national prominence and marked the first major success of the new Committee on Industrial Organization (later the Congress of Industrial Organizations).

Like the textile strike of 1934, the GM sit-down strike was a major test of New Deal labor policy but one that took place at a later stage in another context and with a different outcome. The auto workers were fortunate in that they launched their drive to organize GM at a particularly favorable moment for labor, shortly after President Franklin D. Roosevelt's land-slide reelection in November 1936, when public support for the basic tenets of New Deal labor policy was at its height. Another distinguishing feature of the strike was that President Roosevelt and Michigan's liberal New Deal governor, Frank Murphy, played important roles in mediating the conflict and guiding it to a peaceful conclusion that was highly lauded. At the time, the National Labor Relations Act (NLRA) might have met the fate of the National Industrial Recovery Act (NIRA). Just two years earlier, in 1935, the U.S. Supreme Court had declared the NIRA illegal, thus destroying Section 7 (a) of the act, the basis of the federal government's labor policy. In response, Senator Robert Wagner of New York quickly drafted new legislation to guarantee labor basic rights, including those contained in Section 7 (a), and Congress passed the law, popularly known as the Wagner Act, in July 1935. Because the GM auto strike occurred at a critical point in the 1930s when anti-union employers continued to resist unions and collective bargaining as they awaited the U.S. Supreme Court's ruling on the constitutionality of the NLRA, the strike had a particularly powerful impact. Its outcome encouraged other workers to emulate the auto workers' example by forming unions and engaging in traditional or sit-down strikes to compel union recognition and collective bargaining from their recalcitrant employers. It is probably not an accident that the Supreme Court declared the Wagner Act constitutional in April 1937 in the midst of that labor upsurge and only a few weeks after the historic conclusion of the auto strike.

Large numbers of the nation's auto workers had become dissatisfied long before the strike. The Great Depression had exposed underlying tensions in the prestigious consumer auto industry. During the 1920s, GM and other auto workers had earned high hourly wage rates and received other benefits from prosperous employers. As the depression took its toll, however, they found their livelihoods and job security increasingly threatened. Like other workers, they confronted massive unemployment, wage reductions and layoffs, low annual wages, and the pressures of the speed-up. Most importantly, they had no voice whatsoever about such matters and no way to engage in genuine collective bargaining with their employers through representatives of their own choosing.

In 1933 the auto workers were among those workers who responded enthusiastically to Section 7 (a) and the New Deal government's promise to guarantee workers the right to organize and bargain collectively. However, despite impressive organizing, their hopes were quickly frustrated. The auto industry wrote the National Recovery Administration's Automobile Labor Code, which was unique in containing a "merit clause" that virtually negated Section 7 (a). Employers were accordingly allowed to hire, fire, or promote on the basis of merit, which they alone judged, and which they could, and did, then use as a pretext for discharging union sympathizers en masse. The auto board's decision to endorse a system of "proportional representation" for groups of employees instead of requiring a sole bargaining agent for each company also hindered subsequent attempts to unionize. The result was a plethora of unions, including a handful of craft ones and hundreds of inclusive but ineffective Federal Labor Unions affiliated with the American Federation of Labor (AFL). President Roosevelt delivered yet another blow in 1934, when he approved a GM statement that defined collective bargaining in a narrow, severely limited way and expressed the corporation's preference for company unions over independent ones.

Meanwhile, the inability of mass-production workers to achieve the rights promised by Section 7 (a) was helping to bring the issue of industrial unionism to a head in the U.S. labor movement. The vast majority of auto, rubber, steel, and textile workers were less skilled than the tradesmen traditionally represented by the AFL, and they were increasingly attracted to the notion of an industrial union that included all workers in an industry regardless of skill, craft, or occupation. Many had become disillusioned with the Federation for having squandered organizing opportunities and for insisting that organization of these industries take place only on a craft basis. Militant auto workers, including Wyndham Mortimer, Robert Travis, and the leaders of the Federal Labor Unions in Toledo, Cleveland, and Milwaukee, began to demand the formation of one industrial auto workers' union that could conceivably counter the power of the corporate auto makers. In August 1935, they compelled the reluctant Executive Council of the AFL to charter a new national industrial union, the United Automobile Workers of America (UAW), that the Federation tried, unsuccessfully, to control.

Industrial unionism soon became a fractious issue within the AFL itself. John L. Lewis, member of its executive council and president of the United Mine Workers, the nation's largest industrial union, championed its cause. He garnered some support and fought to bring the issue to a head at the AFL's annual convention in Atlantic City in October 1935. After fierce debates and a well-publicized fistfight with the president of the carpenters' union, Lewis led an exodus of industrial unionists from the convention. The group reconvened elsewhere to plan the formation of the Committee on Industrial Organization (CIO). The CIO leaders, strengthened in their resolve by the passage of the Wagner Act (which had established a new governmental mechanism, the National Labor Relations Board, to ensure collective bargaining rights), made a firm commitment to organize the mass-production industries, including autos, steel, and rubber, on an inclusive industrial basis. In August 1936, the UAW voted to join the CIO, which made the drive to organize the auto industry and achieve collective bargaining a top priority. By then, restless workers in diverse anti-union industries were already spontaneously turning to the sit-down strike as a means to increase their leverage with their employers to gain union recognition and collective bargaining rights.

Such strikes were amazingly effective. As long as the strikers occupied their factories and work sites, employers could not use nonunion employees or strikebreakers to resume production. Also, sit-downs were usually peaceable happenings that reduced violence because the employers were reluctant to use force to disengage the strikers and thereby damage their own property, which the strikers protected. More violence often took place on picket lines during traditional strikes. Sit-downs also raised the morale of the strikers, who shared the same quarters as well as the same cause. The tactic was an old but uncommon one until the mid-1930s. French workers made it famous in 1936 when they used it en masse against fascism during the Popular Front era of Leon Blum. In the United States, in 1936 and 1937, at a critical time when the future status of labor's rights remained unclear, American workers engaged in an unprecedented wave of sit-down strikes. According to the Bureau of Labor Statistics, there were 48 sit-downs involving 87,817 workers in 1936; in 1937 there were 477 involving 398,117 people. The vast majority of these strikers "sat down" to try to secure union recognition from employers who refused to grant it. Auto workers in Flint, Atlanta, Kansas City, Cleveland, and other places were among them.

In this context, UAW and CIO leaders began to develop a strategy for organizing the auto industry in November 1936, after organized labor had helped Roosevelt win a landslide victory in a watershed presidential election that was widely viewed at the time as a mandate for approval of New Deal policies and labor's rights. They decided to organize the Big Three auto companies piecemeal, beginning with General Motors, an economic power that had 110 plants in fourteen states and eighteen countries and that manufactured Chevrolets, Pontiacs, Oldsmobiles, Buicks, and Cadillac-LaSalles, plus Frigidaires. The corporation had made profits every year since 1921, even during the Great Depression. In 1936 its market share of new car sales in the United States was an impressive 43 percent, and its shareholders received record-breaking dividends totaling over $200 million. On the eve of the strike, GM management, which employed 171,711 auto workers, detested the New Deal and refused to abide by the National Labor Relations Act, a law it considered unconstitutional.

GM's disgruntled auto workers' chief grievance was their inability to engage in genuine collective bargaining with their employer through representatives of their own choosing. More specifically, they complained about low annual wages, despite high hourly rates; the speed-up; irregular, seasonal, and extensive unemployment with no seniority rights; and widespread spying and discrimination against union members. On the eve of the strike, only a minority of GM auto workers were unionized, in large part, because of GM's use of detective agencies and spies, a charge later documented by an investigation by the U.S. congressional LaFollette committee on labor and violations of civil rights. This important committee was formed after passage of the Wagner Act to examine employer violations of the new labor law. From 1936 to 1939 it explored unfair employer practices, especially those involving industrial espionage, strikebreaking, private police systems, and the stockpiling of arms and munitions. The massive and shocking evidence it found upheld many of labor's charges against the nation's leading corporations. During and shortly after the GM strike, the committee held public hearings on the labor policies of General Motors and found evidence that GM spies had infiltrated many UAW locals, leading to the discharge of unionists, and otherwise illegally undermined the union's lawful organizing efforts. A detective agency that was located next door to the UAW's central offices in Detroit had even spied on the union's top officers.

The actual showdown between the UAW and GM turned out to be premature. To coordinate an organizing drive and probable strike, UAW and CIO leaders had planned to meet on January 3, 1937, after the turn of the year when Governor Frank Murphy and other elected New Deal officials assumed office. But, ongoing spontaneous sit-down strikes in Atlanta and Kansas City, begun in November and December, had prompted Homer Martin, president of the UAW, to write GM's executive vice president, William S. Knudsen, on December 21, 1936, to ask the corporation's highest management for a conference to discuss collective bargaining, union recognition, and other issues that the union considered national in scope. As Martin awaited a response, workers at a Fisher Body plant in Cleveland launched another sit-down on December 28. Then, two days later, auto workers at Fisher Body No. 1 in Flint sat down to prevent the removal of valuable dies from their plant, dies that could be used by the company to increase production and defeat ongoing strikes in other GM plants. They were soon joined by a sit-down at Fisher Body No. 2 in Flint.

The historic GM strike is usually dated as beginning on December 30 with the first Flint action. From then on, Flint became the focus of the conflict that eventually spread to fifty other plants and involved more than 140,000 workers. For years, GM had ruled the one industry company town where it employed 47,247 workers in its Fisher Body and Chevrolet plants.

The two sides were far apart on collective bargaining—the issue that lay at the heart of the conflict. On December 31, Knudsen replied to Martin's earlier requests for a conference by reasserting the validity of the corporation's policy. Accordingly, GM's central management refused to meet with a union purporting to represent even a fraction of its employees. It further asserted that unhappy workers, union or nonunion, could only take their grievances to local plant managers. In its view, sit-downs were illegal, and all plants had to be vacated before such local conferences could take place.

The UAW leadership responded on January 4 by sending GM a letter listing the strikers' eight grievances. The most contested ones were the UAW's demand for GM to recognize it as the exclusive bargaining agent of the corporation's employees and the demand for a national conference to conclude a national contract. Other grievances concerned the piece-work system, seniority, the work week, minimum pay rates, unjustly discharged workers, and the speed-up. The union stressed its view that it was GM—not the UAW—that was in violation of federal law, specifically the National Labor Relations Act.

On January 5, 1937, GM president Alfred P. Sloan replied to the union's enumeration of grievances by issuing a policy statement. Individual merit would remain GM's criterion for judging work, and GM would never recognize a single union as an exclusive agent for its workers or bargain over national issues. Sloan claimed that the real issue of the conflict was not collective bargaining but who would run GM—a "private group of labor dictators" or GM management.

The stage was set for a long strike, and from December 30 on, the strikers in Fisher Body Plants 1 and 2 organized and prepared for defense against any attempts to eject them. At the outset, the strikers decided that all female workers should leave the plants so that the opposition could not smear them with charges of sexual immorality. Experienced UAW leaders Bob Travis and Victor Reuther managed day-to-day affairs. The strikers held democratic mass meetings and formed committees related to defense, picketing, kitchen duty, sanitation, entertainment, publicity, finances, welfare, and more. On New Year's Eve, fifty Flint women formed a Women's Auxiliary to support the strike by collecting food and money, setting up a nursery to aid female pickets, and organizing a speakers' bureau. Sympathetic veterans, grocers, and others aided the cause.

Meanwhile, GM went to court and, on January 2, secured a temporary injunction that not only authorized the expulsion of the strikers from GM properties but also prohibited picketing and activities that upheld the strike. The injunction quickly became a dead letter when it became known that the judge owned a large amount of GM stock. But GM also received support from the newly created "Flint Alliance for the Security of Our Jobs, Our Homes, and Our Community," an anti-union business and citizens' group that held public meetings and sponsored a "back to work" movement. Craft unionists were divided about the strike, and the presidents of the Metal Trades and Building Trades Departments of the AFL secretly met with, and asked, GM not to recognize the UAW as an exclusive bargaining agent or allow it jurisdiction over craft workers.

The strike remained effective. The existing stalemate between the two contending sides of the class conflict was subsequently broken by two dramatic events. The first was the one real attempt, by force, to remove the strikers from the plants. What later became known as the "Battle of the Running Bulls" took place on the night of January 11, when armed Flint and company police tried to take over Fisher Body No. 2 after GM had turned off the heat in the building. Pickets and strikers struggled to defend the building throughout the night. Victor Reuther directed the defenders from a sound car as they confronted tear gas, buckshot, and bullets. It was a long and confusing battle. At one critical point, Genora Johnson, the young wife of a striker, called upon all the female pickets to join her and place their unprotected bodies between the police and the building to protect the men inside. When the smoke cleared in the morning, numerous people were injured, but no one was dead, and the strikers still had possession of the building. Not long after, Genora Johnson founded the Women's Emergency Brigade, a militant organization of about 350 red-capped women whose purpose was to picket and otherwise defend the sit-downers if anyone should launch another assault on the men in the plants.

The "Battle of the Running Bulls" led to active intervention by the government to try to resolve the conflict in a neutral and peaceful manner. Governor Frank Murphy, who sympathized with the labor movement but considered the sit-down illegal, quickly sent the National Guard to Flint but, in so doing, made it clear that he did so to preserve peace and uphold law and order in a neutral manner that protected the strikers' civil rights as well as property. His efforts to establish a truce on January 15 collapsed, and subsequent attempts by U.S. Secretary of Labor Frances Perkins to bring the contending parties together also failed.

A second clash between the police and strikers took place at another critical point in the strike on February 1, as GM again went to court to seek an injunction. To bolster the strikers' flagging morale and give the union important added leverage to get GM to the negotiating table, a small group of CIO and UAW leaders planned a daring offensive to take over the Chevrolet No. 4 plant. The plan involved creating a diversion by misleading spies into thinking that the strikers would try to take over the Chevrolet No. 9 plant, where unsuspecting strikers did engage police in an actual battle for possession. The plan worked, and the diversion allowed the strikers to seize the more important Chevrolet plant quickly, without opposition.

The seizure of the Chevrolet plant increased public pressure on Governor Murphy to eject the sit-downers and end the strike. Tension mounted, but the concerned New Dealer had been quietly at work with Frances Perkins and Roosevelt behind the scenes. Roosevelt apparently phoned Knudsen, and Murphy also informed the GM executive that the president had authorized him to mediate the conflict. The president wanted GM to negotiate with a CIO committee, and eventually, GM agreed. CIO president John L. Lewis arrived in Detroit on February 2, the very day that GM secured a new injunction that required the strikers to evacuate the two Fisher Body plants. Although harshly criticized by some at the time, Murphy, who wanted to avoid bloodshed, forestalled the forcible ejection of the sit-downers by persuading those in command that such a life-endangering action was unnecessary because negotiations were in progress and a settlement was near.

Murphy personally handled the negotiations, which went on for nine days and nights. GM kept demanding that the strikers leave the plants before any discussion of grievances; Lewis kept insisting on collective bargaining and recognition of the UAW as the employees' exclusive bargaining agent before any evacuation. The frustrated mediator finally read Lewis a formal letter in which he threatened to enforce the court's order to eject the strikers, if they did not evacuate the plants. Lewis defied the governor, and the order was never executed. GM executives, whose company was suffering heavy market losses, then came to Lewis and agreed to settle.

The signing of a written contract on February 11 with GM was, in and of itself, a great union victory. The corporation saved face in the final agreement by recognizing the UAW as the bargaining agent for its members only, but the UAW gained from the important provision that granted exclusive recognition to the young CIO union in twenty struck plants for six months, during which time the union could freely conduct an organizing campaign in preparation for a collective bargaining election. In exchange, the strikers vacated the GM properties. Both parties agreed to begin negotiations on February 16 to resolve the remaining strike grievances.

GM quickly resumed production at its plants and announced an immediate pay raise for its employees. Interestingly, GM, the UAW, and most of the media independently praised Murphy for mediating and ending the sit-down strike peacefully. In many ways, the governor was a prototype New Dealer. His pragmatic approach and active intervention as a mediator were motivated by the belief that the public, the government, had a responsibility to resolve industrial conflicts fairly and peacefully, if at all possible.

At the time, the strike secured the future of the UAW, the CIO, and industrial unionism in the United States. The union's breakthrough at GM turned out to be significant. By the end of May, it succeeded in organizing another one of the Big Three auto companies. According to historian Irving Bernstein, "It was the GM settlement of February 11 that broke the back of resistance at Chrysler."[1] By August 1937, the important and flourishing auto union had a membership of 350,000 and 256 locals, and it had concluded 400 collective bargaining agreements. The UAW's GM victory also brought enormous prestige to the CIO. It immediately went on to plan and conduct a campaign to organize the nonunion steel industry.

The GM strike brought the fundamental issue of the right of workers to organize and engage in collective bargaining into the national spotlight. The strikers achieved their objective, and the Supreme Court's favorable ruling on the Wagner Act in April confirmed such rights for the nation. In this context, the UAW's victory in the GM strike was one of the important events in a turbulent decade that subsequently enabled organized labor to unionize key industrial sectors of the economy that were located primarily in northern states and in the mass-production industries. In a sense, that strike's success, and the textile strike's failure in 1934, marked the emergence of a national pattern of labor relations wherein the North became the geographical center of union strength and the South remained largely unorganized.

The GM strike also brought a secondary issue—the sit-down strike—to the fore, and it became a hotly contested one soon after the strike. John L. Lewis and the CIO never took an official position on the tactic. Meanwhile, business denounced it as a violation of "property rights," while proponents of it claimed that workers had a propertied investment in their jobs. The general public had accepted, or at least tolerated, the sit-down at GM, largely because of GM's anti-union policies and behavior, but the widespread use of it by other workers in subsequent months alienated public opinion and led workers to use it less and less. The public's support of the right to organize and bargain collectively did not necessarily mean approval of the sit-down. The wave of such strikes peaked in March 1937 and then subsided, long before the U.S. Supreme Court declared them illegal in 1939.

NOTE

1. Irving Bernstein, *Turbulent Years: A History of the American Worker, 1933–1941* (Boston: Houghton Mifflin, 1969), p. 553.

DOCUMENTS

8.1. William S. Knudsen, Executive Vice President, General Motors, to Homer Martin, General President, International Union, United Automobile Workers of America, December 31, 1936

In this excerpt from a letter written on December 31, 1936, Knudsen outlined GM's general labor policy. He denounced the sit-down and rejected Martin's request for GM to hold a conference with the UAW and engage in collective bargaining on issues related to the corporation's national policies. By then, the Flint sit-down was underway.

This is in reply to your request for a meeting. . . .

On Dec. 22, 1936, upon receipt of your letter of Dec. 21, I invited you to come to my office for a personal interview and at that time informed you and Mr. George Addes, your secretary-treasurer, that in accordance with the operating policy of General Motors Corporation, the matters you wished to discuss should be taken up with the individual plant managers and if necessary with the general managers having jurisdiction in the location involved.

You say in your letter: "Bona fide collective bargaining is the only workable instrument for the establishment of satisfactory relationship between employers and employes."

General Motors Corporation accepts the principle of collective bargaining and desires to maintain satisfactory relations with all its employes regardless of union or non-union affiliations. To this end it has established a procedure under which employes may bargain collectively with the management. This procedure, dated on Aug. 15, 1934, is well known to the employes, and when you were in my office I showed a copy of it to you. . . .

Obviously, with plants located in thirty-five separate communities in fourteen States, with more than 200,000 employes, and necessarily operating under a variety of conditions peculiar to the manufacture of the products in which they are engaged, grievances of individuals or groups of individuals can only be handled locally where the employes and the plant management are familiar with local conditions, as well as with the basic general policies of the corporation concerning employe relations. . . .

Obviously the managers of these plants cannot bargain collectively with the representatives of a fraction of their employes if these representatives themselves refuse to bargain collectively before a sit-down is called. Yet that is exactly what has been done in each instance. The union itself has refused to bargain collectively and has made real collective bargaining impossible by exercising coercion before the bargaining begins. . . .

The record . . . shows how little regard union representation has for real collective bargaining. Sit-downs are strikes. Such strikers are clearly trespassers and violators of the law of the land. We cannot have bona fide collective bargaining with sit-down strikers in illegal possession of plants. Collective bargaining cannot be justified if one party, having seized the plant, holds a gun at the other party's head. . . .

Our plant managers are at liberty and have authority to meet with your representatives to discuss matters affecting your members who are our employes. Such discussion, however, should precede, not follow, sit-downs. No one can afford to bargain with sit-down strikers or with their representatives until the plants are cleared.

Source: William S. Knudsen to Homer Martin, December 31, 1936, text quoted in *New York Times*, January 1, 1937, p. 10. Copyright © 1937 by The New York Times Co. Reprinted with permission.

8.2.   Homer Martin, General President, International Union, United Automobile Workers of America, to Alfred P. Sloan, President, General Motors, and William S. Knudsen, Executive Vice President, General Motors, January 4, 1937

Martin outlined the strikers' position and basic grievances in this letter to GM executives. The UAW's demands that GM recognize it as the exclusive bargaining agent for GM employees and meet its representatives in a national conference to negotiate a national contract were at the heart of the conflict.

A grave situation has arisen between the employees of the General Motors Corporation and the Management of such Corporation, the seriousness of which you must appreciate. This entire situation not only affects the Corporation and its employees, but also the Public. It is for this reason that I call to your attention again the real issue which exists between the Corporation and the International Union, United Automobile Workers of America.

On December 24, 1936, I forwarded a letter to you requesting that a conference be held between the officers of your Corporation and this organization on behalf of the employees of the General Motors Corporation. I suggested in my letter that this conference be held for the purpose of discussing and negotiating certain fundamental issues which had arisen between the employees and the Management. These issues, as I indicated, cover the recognition of the Union by the Corporation for the purpose of collective bargaining, recognition of seniority rights for the purpose of maintaining job security for the employees, the elimination of the speedup system, and the establishment of a minimum wage which would assure a decent standard of living to your employees.

In your reply, dated December 31, 1936, you suggested that the employees of the General Motors Corporation should discuss any of their grievances with the plant managers. This procedure you term the system of "collective bargaining". The justification for your proposal was that there is such a diversity of factors among your various plants that it is impossible to have any national agreement between this organization and the General Motors Corporation.

There are two basic reasons why your proposal cannot meet the problem at hand:

First, the employees throughout the plant of the General Motors Corporation have encountered widespread discrimination and wholesale discharges because of their mere affiliation with the union at the hands of the plant managers. In other words, there apprears [*sic*] to be a nation-wide policy on the part of the General Motors Corporation not to permit the organization of a union among the employees. This policy had been in practice in absolute violation of the National Labor Relations Act, and also in contravention of the accepted principles in the United States today. Not until there has been a discontinuance of such a policy can there be any effective discussion of grievances between the employees and the respective plant managers.

Second, of course, there are diverse factors among the various plants of the General Motors Corporation. But it must also be recognized that with respect to certain fundamental policies, they are adopted and fixed by the National Executive Officers of your Corporation. It is with respect to a few such fundamental issues, which can only be accepted by the Executive Officers of your Corporation, that this organization demands a conference with you for the purpose of negotiating the same, looking toward a national agreement between the International Union, United Automobile Workers of America, and the General Motors Corporation.

The fundamental issues, for which there must be a national policy fixed by your corporation, are the following:

1. National Conference between responsible heads of General Motors Corporation and the Chosen representatives of the International Union,

United Automobile Workers of America. Such conference to discuss and bargain collectively on the following points as a basis for national agreement between the General Motors Corporation and its employees, as represented by the International Union, United Automobile Workers of America.

2. Abolition of all piece work systems of pay, and the adoption of straight hourly rate in its place.

3. 30 hour work week and six hour work day and time and one-half for all time worked over the basic work day and work week.

4. Establishment of a minimum rate of pay commensurate with an American standard of living.

5. Reinstatement of all employees who have been unjustly discharged.

6. Seniority, based upon length of service.

7. Recognition of the International Union, United Automobile Workers of America as the sole bargaining agency between the General Motors Corporation and its employees, for the establishment of joint tribunals and joint rules of procedure for the adjusting of any or all disputes that may arise from time to time between employees of General Motors Corporation and the management.

8. Speed of production shall be mutually agreed upon by the management and the union committee in all General Motors plants.

Again, it is with respect to the foregoing problems that I demand that an immediate conference be held between the officers of this Organization and the officers of the General Motors Corporation, looking toward a national agreement relating to such issues. It is absurd for your Corporation to suggest that with respect to basic problems of this sort the determination of their acceptance be left to the individual plant managers.

The failure on the part of your Corporation to accept the fundamental doctrine of collective bargaining with its employees is the sole and only cause for the serious situation that has resulted. This Organization, on behalf of the employees of the General Motors Corporation has merely requested the opportunity to confer with the Executive Officers of the General Motors Corporation to negotiate and reach an agreement with regard to certain problems which affect your corporation on a national scale.

Source: Homer Martin to Alfred P. Sloan Jr. and William S. Knudsen, January 4, 1937, Henry Kraus Collection, Reuther Archives of Labor and Urban Affairs, Wayne State University, Detroit, Michigan, Box 9, Folder 1. Used with permission of the Reuther Archives.

**8.3.   Alfred P. Sloan Jr., President, General Motors, "To
           All Employes of General Motors Corporation,"
           January 5, 1937**

> *The anti-union motivation of GM's collective bargaining pol-
> icy clearly emerges in a statement Sloan issued to employees on
> January 5. This excerpt clarifies GM's position. Especially note-
> worthy is Sloan's description of the real issue of the strike. In his
> view, collective bargaining, as sought by the union, threatened
> to subvert corporate power.*

. . . efforts are being made, in various ways, to make you as well as the
public believe that General Motors refuses to bargain collectively with its
workers and exercises discrimination against men who elect to join one
organization or another. Nothing could be farther from the truth.

But, after all, this is not the real issue that has brought about the situation that we face today. That real issue is perfectly clear, and here it is:

Will a labor organization run the plants of General Motors Corporation
or will the management continue to do so? On this issue depends the
question as to whether you have to have a union card to hold a job, or
whether your job will depend in the future, as it has in the past, upon
your own individual merit. In other words, will you pay to a private
group of labor dictators for the privilege of working, or will you have the
right to work as you may desire. Wages, working condition, honest collective bargaining, have little, if anything, to do with the underlying situation. They are simply a smoke screen to cover the real objective.

Now, you are entitled to know what General Motors position is. That
is the real purpose of this message to you. Here it is:

1. General Motors will not recognize any union as the sole bargaining
agency for its workers, to the exclusion of all others. General Motors will
continue to recognize, for the purpose of collective bargaining, the representatives of its workers, whether union or non-union.

2. Work in General Motors plants will continue to depend on the ability and efficiency of the worker—not on the membership or non-
membership in any labor organization whatsoever. This means that you
do not have to pay tribute to any one for the right to work.

3. General Motors will continue to pay the highest justifiable wages in
the future, as it has in the past, and just as it is doing at present. It believes in high wages. It is justly proud of its record in that respect.

4. General Motors standard work-week will continue to be forty hours.
Time and a half will be paid for over-time.

5. Seniority rights will be observed under the rules laid down by the Automobile Labor Board appointed by the President of the United States in March, 1934. These rules are recognized as fair and just to all workers and permit no discrimination against any worker on account of any organization membership.

Source: Alfred P. Sloan Jr., "To All Employes of General Motors Corporation," text quoted in *New York Times*, January 5, 1937, p. 17. Copyright © 1937 by The New York Times Co. Reprinted with permission.

8.4.   Genora Johnson, Affidavit, Genessee County, Michigan, January 28, 1937

In this affidavit, Johnson, a female strike supporter, described her experiences during the "Battle of the Running Bulls" at Fisher Body No. 2 on the night of January 11, 1937, when she rallied the women to defend their brothers and husbands. The violent attempt by the police to dislodge the strikers that night subsequently led her to found the Women's Emergency Brigade.

On Monday, January 11th, 1937, at about 6 P.M. I was at the Pengelly Bldg. [strike headquarters] rehearsing a play, with my husband, my sister, and two friends. After rehearsal was over and we were ready to go home, we were told that food and heat had been shut off from our boys in Fisher #2 plant. So, instead of going directly home, we drove over to Fisher #2 on Chevrolet Ave. There was a picket line in front of the plant. The picketeers [*sic*] were singing and marching, and everything was peaceful. However, the boys inside were not singing; they seemed anxious and kept hollering down, "We are having a meeting and electing a committee to see about getting our meals through". After marching and singing awhile, my sister and her friend said they had to go home, so we all drove home together. But my husband, our friend, and myself decided to return to Fisher #2 and do picket duty; so we hurried back. After parking our car 2 blocks away around the corner from the Chevrolet office bldg., and starting to walk towards the plant I heard gun shots. At that I began to run—and in running toward the plant I noticed that nearly everyone was running toward us, and bullets were being shot, and missles [*sic*] being hurled very close to me; although I did not see who the bullets hit. Fred Stevens was carried past me on the shoulders of 2 men; and another man who was carried in the arms of 2 comrades was soaked with blood, his head hanging limply. The third man that I saw shot was bleeding from the shoulder.

From the beginning the air was clouded with tear gas, and smarted my eyes. The loud speaker in the Union sould [*sic*] car carried Victor Reuther's voice, urging the men to keep their heads and to think very clearly. Although several Union men urged me to go to a safer place because I was a woman I wanted to remain, and I called up encouraging words to the fellows in the windows. Beneath the windows I found a bar of solder which I carried the rest of the night. The streets were being blocked off at that time with cars at each end of the block in front of Fisher #2. Windows and doors in the plant had been smashed; broken bottles and stones were strewn around. Still Victor Reuther's voice was not excited, and consequently it calmed my nerves. Tear gas bombs were still being hurled but the men directing the water hose from the plant helped considerably by rendering much of it ineffective. The police on the bridge threw bombs and gas grenades. The bombs reported loudly, and every once in awhile I heard a gun report. I picked up and examined shells. I walked in the picket line and sang. Very soon I saw a man in a police uniform on the other side of the street in front of Chevrolet plant #2. The sound car was exposed to him and I yelled. Someone heard me and men began to throw stones and rocks at him. He escaped unhurt into the side entrance of Chev. #2. From then on I remained close to the sound car, because the directions we received from it kept us calm, orderly, and prepared. For a very long period of time the bombs kept bursting; whots [*sic*] rang out intermittantly [*sic*], and tear gas stung my eyes. I would say that for 4 hours this situation kept up. During this time I did not know fear. I knew only surprise, anguish, and anger. I had never seen anything like this situation before. The police kept advancing slowly—dispersing the crowds behind them with tear gas, and keeping union men and sympathizers who were trying to get through to help us from doing so.

At one point I saw my husband, my friend and another man walk toward the Sheriff Dept.'s car which had been overturned. I heard shots. The men ran. One of them kept crying out, "I'm shot", "I'm shot". I was standing directly in back of the men at a further distance from the car. The man who had been shot ran until he fell. My husband came up to me and said, "Some of that buckshot hit me in the head, I'm glad I wore this leather helmet". At a later period in the night I saw one of the men pick up an empty buckshot carton, and I examined it.

I saw Victor Reuther get out of the sound car twice and expose himself, and I pleaded with him to remain inside the sound car and to direct us in that calm manner.

During this period I saw cops and men going into Chevrolet plant #2. After watching closely we saw the shadows of many men moving back and forth on all three floors of Chev. #2. Expecting a rush from Chev. #2 across the overhead bridge, I saw the men in Fisher #2 block up the entrance of the bridge through the bridge windows.

Toward the end I asked if I might speak over loudspeaker to the people on the lines in back of the city police. I received permission, and I told the people standing in the lines that the men had no firearms and were defenseless in the face of firearms. I asked the women in the lines to break through and come down and stand with their husbands and brothers. I said if the police were cowards enough to shoot defenseless men, they would be cowards enough to shoot down women. After I finished, women from both sides walked down the streets and sidewalks to the front of Fisher #2. There was no more shooting of buckshot or bullets after that. However, they still threw bombs and tear gas.

Source: Genora Johnson, Affidavit of Genora Johnson, Genessee County, Michigan, January 28, 1937, National Archives, Records of the U.S. Senate, Record Group 46, Sen. 78A-F9, Box 126.

8.5.   John L. Lewis, Speech Delivered at the Fifth Annual Convention of the International Union, United Automobile Workers of America, July 30, 1940

In this excerpt from his speech, Lewis, CIO president, graphically traced the history of the negotiations that concluded the landmark GM strike. Especially noteworthy is his vivid description of his reaction to Governor Murphy's letter and threat to enforce the court's writ to evacuate the struck plants.

On February 1, 1937, in behalf of the C.I.O., in behalf of the United Automobile Workers, in behalf of the men on strike in the General Motors plants, I conferred with the President of the United States, and the proposals which were adduced for settlement at that time were so unsatisfactory that I declined to present them to the United Automobile Workers' Union, and on the following day, February 2nd, I took a train for Detroit with no further conference arranged, determined to contribute my strength to the cause of the workers in the General Motors plants and determined to rise or fall with these men and that organization.

ULTIMATUM

I do not know what happened in the night, but on leaving the train in Detroit the following morning I was waited on by representatives of the Governor of Michigan and summoned forthwith into a conference which resulted later in the day in a joint meeting of three representatives of the General Motors Corporation and the Governor of the State. Those conferences lasted nine days and a large part of nine nights, and during that entire period the constant refrain of the manufacturers' representatives and the constant request of the Governor of the State was that I order an evacuation of the plants, and submit to the hazard of negotiations following that evacuation. My reply was every day and every night to this effect: "Those men, out of a sense of their own grievous injustices, voluntarily elected to take that step, and I would be a fool indeed and a traitor indeed if I asked those men to evacuate their position of strength, knowing that in Flint and elsewhere they would be shot down in the streets by the murderous agents of General Motors Corporation, and the chances of getting a satisfactory settlement would be entirely dissipated and thrown away."

It is a matter of public knowledge now that the Governor of this State read me a formal letter in writing demanding that this action be taken by me, and my reply to the Governor of the State when he read that letter, with the knowledge of the President of the United States—and the approval—was this: "I do not doubt your ability to call out your soldiers and shoot the members of our union out of those plants, but let me say that when you issue that order I shall leave this conference and I shall enter one of those plants with my own people."

(Applause.)

(continuing) "And the militia will have the pleasure of shooting me out of the plants with you." The order was not executed.

VICTORY

And one morning about 3 o'clock, after nine days of constant, wearisome negotiations, a vice-president of General Motors Corporation who owned $13,000,000 worth of the stock came up himself to my bedroom in the hotel and told me that General Motors would sign on the dotted line. And they did, and I did, and you did, and the Union was born beyond peradventure. They had executed collective bargaining contracts with the mightiest corporation of them all.

Source: "Address of John L. Lewis," in *Proceedings of the Fifth Annual Convention of the International Union, United Automobile Workers of America, Convened July 29 to August 6, 1940, St. Louis, MO* ([Detroit]: The Union, 1940), pp. 104–5. Used with permission of the International Union, United Automobile Workers.

8.6.   "Strike, A Fair Compromise," *Washington Post*, February 14, 1937

At the conclusion of the strike, the Washington Post *praised the settlement and Governor Murphy's mediating role in it, as this excerpt from an editorial indicates. Many other newspapers expressed similar sentiments at the time.*

A "peace without victory" ended the costliest strike in American industrial history last week. The 44-day struggle for power between the giant General Motors Corporation, producer of half the country's automobiles, and the United Automobile Workers, vanguard in John L. Lewis's fight for industrial unionism, was terminated Thursday morning with the signing of a "peace treaty" that brought honor to both sides and left no room for gloating. . . .

Nation-wide praise was showered on Gov. Murphy for his success in bringing about a peaceful settlement of the bitter struggle. The President sent his "heartiest congratulations" for a "high public service nobly performed," and the Nation in general agreed with that verdict. Michigan's red-haired Governor was lauded for his tenacity in holding both sides together during the eight days of wearying conferences, for his patience, tact and diplomacy in dealing with two seemingly adamant forces; for his absolute impartiality, and for his wise handling of the explosive situation in Flint, where feeling between strikers and nonunion men ran high, but violence was held down to a minimum. Some uncompromising defenders of legal rights felt that Gov. Murphy should have used troops to evacuate the sit-down strikers, no matter what the cost, but the general opinion was that the Governor had taken the best course to bring about a peaceful agreement built on mutual respect, and not a settlement forced by violence or bloodshed.

Source: "Strike, A Fair Compromise," *Washington Post*, February 14, 1937, p. B3. © 1937, The Washington Post. Reprinted with permission.

8.7.   "Sit-Down on Trial," *Christian Science Monitor,* **February 1, 1937**

The GM strike made the sit-down strike famous and an issue in labor relations. While the strike was still in progress, the Christian Science Monitor *published "Sit-Down on Trial" and explored some of the conflicting and ambiguous ways the tactic was viewed at the time. As this excerpt indicates, the newspaper considered the sit-down in relationship to broader issues such as the role of unions, government, and collective bargaining in U.S. labor policy. At this date, the public had not yet developed a fixed position on the new tactic.*

The conscience of the American people is still weighing the sit-down strike.

To the many imponderables, the many behind-the-scenes factors, which make hasty judgments unwise in the ordinary labor dispute are now added a new method and many unweighed influences. Many Americans are suspending judgment on the new and seemingly very powerful weapon labor has discovered. . . .

Failing to win public support, the ousting of workers from the plants may prove no more feasible than the foreclosing of mortgages did when farm communities blocked sheriffs' sales during the depression. Public approval or rejection of the sit-down, not only in the present test but in the whole field of labor relations, will largely be determined by how it is used. If it is used responsibly and a majority of employees either support it or show no strong objection, the public may consider it a legitimate method of matching the power of employers.

This may explain why there has been no popular protest against the plainly illegal occupation of company property in the motor strike. General Motors has stated the legal position clearly but after one attempt to dislodge the Flint strikers has appeared unwilling to again risk violence. The sit-down gives the strikers the advantage of appearing on the defensive. Any move which precipitates violence seems to come from the employer.

For that reason the public, conscious that many employers while recognizing collective bargaining "in principle" are by no mean facilitating its operation in practice, may be willing to tolerate the sit-down. Americans may not object to the sit-down as an encourager of collective bargaining. But if it is to be employed by an irresponsible minority which does not ask for elections to prove its right to represent workers in collective bargaining, public opinion may quickly reject it.

In the last few days there have been signs that the public was becoming impatient with John L. Lewis and his dictatorial position, if not with the Flint strikers. The refusal of the company even to discuss peace terms until the plants are evacuated checked a swing of popular sympathy toward the company and its employees who want to work. Yet it is clear that the sit-down is far from an accepted method.

In France this sharp and double-edged weapon forced a system of compulsory arbitration. America is likely to be slow to adopt such a drastic control, but the present tests of the sit-down will impel the study of better means for preventing and settling strikes. In that process we may expect a more complete unionization of workers, a more ready acceptance of collective bargaining by employers, and a more positive effort at early mediation by the Government.

Source: "Sit-Down on Trial," *Christian Science Monitor*, February 1, 1937, p. 18. Reprinted with permission.

SELECTED ANNOTATED BIBLIOGRAPHY

Books

Bernstein, Irving. *Turbulent Years: A History of the American Worker 1933–1941.* Boston: Houghton Mifflin, 1969. For a brief description of the strike and surrounding events, see Chapter 11, "The Emergence of the UAW."

Dollinger, Sol and Genora Johnson Dollinger. *Not Automatic: Women and the Left in the Forging of the Auto Workers' Union.* New York: Monthly Review Press, 2000. Contains a valuable oral history of the strike by the founder of the Women's Emergency Brigade.

Fine, Sidney. *The Automobile Under the Blue Eagle: Labor, Management, and the Automobile Manufacturing Code.* Ann Arbor: University of Michigan Press, 1963. Important account of the auto industry and events under the NIRA.

———. *Sit-Down: The General Motors Strike of 1936–1937.* Ann Arbor: University of Michigan Press, 1969. Indispensable and classic scholarly account of the strike.

Kraus, Henry. *Heroes of Unwritten Story: The UAW, 1934–39.* Foreword by Nelson Lichtenstein. Urbana: University of Illinois Press, 1993. A useful narrative of the union's early days, as seen by a radical union activist and strike participant.

———. *The Many and the Few: A Chronicle of the Dynamic Auto Workers.* 2nd ed. Urbana: University of Illinois Press, 1985. An essential rank-and-file narrative of the strike, written by the strike participant who edited the UAW's newspaper.

Levinson, Edward. *Labor on the March.* New York: Harper & Brothers, 1938. See Chapter 7, "Akron and Flint," in this labor journalist's classic description of the rise of the CIO.

Meier, August and Elliott Rudwick. *Black Detroit and the Rise of the UAW.* New York: Oxford University Press, 1979. The strike receives attention in this valuable study of how labor and race relations changed in Detroit during the 1930s and early 1940s.

Perkins, Frances. *The Roosevelt I Knew.* New York: Viking Press, 1946. For President Roosevelt's role in the strike, see the Secretary of Labor's memoir, pages 319–25.

Pesotta, Rose. *Bread Upon the Waters.* Edited by John Nicholas Beffel. New York: Dodd, Mead & Company, 1945. For an organizer's depiction of events, see Chapter 22, "Auto Workers Line Up For Battle," and Chapter 23, "General Motors Capitulates."

Sloan, Alfred P., Jr. *My Years with General Motors.* Edited by John McDonald with Catharine Stevens. Garden City, NY: Doubleday & Company, 1964. This GM executive's memoir contains brief allusions to the strike's significant impact on GM.

———. *The Story of the General Motors Strike, Submitted to Stockholders by Alfred P. Sloan, Jr., President General Motors Corporation, April, 1937* [New York, 1937]. Valuable documents and narrative of the strike, as seen by the GM executive.

U.S. Congress. Senate, Committee on Education and Labor. *Violations of Free Speech and Rights of Labor; Hearings before a Subcommittee of the Committee on Education and Labor, United States Senate, 75th Congress, 1st session pursuant to S. Res. 266.* 2 vols. Parts 6 and 7, *Labor Espionage, General Motors Company.* Washington, DC: GPO, 1937. Contains testimonies and rare documents from the LaFollette committee's investigation.

Web Sites

Teachers, students, and researchers will find "The Great Flint Showdown," a useful introduction and overview of the strike, at the Reuther Library, Wayne State University site, http://www.reuther.wayne.edu/exhibits/sitdown.html. Excerpts from Genora Johnson's oral histories are conveniently located in the Sol Dollinger American Socialist Collection at http://www.marxists.org/history/etol/newspape/amersocialist/other_documents.htm. Note especially "Striking Flint: Genora (Johnson) Dollinger Remembers the 1936–37 General Motors Sit-Down Strike . . . as told to Susan Rosenthal" (1993) and Sharon Gluck's "Oral History on Genora Johnson's Role in 1937 Strike" (1976). "This Is the Pressure That They Used" and "I Was Able to Make My Voice Really Ring Out," two excerpts from Gluck's interview, are also available at the History Matters site, www.historymatters.gmu.edu/all.html. "Remembering the Flint Sit-Down Strike, Audio Gallery," another useful collection of oral histories, is available at Michigan State University's site, http://www.historicalvoices.org/flint/strike.php. See the Michigan Department of Education's Michigan Education Portal for Interactive Content site at www.michiganepic.org/flintstrike/ for photos, articles, a timeline, audio and movie clips.

The New Deal Network, established by the Franklin and Eleanor Roosevelt Institute and located at http://newdeal.feri.org, provides other valuable documents. They include contemporary strike articles such as "Detroit Digs In" by Edward Levinson, *The Nation,* January 16, 1937; "Profile of General Motors" by Samuel Romer, *The Nation,* January 23, 1937; "A G.M. Stockholder Visits Flint" by Robert Morss Lovett, *The Nation,* January 30, 1937; "Flint Faces Civil War" by Charles R. Walker, *The Nation,* February 13, 1937; and an editorial, "Relief in the Sit-Down Strike," *Survey,* March 1937.

Of the many other strike sites, note especially "Remembering Flint," an excerpt from *Who Built America?* at http://a4a.mahost.org/uaw.html; a Progressive Labor Party pamphlet, *How Industrial Unionism Was Won. The Great Flint Sit-Down Against GM 1936–37,* by Walter Linder (1965) at http://www.plp.org/pamphlets/flintstrike.html; and "The Flint Sit-Down Strike" by Monica Link and Larry Gabriel, UAW *Solidarity,* at http://www.uaw.org/solidarity/03/0103/feature07.html.

Video

With Babies and Banners: Story of the Women's Emergency Brigade. Produced by Lorraine Gray and Lyn Goldfarb. 47 minutes. New York: New Day Films, 1990

[1978]. This excellent documentary, originally produced in 1978, explores the role of women in the strike and the formation of the Women's Emergency Brigade. The 1990 edition includes interviews with strike participants on the fortieth anniversary of the strike. Ideal for classes, groups, and general viewing.

9

The Labor Management Relations (Taft-Hartley) Act of 1947

In 1947 industrial representatives and proponents of the Labor Management Relations Act, popularly known as the Taft-Hartley Act, hailed it as a "bill of rights" for workers while many in the labor movement and critics blasted it as a "slave-labor" statute. The controversial law enacted after World War II by the conservative Republican 80th Congress over President Harry Truman's veto may not have justified either epithet, but it did, without doubt, redefine labor relations in the United States. In fundamental ways, it amended the National Labor Relations Act of 1935 (the Wagner Act) and imposed stringent new restrictions on trade unions. It remains the basic law governing U.S. labor relations today. Labor's sporadic efforts over the years to repeal it have failed, but the controversy over the 1947 statute has not ended. In 2000, for example, Ralph Nader, the Green Party's presidential candidate, made its repeal a central issue during his campaign, and in 2002, in a controversial decision, President George W. Bush invoked the "national emergency" provisions of the law during the Pacific Maritime Association's lockout of West Coast dock workers. The Taft-Hartley Act continues to arouse ongoing debate and fierce resentment.

What the Taft-Hartley Act did was establish new parameters for labor relations and collective bargaining. Although it retained the workers' right to organize and bargain collectively through representatives of their own choosing, it included many changes that marked a departure from the path-breaking Wagner Act that the labor movement had hailed as its "Magna Carta," a law that subsequently helped organized labor grow from about 3 million members in 1935 to 15 million in 1946. On the eve of the new law's passage, Senator Robert A. Taft, prominent Republican sponsor of the bill, asserted that its central purpose "was to 'equalize' the bargaining power of employer and union by increasing it for the one and decreasing it for the other."[1] For labor and its supporters, however, the new bill was not a neutral or fair one that "equalized" bargaining power but a deliberate attempt by business interests to create a new imbalance and destroy the labor movement or render it as weak and powerless as it had been before the New Deal.

Among the most important provisions of the complex new law were the following:

1. It banned the "closed shop." Closed shop agreements between employers and employees stipulated that only union members in good standing could be hired or retained as employees. At the time the law was passed, thousands of workers in industries such as shipping and pottery making were covered under such agreements.

2. It retained the "union shop" but substantially restricted it. In union shop contracts, employers agreed to keep only union members on their payrolls; the employers were permitted to hire nonunion workers, but those workers had to join the union within a specified time period, usually thirty days. This general acceptance in the law of the union shop was muted and contradicted by section 14 (b), which allowed states to pass "right to work" laws that prohibited union shops and made them illegal.

3. It banned jurisdictional strikes, sympathy strikes, and secondary boycotts. Jurisdictional strikes involved rivalries between different unions who often claimed entitlement to the particular jobs involved, along with representation rights.

4. It outlawed all strikes by employees of the federal government.

5. It granted authority to the president to go to court to get an injunction against a labor stoppage or an employer's lockout, that is, the closing down of a business by management to pressure workers to agree to its terms, whenever the chief executive thought the disruption jeopardized the nation's health or safety. In such "national emergencies," courts could then order an eighty-day, "cooling off" period during which the two sides would negotiate under the auspices of a federal mediator. At the end of that time, if the two parties had not reached an agreement, the workers could strike or management could lock them out.

6. It compelled unions to furnish detailed financial and other data to the U.S. government, prohibited union contributions to political campaigns in federal elections, and required union officers to sign non-communist oaths, thereby bringing the federal government into the internal affairs of labor organizations in new ways.

7. It granted employers the right to go to court and sue unions for violation of contracts.

8. It granted employers as well as workers the right to ask for an election to determine if employees wanted a given union to represent them so long as such certification or decertification elections were held only once a year.

9. It incorporated a list of "unfair practices" by unions to supplement and complement the list of "unfair practices" by employers that was contained in the Wagner Act.

10. It retained collective bargaining as a fundamental goal but redefined terms such as "employee," "supervisor," and "collective bargaining," thereby restructuring bargaining units in ways that undercut labor support and favored business interests.

11. It preserved the National Labor Relations Board but redefined and enlarged it from three to five members who were to be appointed by the president, subject to Senate confirmation.

12. It removed federal mediation and conciliation services from the Department of Labor, considered biased by the law's proponents, and established an independent Federal Mediation and Conciliation Service.

To understand where the Taft-Hartley Act came from, it is useful to go back to 1935 and the passage of the Wagner Act, which guaranteed workers the basic right to organize and bargain collectively and established the National Labor Relations Board (NLRB) to enforce those rights. As we have seen, General Motors and other major anti-union employers did not like the law at the time and refused to abide by it in the belief that it was unconstitutional. Nor did corporate opposition cease after the Supreme Court declared the labor law constitutional in 1937. Hostile employers such as Ford Motor Company and Republic Steel continued to oppose collective bargaining, and in 1939, the National Association of Manufacturers (NAM), an important trade organization that espoused the open shop and represented thousands of large and small employers, led an unsuccessful drive to alter, or repeal, the Wagner Act. After World War II, NAM again led a concerted drive, this time successfully, to amend the labor law in significant ways. In the interim from 1935 to 1947, many U.S. businesses had come to accept collective bargaining, but others had not. As Senator Wayne Morse, the independent Oregon Republican noted, after hearing industrialists testify about the proposed labor legislation in 1947: "I think it is important that voices be heard in America these days pointing out that there are still many employers who have not learned— or who are not willing to admit—that collective bargaining through the elected representatives of the workers is here to stay."[2]

Industrial strife emerged as a key domestic issue after World War II and set the stage for those classes and interests who favored the Taft-Hartley Act. Earlier, during the war, a coal strike led by John L. Lewis in 1943 had fueled public anger and led Congress to pass the Smith-Connally Act to restrict work stoppages in essential industries for the duration. Then, in

1946, the ending of the war and wartime restrictions brought about one of the most impressive strike waves in U.S. history. Rank-and-file workers who continued to suffer from spiraling inflation and who had refrained from striking during the war began unprecedented work stoppages for improved wages and working conditions. There were national strikes in the auto, meat-packing, electrical, steel, rail, and coal industries. What caused the strikes? In general, NAM and the business community blamed a "labor monopoly" and bad legislation, while organized labor blamed inflation and recalcitrant employers. The critical battle for labor legislation depended on what the public thought and who it blamed for the strife.

The wave of postwar strikes created immense problems for Harry S. Truman. In the summer of 1946, after dealing with the national rail and coal strikes, the exasperated president startled labor with a proposal that strikers in essential industries be drafted. But soon after, when a conservative Congress responded to the strike wave by passing the Case bill, which resembled the future Taft-Hartley Act, the conflicted New Deal Democrat vetoed it, and the veto was sustained. The domestic political climate for passage of punitive labor legislation greatly improved after the congressional elections of 1946, when a predominantly conservative Republican Congress—the first Republican majority elected since the New Deal—openly espoused curbing labor's power severely.

It was Truman himself who opened the door for the subsequent legislation. During his "State of the Union" speech before Congress on January 6, 1947, he suggested the need for new, nonpunitive, labor legislation. Stressing that management and labor shared responsibility for industrial strife, he emphasized that collective bargaining would remain the official policy of the United States. To correct abuses, he advocated new laws to restrict jurisdictional strikes and secondary boycotts; greater financial support for the Department of Labor; the expansion of New Deal social programs to create economic security for workers; and the formation of a joint committee to study labor–management relations. Immediately, the *New York Times* and much of the mainstream media editorialized that Truman had not gone nearly far enough to curb the labor "monopoly," which they blamed, single-handedly, for the strikes. NAM took out newspaper ads to oppose Truman's study commission and advertise its own proposals, while labor leaders confined their comments to mild acceptance or criticism of Truman's proposals.

Curbing the power of labor was the talk of the day, however. In the first week of the 80th Congress, over thirty bills were introduced to restrict labor and amend the Wagner Act. Senators Robert A. Taft of Ohio, Joseph H. Ball of Minnesota, and H. Alexander Smith of New Jersey had already drafted a major bill and were working with Rep. Philip A. Hartley of the House Labor Committee. Their insistence that Congress pass an omnibus bill that contained all labor reforms within one comprehensive bill was designed to force Truman, who wanted some legislation, to accept or veto the bill in its entirety, no matter what provisions it contained.

From January 23 to March 15, House and Senate committees held hearings on proposed legislation. Representatives from business, labor, the public, and government testified. Much of the testimony revolved around specific issues or bills. Ira Mosher, Chairman of the Executive Committee of NAM, led an array of corporation presidents and corporate lawyers favoring the most extreme restrictions. NAM advocated bans on any form of "compulsory unionism," including the closed shop and union shop, and on industrywide bargaining, which meant that national unions would be reduced to small, weaker units that could only negotiate at the local level. It sought severe limits on the right to strike and the collective bargaining process.

AFL President William Green, CIO President Philip Murray, and other labor leaders also testified. It is significant to note that the Taft-Hartley Act was passed at a time when the AFL and CIO were rival organizations and that many jurisdictional strikes, an important issue that fueled the drive for restriction, were related to that rivalry. Despite their differences, the labor representatives all took the position that they did not want *any* changes in the Wagner Act and that they wanted *less*—not more—government intervention so that collective bargaining could work. Advocates of moderate reform such as Senator Wayne Morse, who stressed that the 80th Congress was going to enact some sort of labor legislation, criticized organized labor for failing to offer constructive suggestions on how to change the laws to help reduce industrial conflict.

Underlying the congressional debates on specific provisions of the future Taft-Hartley Act was the more fundamental and contentious issue of the proper role of organized labor in a democratic nation. The House Majority and Minority Committees' reports on H.R. 3020, subsequently the core of the Taft-Hartley Act, are especially revealing in this respect. The House majority justified the bill in this way: "During the last few years, the effects of industrial strife have at times brought our country to the brink of general economic paralysis. Employees have suffered, employers have suffered—and above all the public has suffered."[3] But it was not an impartial report. It went on to condemn the Wagner, Clayton, and Norris-LaGuardia acts as "ill-conceived"; it ignored the causes of labor unrest, condemned labor "bosses" without saying anything favorable about unions or collective action, blasted the NLRB for biased and unfair rulings, and indiscriminately criticized all strikes that had occurred since the Wagner Act. It presented its case in terms of "a bill of rights" for workers—as individuals—and their employers.

By contrast, the House Minority report on H.R. 3020 viewed the bill as a fierce attack on American industrial democracy. Unions were an essential "citadel of democracy," and the right to strike was essential. The report noted that not only did the bill repeal the Wagner Act and other important labor legislation; it also threatened the status of workers as "free men." Adam Clayton Powell, a black labor and civil rights representative from New York, stressed the minority's bleak conclusions about the bill's impact on free working people and democratic freedoms: "Those who support this measure shout a single refrain: 'What about big strikes?' There is an answer to big strikes; indeed, there are two answers. One is the Russian answer of destroying all businesses and making labor an implement of the state. . . . The other is the Nazi and Fascist answer of destroying trade unions and forbidding strikes."[4]

On April 17, the House passed H.R. 3020 by a veto-proof majority. On May 13, the Senate also approved the House bill, but, to make it appear more moderate, substituted softer language to replace its extreme wording. A joint conference met to resolve differences. The media misleadingly portrayed the final bill as much more moderate than the House's. Although the House did ultimately drop its demands for abolition of the NLRB and a total ban on industrywide bargaining, it did so only because such concessions were deemed necessary to retain the votes needed to override a veto. Moreover, as Hartley informed the press, if labor conflict continued, Congress would enact more drastic legislation. *The Nation* was one of the few mainstream journals that ridiculed the idea that this was a "moderate" bill and openly called it "class legislation" designed to destroy the labor movement.

Meanwhile, the AFL, CIO, and independent unions mobilized their constituencies, held rallies, and conducted petition drives to support a presidential veto. The *United Mine Workers Journal* was one of the many labor journals that scathingly attacked the bill and spelled out its implications to its members. On June 15, the *UMWJ* argued that "N.A.M.-Taft-Hartley" meant the liquidation of collective bargaining and the probable end of free enterprise. It especially deplored the ban on political contributions as a violation of free speech and the union's constitutional rights. It singled out Section 14 (b) as an invitation to open-shop employers in the South, and it viewed the complicated law as a heyday for lawyers and government bureaucrats.

Labor got its wish, and Truman did veto the Taft-Hartley bill on June 20. But the House overrode the veto by a vote of 331 to 83 that same day, and on June 23, the Senate overrode it by a vote of 68 to 25. In response, coal miners in Pennsylvania and elsewhere went out on strike to protest the new "slave-labor" law. Soon thereafter, unions were rallying and vowing to defeat those who had supported the measure in the 1948 congressional elections.

Truman made the "do nothing" 80th Congress and repeal of the Taft-Hartley Act prime issues in the 1948 presidential election. His upset victory over Thomas Dewey and the return of a Democratic Congress led organized labor to believe the law would be repealed in 1949. Even *Business Week*, sobered by the election results, expected repeal and reassessed the labor legislation: "What was wrong was that the Taft-Hartley act went too far. It crossed the narrow line separating a law which aims only to regulate from one which could destroy."[5] Yet, despite such expectations, there still weren't enough votes in the 81st Congress to repeal the law.

The Taft-Hartley Act did not produce the most dire consequences labor feared, but, without a doubt, it did profoundly damage the labor movement and alter the balance of power in labor relations to favor business. Comparison of the text of the Taft-Hartley Act with the Wagner Act suggests the profound shift that occurred. The 1947 law undercut the momentum and power of a rank-and-file social movement that had flourished under the New Deal and that was inherent in the postwar strike wave. Born in the context of political reaction against the New Deal and the extension of social programs, in the midst of an emerging Cold War and the precursors of full-scale "McCarthyism," it made dissent and radical ideas victims. "The Taft-Hartley statute is the first ugly savage thrust of Fascism in America,"[6] warned John L. Lewis in October 1947 when he urged AFL leaders to do as he did, and refuse, out of principle, to sign the mandatory non-communist affidavit. Instead, the AFL quickly complied with the law, and the CIO followed suit, shortly before purging itself of all communist and noncomplying unions. The result was that not only communists but all those labor leaders who had championed radical or progressive causes, including civil rights, were effectively silenced or marginalized. Then, too, states responded to the labor restrictions by reducing workers' compensation and passing additional anti-labor laws, including "right to work" laws. The South remained a bastion of the open shop. Nor did the law end labor strife. In the first year of its effectiveness, Truman himself used the law to get injunctions against work stoppages on seven occasions, and, to date, presidents have invoked the "national emergency" provisions of the law thirty-six times.

Over the years the Supreme Court and federal courts have upheld most of the law's provisions except the ban on political contributions. Organized labor and business have learned to live with the law that many say is deeply flawed, if not unfair. In 1948 *Business Week* suggested that the administration of the law was dependent on the proclivities of the particular administration in power and that, under certain conditions such as mass unemployment, a hostile government could use the law to destroy the labor movement. Today, much to the chagrin of organized labor and to the delight of anti-union businesses, the Taft-Hartley Act is often mentioned as a contributing factor in the ongoing decline of organized labor.

NOTES

1. *New York Times*, May 30, 1947, p. 14.

2. Wayne Morse, Speech on Labor Legislation, 80th Cong., 1st sess., Senate, *Congressional Record* (March 10, 1947), vol. 93, pt. 2, p. 1826.

3. Congress, House, House Report No. 245 on H.R. 3020, in U.S. National Labor Relations Board, *Legislative History of the Labor Management Relations Act*, commemorative ed., 2 vols. (Washington, DC: GPO, 1985, 1959), 1:294.

4. Adam Clayton Powell, Speech on Labor Legislation, 80th Cong., 1st sess., House, *Congressional Record* (April 16, 1947), vol. 93, pt. 3, pp. 3526–27.

5. "Why the Taft-Hartley Act Failed," *Business Week* 56 (December 18, 1948): 124.

6. John L. Lewis, *Speech by John L. Lewis in Opposition to Taft-Hartley Statute, Delivered Before A.F.L. Convention, October 14, 1947, San Francisco, California* (Washington, DC: n.p., 1947), p. 2.

DOCUMENTS

9.1. Harry S. Truman, Annual Message to the Congress on the State of the Union, January 6, 1947

In this speech before the new conservative Republican Congress, the Democratic president outlined his views on labor legislation and proposed a moderate four-point program to improve them. His limited suggestions for legal change did not satisfy the Congress or please organized labor.

The year just past—like the year after the First World War—was marred by labor-management strife.

Despite this outbreak of economic warfare in 1946, we are today producing goods and services in record volume. Nevertheless, it is essential to improve the methods for reaching agreement between labor and management and to reduce the number of strikes and lockouts.

We must not, however, adopt punitive legislation. We must not, in order to punish a few labor leaders, pass vindictive laws which will restrict the proper rights of the rank and file of labor. We must not, under the stress of emotion, endanger our American freedoms by taking ill-considered action which will lead to results not anticipated or desired.

We must remember, in reviewing the record of disputes in 1946, that management shares with labor the responsibility for failure to reach agreements which would have averted strikes. For that reason, we must realize that industrial peace cannot be achieved merely by laws directed against labor unions.

During the last decade and a half, we have established a national labor policy in this country based upon free collective bargaining as the process for determining wages and working conditions.

That is still the national policy.

And it should continue to be the national policy!

But as yet, not all of us have learned what it means to bargain freely and fairly. Nor have all of us learned to carry the mutual responsibilities that accompany the right to bargain. There have been abuses and harmful practices which limit the effectiveness of our system of collective bargaining. Furthermore, we have lacked sufficient governmental machinery to aid labor and management in resolving their differences.

Certain labor-management problems need attention at once and certain others, by reason of their complexity, need exhaustive investigation and study.

We should enact legislation to correct certain abuses and to provide additional governmental assistance in bargaining. But we should also concern ourselves with the basic causes of labor-management difficulties.

In the light of these considerations, I propose to you and urge your co-operation in effecting the following four-point program to reduce industrial strife:

Point number one is the early enactment of legislation to prevent certain unjustifiable practices.

First, under this point, are jurisdictional strikes. In such strikes the public and the employer are innocent bystanders who are injured by a collision between rival unions. . . .

A second unjustifiable practice is the secondary boycott, when used to further jurisdictional disputes or to compel employers to violate the National Labor Relations Act.

Not all secondary boycotts are unjustified. We must judge them on the basis of their objectives. . . . The structure of industry sometimes requires unions, as a matter of self-preservation, to extend the conflict beyond a particular employer. There should be no blanket prohibition against boycotts. The appropriate goal is legislation which prohibits secondary boycotts in pursuance of unjustifiable objectives, but does not impair the union's right to preserve its own existence and the gains made in genuine collective bargaining.

A third practice that should be corrected is the use of economic force, by either labor or management, to decide issues arising out of the interpretation of existing contracts. . . .

. . . Legislation should be enacted to provide machinery whereby unsettled disputes concerning the interpretation of an existing agreement may be referred by either party to final and binding arbitration.

Point number two is the extension of facilities within the Department of Labor for assisting collective bargaining. . . .

Point number three is the broadening of our program of social legislation to alleviate the causes of workers' insecurity. . . .

. . . The solution of labor-management difficulties is to be found not only in legislation dealing directly with labor relations, but also in a program designed to remove the causes of insecurity felt by many workers in our industrial society. In this connection, for example, the Congress should consider the extension and broadening of our social security system, better housing, a comprehensive national health program, and provision for a fair minimum wage.

Point number four is the appointment of a Temporary Joint Commission to inquire into the entire field of labor-management relations. . . .

The Commission should be charged with investigating and making recommendations upon certain major subjects, among others:

First, the special and unique problem of nationwide strikes in vital industries affecting the public interest. In particular, the Commission should examine into the question of how to settle or prevent such strikes without endangering our general democratic freedoms. . . .

Second, the best methods and procedures for carrying out the collective bargaining process. This should include the responsibilities of labor and management to negotiate freely and fairly with each other, and to refrain from strikes or lockouts until all possibilities of negotiation have been exhausted.

Third, the underlying causes of labor management disputes.

Source: Office of the Federal Register, *Public Papers of the Presidents of the United States: Harry S. Truman, Containing the Public Messages, Speeches, and Statements of the President, January 1 to December 31, 1947* (Washington, DC: GPO, 1963), pp. 3–6.

9.2.   "The President's Message," *New York Times,* **January 7, 1947**

This editorial response to Truman's speech from a leading U.S. newspaper is representative of the media's prevailing opinion about unions, industrial strife, and the need for new restrictive labor legislation.

We come, finally, to the important question of labor legislation. Here the President is ready to go further than he has gone before; ready, in fact, to invite the enactment of new legislation dealing with such problems as jurisdictional strikes, secondary boycotts, and lack of respect for existing contracts. He also wants more effective machinery of conciliation and a year's study to be made of the more fundamental "underlying causes of labor-management disputes." But we know enough now, on the basis of the bitter experience of the hundred million man-days of work lost in 1946, to know that one of these "underlying causes" is a present unbalance in labor legislation which has had the effect of creating a monopoly power and putting a premium on strikes and threats of strikes. The President is right when he says that we should not adopt "punitive legislation" or "vindictive laws" or measures that will "endanger American freedom." But all this is one thing. It is quite another thing, and a very necessary thing, to overhaul existing Federal labor legislation—beginning with the Wagner Act—in order to weaken the power of artificially created monopolies and create the conditions which will foster more even-handed collective bargaining.

Source: "The President's Message" [Editorial], *New York Times*, January 7, 1947, p. 26. Copyright © 1947 by The New York Times Co. Reprinted with permission.

9.3. National Association of Manufacturers, "Basic Principles Behind Good Employee Relations and Sound Collective Bargaining," December 3, 1946

In December 1946, after the congressional elections, NAM adopted these "basic principles," a revised version of its anti-union program, to increase public support for restrictive labor legislation. This excerpt, taken from the written statement Ira Mosher, Chairman of NAM's Executive Committee, submitted to Congress at the Senate hearings on February 15, 1947, suggests the influence the NAM program subsequently had on shaping the Taft-Hartley Act.

1. The union as well as the employer should be obligated, by law, to bargain collectively in good faith, provided that a majority of the employees in the appropriate unit wish to be represented by the union.

2. The union as well as the employer should be obligated, by law, to adhere to the terms of collective bargaining agreements. Collective bargaining agreements should provide that disputes arising over the meaning or interpretation of a provision should be settled by peaceful procedures.

3. Monopolistic practices in restraint of trade are inherently contrary to the public interest, and should be prohibited to labor unions as well as to employers. It is just as contrary to the public interest for a union or unions representing the employees of two or more employers to take joint wage action or engage in other monopolistic practices as it is for two or more employers to take joint price action or engage in other monopolistic practices.

4. If a legitimate difference of opinion over wages, hours or working conditions cannot be reconciled through collective bargaining or mediation, employees should be free to strike where such strike is not in violation of an existing agreement. However, the protection of law should be extended to strikers only when the majority of employees in the bargaining unit, by secret ballot under impartial supervision, have voted for

a strike in preference to acceptance of the latest offer of the employer. Employees and employers should both be protected in their right to express their respective positions.

5. No strike should have the protection of law if it involves issues which do not relate to wages, hours or working conditions, or demands which the employer is powerless to grant. Such issues and demands are involved in jurisdictional strikes, sympathy strikes, strikes against the Government, strikes to force employers to ignore or violate the law, strikes to force recognition of an uncertified union, strikes to enforce featherbedding or other work—restrictive demands, or secondary boycotts.

6. No individual should be deprived of his right to work at an available job, nor should anybody be permitted to harm or injure the employee, or his family, or his property, at home, at work or elsewhere. Mass picketing and any other form of coercion or intimidation should be prohibited.

7. Employers should not be required to bargain collectively with foremen or other representatives of management.

8. No employee or prospective employee should be required to join or to refrain from joining a union, or to maintain or withdraw its membership in a union, as a condition of employment. Compulsory union membership and interference with voluntary union membership both should be prohibited by law.

9. Biased laws and biased administration of laws have made a contribution to current difficulties, and should be replaced with impartial administration of improved laws primarily designed to advance the interests of the whole public while still safeguarding the rights of all employees. The preservation of free collective bargaining demands that government intervention in labor disputes be reduced to an absolute minimum. The full extent of government participation in labor disputes should be to make available competent and impartial conciliators. . . .

In brief, the entire program outlined above is rooted in the knowledge that management and its employees can join together to regulate their relationships if we take steps to remove those external and arbitrary obstacles which interfere with a sound relationship between them. Speaking broadly, these external obstacles can be classified in the following categories:

1. Government intervention, whether it be through compulsory arbitration, permanent mediation boards, or politically directed fact-finding.

2. The external influence of industry-wide bargaining and of secondary boycotts.

3. The conflict between union objectives and the best interests of the employees, as evidenced by strikes which cannot improve the status of the employees, which are promulgated without giving the employees a chance to vote on them and which are forced upon the employees through compulsory unionism.

4. The inequities, resulting from one-sided obligations and responsibilities under existing laws.

Source: Statement of Ira Mosher, Congress, Senate, Committee on Labor and Public Welfare, *Labor Relations Program: Hearings Before the Committee on Labor and Public Welfare, United States Senate, Eightieth Congress, First Session on S. 55 and S. J. Res. 22*, 5 vols. (Washington, DC: GPO, 1947), 2:950–51.

9.4.   House Majority Report No. 245 on H.R. 3030, April 11, 1947

On April 11, 1947, Representative Philip Hartley submitted the majority's favorable report on the bill from the House Committee on Education and Labor. The bitter anti-union sentiments that lay behind the bill stand out in this excerpt. Along with the list of the bill's accomplishments, the strident language and scathing assessments of the Wagner Act and the NLRB are especially notable.

. . . The bill herewith reported has been formulated as a bill of rights both for American workingmen and for their employers.

For the last 14 years, as a result of labor laws ill-conceived and disastrously executed, the American workingman has been deprived of his dignity as an individual. He has been cajoled, coerced, intimidated, and on many occasions beaten up, in the name of the splendid aims set forth in section 1 of the National Labor Relations Act. His whole economic life has been subject to the complete domination and control of unregulated monopolists. He has on many occasions had to pay them tribute to get a job. He has been forced into labor organizations against his will. At other times when he has desired to join a particular labor organization he has been prevented from doing so and forced to join another one. He has been compelled to contribute to causes and candidates for public office to which he was opposed. He has been prohibited from expressing his own mind on public issues. He has been denied any voice in arranging the terms of his own employment. He has frequently against his will been called out on strikes which have resulted in wage losses representing years of his savings. In many cases his economic life has been ruled by Communists and other subversive influences. In short, his mind, his soul, and his very life have been subject to a tyranny more despotic than one could think possible in a free country.

The employer's plight has likewise not been happy. He has witnessed the productive efficiency in his plants sink to alarmingly low levels. He has been required to employ or reinstate individuals who have destroyed his property and assaulted other employees. When he has tried to discharge Communists he has been prevented from doing so by a board which called this valid reason for the discharge a mere pretext. He has seen the loyalty of his supervisors undermined by the compulsory unionism imposed upon them by the National Labor Relations Board. He has been required by law to bargain over matters to which it was economically impossible for him to accede, and when he refused to accede has been accused of failing to bargain in good faith. He has been compelled to bargain with the same union that bargains with his competitors and thus to reveal to his competitors the secrets of his business. He has had to stand helplessly by while employees desiring to enter his plant to work have been obstructed by violence, mass picketing, and general rowdyism. He has had to stand mute while irresponsible detractors slandered, abused, and vilified him.

His business on occasions has been virtually brought to a standstill by disputes to which he himself was not a party and in which he himself had no interest. And finally, he has been compelled by the laws of the greatest democratic country in the world—or at least by their administrators—to treat his employees as if they belonged to a different class or caste of society. . . .

. . . In brief outline, the bill accomplishes the following:

(1) It abolishes the existing discredited National Labor Relations Board, and creates in lieu thereof a new board of fair-minded members to exercise quasi-judicial functions only.

(2) It establishes a new official to exercise the various prosecuting and investigative functions under the National Labor Relations Act, to be entirely independent of the Board.

(3) It requires the Board to act only upon the weight of credible legal evidence, and it gives to the courts of the United States a real, rather than a fictitious, power to review decisions of the Board.

(4) It outlaws the closed shop and monopolistic industry-wide bargaining.

(5) It exempts supervisors from the compulsory features of the National Labor Relations Act.

(6) It imposes on both parties to labor disputes the duty of bargaining and requires that the employees themselves be given a voice in the bargaining arrangements through the device of providing for a secret ballot of the employees on their employer's last offer of settlement of the dispute.

(7) It protects the existence of labor organizations which are not affiliated with one of the national federations.

(8) It prohibits certification by the Board of labor organizations having Communist or subversive officers.

(9) It prescribes the rights which an individual member of a labor organization can justly claim of his union, and gives him protection in the exercise of those rights.

(10) It outlaws sympathy strikes, jurisdictional strikes, illegal boycotts, collusive strikes by employees of competing employers, as well as sitdown strikes and other concerted work interferences conducted by remaining on the employer's premises.

(11) It outlaws strikes to remedy practices for which an administrative remedy is available under the bill or to compel an employer to violate the law.

(12) It outlaws mass picketing and other forms of violence designed to prevent individuals from entering or leaving a place of employment.

(13) It outlaws picketing of a place of business where the proprietor is not involved in a labor dispute with his employees.

(14) For unlawful concerted activities it gives the person injured thereby a right to sue civilly any person responsible therefor.

(15) It prescribes unfair labor practices on the part of employees and their representatives as well as by employers.

(16) It creates a new and independent conciliation agency.

(17) It removes the exemption of labor organizations from the antitrust laws when such organizations, acting either alone or in collusion with employers, engage in unlawful restraints of trade.

(18) It makes labor organizations equally responsible with employers for contract violations and provides for suit by either against the other in the United States district courts.

(19) It provides a means for stopping strikes which imperil or threaten to imperil the public health, safety, or interest.

(20) It guarantees to employees, to employers, and to their respective representatives, the full exercise of the right of free speech.

Source: National Labor Relations Board, *Legislative History of the Labor Management Relations Act, 1947*, commemorative ed., 2 vols. (Washington, DC: GPO, 1985, 1959), 1:295–97.

9.5.   House Minority Report No. 245 on H.R. 3020, April 1947

Six members of the House Committee on Labor and Education, including John F. Kennedy, protested the majority's tactics and the proposed legislation. In this excerpt from their strongly worded report, they conveyed some of their major objections to a bill they considered extreme, un-American, and unjust.

It does not . . . require mature reflection to realize that these proposals are deliberately designed to wreck the living standards of the American people. Under the false guise of "correcting labor abuses" this bill is designed to so weaken, as in effect to repeal, the National Labor Relations Act. By making practically all strikes unlawful it repeals the Norris-LaGuardia Act, signed by President Hoover. By removing the protection of the Clayton Act from practically all trade-union activity, it makes trade-unions and their members subject to suits for treble damages under the Sherman Antitrust Act of 1890. It revives the common law doctrine of conspiracy against workers who band together to protect their living standards and thereby throws the law back to where it was in England in the late 1700's. This bill does not merely wipe out labor's gains under the beneficent administration of President Roosevelt; it turns the clock of history back at least a century and a half and eliminates safeguards and protections which both Republican and Democratic Congresses have sponsored for generations.

It undertakes to do this at a time when rising price levels have begun to squeeze the American worker dry. It does not propose, as the answer to our economic problems, the hope of a rising standard of living made possible by our enormously increased productivity. It does not propose to treat with fairness those millions of American workers who contributed so signally to our victory in war and our reconversion to peace. It only proposes to swell the coffers of gigantic industrial combinations by rendering labor impotent.

By placing heavy penalties upon industry-wide bargaining this bill forces workers to compete with each other to see which can work for the lowest wages. It forces the fair-minded employer to cut his wages to the level of his worst sweat-shop competitor. It strikes from the hand of labor its most effective weapon—the right to strike. It discourages collective bargaining by encouraging individual bargaining, though our experience from 1920 to 1929 proved that individual bargaining can only result in reduction of wages and consequent depression. It revives company unionism as a method by which the employer may sit on both sides of the bargaining table. It lumps together for punitive action the criminal or slothful employee and the honest and conscientious worker; it deprives the patriotic citizen of long-established rights in order to punish the misguided. The bill is not designed to help employers but to punish labor. It strikes at the established Federal policy of encouraging collective bargaining, to make of the Federal Government a mere police court, taking over functions which have, with few exceptions, been well handled by States and local communities.

While preaching economy, the majority would enormously increase the size of the Federal establishment devoted to the handling of labor problems. While denouncing bureaucracy, the majority would set up two new independent agencies within the executive branch of the Government. While they decry Federal intervention in local affairs, the majority would transfer from State and local authority to the Federal Government, or would duplicate within the Federal Government, matters traditionally left to State action. While purporting to defend free enterprise and free collective bargaining, the majority would throw about employers, employees, and trade-unions shackles not heretofore proposed in any legislative assembly in the country. While pretending to seek industrial peace, the majority have included in their bill proposals which would unsettle labor relations, make illegal countless heretofore accepted industrial practices, destroy many well-recognized legal rights, and bring to labor relations a confusion and chaos which must result in bitter and costly strikes. . . .

[The committee then analyzed the bill section by section before concluding:]

This bill is aimed at the heart of American industrial democracy. If it is permitted to hit that target, the working people of this country will not soon recover their status as free men. The Fascists and Communists learned early that a strong trade-union movement was inconsistent with their objectives and an obstacle to the achievement of those objectives. As a means of securing power, the Fascists and the Communists destroyed the labor movement in other countries, because they recognized that trade-unions were a citadel of democracy which they must batter down in order to achieve their evil purposes.

Source: National Labor Relations Board, *Legislative History*, 1:355–56, 403.

9.6.   [Taft-Hartley Act Editorial], *The Nation*, May 31, 1947

> *This editorial in a liberal mainstream journal was one of the few that deplored the new law and considered it class legislation that Truman should veto.*

THE SENATE'S SUPPOSEDLY "MODERATE" anti-labor bill will probably be on the President's desk by the time this comment appears in print. Its moderation, of course, is merely relative, and can be seen only when it is placed against the measure originally passed by the House—the kind of moderation that characterizes hanging as compared with boiling in oil. The President, we earnestly hope, will not allow himself to be taken in by a brazen campaign now raging in the press to make the bad look good by contrast with the worst. The fact is that the Senate version, to which the House will in all likelihood give its assent, is one of the most dangerously drawn bills ever to be offered for a President's signature. The danger lies in its deviousness. Killing the closed shop outright, for example, it pretends to compensate by upholding the union shop, but the right to this form of security is so fenced about with provisos that in practice it would soon be meaningless. Indeed, the entire process of collective bargaining, which the bill piously defends in the abstract, would be made enormously difficult by provisions for hectoring the unions and denying them recognition for a variety of frivolous and implausible reasons, while making their internal disruption a progressive certainty. The President will enhance his prestige enormously if he accompanies his veto with a message that clearly and soberly exposes the bill as the hypocrisy it is— a piece of class legislation that pretends to correct abuses but is coolly calculated to destroy the nation's trade-union movement.

Source: [Taft-Hartley Act Editorial], *The Nation* 164 (May 31, 1947): 644. Reprinted with permission from the May 31, 1947 issue of *The Nation*. For subscription information, call 1-800-333-8536. Portions of each week's Nation magazine can be accessed at http://www.thenation.com.

9.7.   "NAM-Taft-Hartley Bill Designed to Liquidate Unions and Free Enterprise," *United Mine Workers Journal*, June 15, 1947

This angry and dire editorial was representative of organized labor's opinion when it appeared in the UMWJ after congressional passage of the Taft-Hartley Act, but before Truman's veto. This excerpt reveals the union's anger and its views on the serious potential, immediate, and real consequences of the law. The boldface type and italics are as they appeared in the original publication.

The N.A.M.-Taft-Hartley bill is a throw-back to uneconomic industrial relations—below standard labor rates and cutthroat competition. The claimants of credit for sponsoring the bill and the disclosure of the powers behind its promotion tell as much.
Those who state that the bill as finally agreed upon in conference is a *"mild" measure* to equalize the rights of employers and employes [*sic*] *falsify* the intent and purpose of the bill. Simply stated, the bill is designed to *liquidate collective bargaining.*
The N.A.M.-Taft-Hartley bill is the most cleverly designed legislative aid to the promotion of a regimented economy that was ever enacted dur-

ing peace or war in the history of the Nation. It creates a government bur-rocracy [a satirical term the journal used to mean bureaucracy] that will be buttressed by *judicial interpretations* which can and will, if the provisions of the act are submitted to by the American people, terminate *free enterprise.* . . .

At this time the full impact of the *N.A.M.-Taft-Hartley union liquidation bill* cannot be fully determined, even by the most learned attorneys. The reason is plain. The ramifications of the all-embracing *N.A.M.-Taft-Hartley bill* are so far reaching and will be subject to so many possible and probable judicial interpretations that reporting agencies professionally engaged in interpreting federal legislation are unable to *digest and fix the terminal facilities of the loaded measure.*

Section 14 (b) is proof positive of the uncertainties of the provisions because it is provided in this section that state laws will supersede the act in outlawing wage contracts requiring membership in trade unions as a condition of employment or even union security. What good is the alleged guarantee publicly stated by the N.A.M.-Taft-Hartley sponsors of the bill that the measure provides union security when the scheming politicians of the cotton states of the South and the Midwest make state labor laws that will go even farther in curtailing the limited rights and privileges provided under the *N.A.M.-Taft-Hartley bill.*

The bill *emasculates the Wagner Act* by providing a criss-cross of procedure, hedged authority and limitation of power that bids fair to create a worse condition in industrial relations than existed without a labor code prior to the enactment of the Wagner Act.

Strictly enforced, it will create turmoil and work stoppages in industries where labor conditions have long been stabilized, and where both employes and management desire to continue their satisfactory collective bargaining unimpaired.

The *N.A.M.-Taft-Hartley bill* provides injunctions to protect employers. No such provision is made for unions to obtain injunctions against the employers who violate wage agreements and promote systematic union destruction.

Unions and individual members can be sued by unscrupulous employers for the slightest infraction of a union contract, for engaging in jurisdictional strikes and secondary boycotts, but again no such provision is made for unions to sue employers who combine in a conspiracy, municipal, county, statewide or national, to promote work stoppages, hold wages down and violate wage contracts.

The high point of the measure's abrogation of constitutional rights and privileges of organized labor is the outright prohibition of union participation in political campaigns, *even to the extent of editorially expressing a preference for or attacking a candidate in the official publication owned and published by a district or national union. Under this provision, unions are prohibited from contributing to candidates and politi-*

cal parties, publishing pamphlets or supporting any man or measure by contributions out of union funds. The penalty for violation is a year's imprisonment and a $1,000 fine for individuals and a $5,000 fine for labor organizations.

This is in fact an attack upon the freedom of the press. And if this curtailment of the freedom of the labor press is permitted to stand, it will apply with equal force later on to newspapers and radio alike. . . .

We may not know where we are going, but we are on our way. Just how far we will travel the road back to *industrial serfdom, economic woe, industrial paralysis and indiscriminate political burrocratic controls, no one can tell. But from where we sit, it looks like we are in for a decade of industrial, political and economic hell unless the Supreme Court throws the N.A.M.-Taft-Hartley bill into the discard.*

Source: "NAM-Taft-Hartley Bill Designed to Liquidate Unions and Free Enterprise," *United Mine Workers Journal* 58 (June 15, 1947): 10–11. Used with permission of the *United Mine Workers Journal*.

9.8.   National Labor Relations Board, Comparison of the National Labor Relations Act of 1935 with Title I of the Labor Management Relations Act of 1947

After the law's passage, the NLRB published a comparison of the precise wording of the Wagner and Taft-Hartley Acts. This excerpt from the legal documents includes the introductory sections of the two laws, in order to highlight their respective purposes, and three of the most contested provisions.

Key to Comparison

Portions of the National Labor Relations Act which have been eliminated by the Labor Management Relations Act are enclosed in black brackets; provisions which have been added to the National Labor Relations Act are in italics; and unchanged portions of the National Labor Relations Act are shown in roman.

NATIONAL LABOR RELATIONS ACT

[AN ACT]

[To diminish the causes of labor disputes burdening or obstructing interstate and foreign commerce, to create a National Labor Relations Board, and for other purposes.]

FINDINGS AND POLICIES

SECTION 1. The denial by *some* employers of the right of employees to organize and the refusal by *some* employers to accept the procedure of collective bargaining lead to strikes and other forms of industrial strife or unrest, which have the intent or the necessary effect of burdening or obstructing commerce by (a) impairing the efficiency, safety, or operation of the instrumentalities of commerce; (b) occurring in the current of commerce; (c) materially affecting, restraining, or controlling the flow of raw materials or manufactured or processed goods from or into the channels of commerce, or the prices of such materials or goods in commerce; or (d) causing diminution of employment and wages in such volume as substantially to impair or disrupt the market for goods flowing from or into the channels of commerce.

The inequality of bargaining power between employees who do not possess full freedom of association or actual liberty of contract, and employers who are organized in the corporate or other forms of ownership association substantially burdens and affects the flow of commerce, and tends to aggravate recurrent business depressions, by depressing wage rates and the purchasing power of wage earners in industry and by preventing the stabilization of competitive wage rates and working conditions within and between industries.

Experience has proved that protection by law of the right of employees to organize and bargain collectively safeguards commerce from injury, impairment, or interruption, and promotes the flow of commerce by removing certain recognized sources of industrial strife and unrest, by encouraging practices fundamental to the friendly adjustment of industrial disputes arising out of differences as to wages, hours, or other working conditions, and by restoring equality of bargaining power between employers and employees.

Experience has further demonstrated that certain practices by some labor organizations, their officers and members have the intent or the necessary effect of burdening or obstructing commerce by preventing the free flow of goods in such commerce through strikes and other forms of industrial unrest or through concerted activities which impair the interest of the public in the free flow of such commerce. The elimination of such practices is a necessary condition to the assurance of the rights herein guaranteed.

It is hereby declared to be the policy of the United States to eliminate the causes of certain substantial obstructions to the free flow of commerce and to mitigate and eliminate these obstructions when they have occurred by encouraging the practice and procedure of collective bargaining and by protecting the exercise by workers of full freedom of association, self-organization, and designation of representatives of their own choosing, for the purpose of negotiating the terms and conditions of their employment or other mutual aid or protection.

DEFINITIONS

SEC. 2. When used in this Act . . .

(3) The term "employee" shall include any employee, and shall not be limited to the employees of a particular employer, unless the Act explicitly states otherwise, and shall include any individual whose work has ceased as a consequence of, or in connection with, any current labor dispute or because of any unfair labor practice, and who has not obtained any other regular and substantially equivalent employment, but shall not include any individual employed as an agricultural laborer, or in the domestic service of any family or person at his home, or any individual employed by his parent or spouse [.], *or any individual having the status of an independent contractor, or any individual employed as a supervisor, or any individual employed by an employer subject to the Railway Labor, Act, as amended from time to time, or by any other person who is not an employer as herein defined.* . . .

RIGHTS OF EMPLOYEES

Sec. 7. Employees shall have the right to self-organization, to form, join, or assist labor organizations, to bargain collectively through representatives of their own choosing, and to engage in *other* concerted activities for the purpose of collective bargaining or other mutual aid or protection, *and shall also have the right to refrain from any or all of such activities except to the extent that such right may be affected by an agreement requiring membership in a labor organization as a condition of employment as authorized in section 8 (a) (3).* . . .

LIMITATIONS. . . .

Section 14 *(b) Nothing in this Act shall be construed as authorizing the execution or application of agreements requiring membership in a labor organization as a condition of employment in any State or Territory in which such execution or application is prohibited by State or Territorial law.*

Source: National Labor Relations Board, *Legislative History*, 2:1661–62, 1666, 1679.

SELECTED ANNOTATED BIBLIOGRAPHY

Books

Dubofsky, Melvyn. *The State and Labor in Modern America*. Chapel Hill: University of North Carolina Press, 1994. Useful narrative of the national government's labor policies from 1870 to 1973, with a provocative analysis about the role of the state.

Gall, Gilbert J. *The Politics of Right to Work: The Labor Federations as Special Interests, 1943–1979*. Westport, CT: Greenwood Press, 1988. Important political study of a major union security issue, and of labor's alliance with the Democratic Party.

Green, James R. *The World of the Worker: Labor in Twentieth-Century America*. 1980. Reprint, Urbana: University of Illinois Press, 1998. Especially valuable survey for its focus on working people—not just unions—and for its perspective on the 1940s.

Gross, James A. *Broken Promise: The Subversion of U.S. Labor Relations Policy, 1947–1994*. Philadelphia: Temple University Press, 1995. Volume 3 in the author's three-volume history of the NLRB continues the board's story after Taft-Hartley.

————. *The Reshaping of the National Labor Relations Board: National Labor Policy in Transition, 1937–1947*. Albany: State University of New York Press, 1981. Argues Taft-Hartley was the result of years of effort by a conservative alliance of employers, politicians, and the AFL to undermine board enforcement of the Wagner Act.

Harris, Howell John. *The Right to Manage: Industrial Relations Policies of American Business in the 1940s*. Madison: University of Wisconsin Press, 1982. Explores business responses to union challenges to their prerogatives and authority in the 1930s and 1940s.

Hartmann, Susan M. *Truman and the 80th Congress*. Columbia: University of Missouri Press, 1971. Worthy political analysis and insight into the context of the law.

Lee, R. Alton. *Truman and Taft Hartley; A Question of Mandate*. Lexington: University Press of Kentucky, 1966. Informative and readable introduction to the subject.

Lichtenstein, Nelson. *Labor's War at Home: The CIO in World War II*. Cambridge, Eng.: Cambridge University Press, 1982. Important work argues that the war was the critical era during which CIO leaders made questionable decisions that defused labor's militancy, thereby precipitating the Taft-Hartley Act and labor's subsequent decline.

Millis, Harry A. and Emily Clark Brown. *From the Wagner Act to Taft-Hartley: A Study of National Labor Policy and Labor Relations*. Chicago: University of Chicago Press, 1950. Remains a classic study by a former chair and former analyst for the NLRB.

National Association of Manufacturers. *Why and How the Wagner Act Should Be Amended*. [New York]: NAM, 1939. Valuable for comparing NAM's 1939 and 1947 programs.

Tomlins, Christopher L. *The State and the Unions: Labor Relations, Law, and the Organized Labor Movement in America, 1880–1960*. Cambridge, Eng.: Cambridge University Press, 1985. Essential reading and provocative argument that the Wagner Act—not Taft-Hartley—was the watershed legal event that led to the decline of the labor movement.

U.S. Congress. Senate. Committee on Labor and Public Welfare. *Hearings before the Committee on Labor and Public Welfare, United States Senate, Eightieth Congress, First Session, on S. 55 and S.J. 22*. 5 vols. Washington, DC: GPO, 1947. Essential primary source.

U.S. Department of Labor, Bureau of Labor Statistics. *National Emergency Disputes under the Taft-Hartley Act, 1947–77*. Report 542. Washington, DC: GPO,

1977. Brief overview of thirty years, with statistics, on the thirty-five work stoppages that led U.S. presidents to invoke the law.

U.S. National Labor Relations Board. *Legislative History of the Labor Management Relations Act, 1947.* 1959. Commemorative ed. 2 vols. Washington, DC: GPO, 1985. Primary source contains the text of the law, bills, debates, and reports.

Web Sites

The complete text of the Labor Management Relations (Taft-Hartley) Act is available at http://www.law.cornell.edu/topics/labor.html, Cornell University's Legal Information Institute site. Truman's veto speech and other public addresses can be found at the Truman Presidential Museum & Library's site at http://trumanlibrary.org/publicpapers/index.

Teachers and students will find the Holt Labor Library's online exhibit, "Pamphlets in the Fight Against Taft-Hartley 1947–1948," of special interest. Its informative Web site at http://www.holtlaborlibrary.org/tafthartley.html also includes related topical links. Lewis's speech to the AFL convention in October 1947 appears on the Labor Standard site at http://www.laborstandard.org/Vol4No2/John_L_Lewis_Speech.htm. Speeches by Robert Taft and others about the law are available in libraries where the journal, *Vital Speeches of the Day*, is online. Ralph Nader's views on repealing the law can be read at The Voice News site at http://www.thevoicenews.com/News/2002/0802/Features/F01_Nader-Taft-Hartley.html.

10

The Memphis Sanitation Strike of 1968

"This is a significant turn in the civil rights movement and a new chapter in labor history,"[1] declared the Reverend James M. Lawson, Jr., an
African-American civil rights leader, in March 1968, during the fifth week
of a momentous sixty-four-day-long strike by Memphis sanitation workers. Lawson's assessment was ultimately an accurate and prophetic one.
The relatively minor municipal dispute that began on February 12 had
served as a catalyst to unify a fractured African-American community on
behalf of the city's garbage collectors, 95 percent or more of whom were
black men. It had also mobilized the international offices of one of the nation's fastest growing public-sector unions, the American Federation of
State, County, and Municipal Employees (AFSCME), whose members in
Memphis Local 1733 had launched the wildcat strike. The sanitation
workers' quest for dignity—the central issue of the strike—had transcended narrow racial or labor lines and brought into being an effective
labor and civil rights coalition, the kind of coalition that the most progressive trade unionists and key black leaders such as A. Philip Randolph,
Bayard Rustin, and Martin Luther King, Jr., had long advocated.

This strike of poorly paid African-American workers is most often
remembered today because of the national tragedy that occurred in its
midst. On April 4, 1968, King was assassinated in Memphis as he was
preparing to lead a nonviolent march in support of the strikers. Focus
upon his tragic death has often distracted attention away from the sanitation strike, a worthy subject in its own right.

Memphis sanitation workers had been trying to organize and gain the city's recognition of their union for at least five years before the strike. Participants, many of whom were older family men, later explained that they had confronted discriminatory occupational limits in their lifetimes. They could either choose to pick cotton somewhere in the Mississippi Delta or take a dirty, dead-end job and collect garbage in the city—one of the few jobs open to unskilled rural black migrants. Until the mid-1960s these men were expected to go into people's yards and carry tubs of refuse on their heads or shoulders to antiquated trucks and equipment. There was no formal grievance procedure, and unlike other municipal employees, the city considered them "unclassified." That meant that they were paid the minimum wage or slightly more, had no security, and were ineligible for paid vacations, overtime pay, or workers' compensation. Before the strike, 40 percent of the men qualified for welfare and food stamps.

Such conditions led Thomas Oliver (T. O.) Jones, who had been a sanitation worker since 1958, to try to form a union. In 1963 he and others were quickly fired after they took part in a failed strike. But Jones persisted, and the men formed an independent union that became AFSCME Local 1733 in 1964. The public sector was a growing industry, and, by 1966, AFSCME was an up-and-coming union whose members included over 300,000 blue-collar, white-collar, and professional people employed by state, county, or municipal governments.

AFSCME had been founded in Madison, Wisconsin, in 1932 by a small group of professional white-collar state employees. The union's basic tactic was lobbying, and by the 1950s, it was actively advocating collective bargaining rights for public employees. AFSCME rose to prominence in 1958 when New York City Mayor Robert Wagner granted those rights to the city's public unions. Jerry Wurf and others in New York City's District Council 37 of AFSCME then led successful drives for collective bargaining rights, and, in 1964, Wurf was elected president of the international union, in large part because of his militancy.

By the mid-1960s the legal rights of public-sector unions and public employees, who were not subject to the protections of the nation's labor laws, were also being redefined. President John F. Kennedy provided an impetus for the growth of public unions when he issued Executive Order 10988 in 1962. The order allowed federal employees to form unions and engage in collective bargaining but did not permit strikes against the federal government. State and municipal employees then actively sought to achieve such rights. By 1969 they had secured the right to organize in twenty-nine states, along with collective bargaining rights in sixteen.

Although most states—thirty-five in 1969—prohibited strikes against the government, teachers, garbage collectors, transit workers, and other public employees began to strike for higher wages and other demands in increasing numbers throughout the 1960s. AFSCME president Jerry Wurf argued that denying nonessential government workers the right to strike in a democracy was a way for employing governments to subvert legitimate collective bargaining rights. To counter criticism that public-sector strikes endangered the public's health or safety, AFSCME forbade strikes by the police, fire fighters, and prison guards, and, in 1966, its International Executive Board issued an important statement, "Public Employee Unions: Their Rights and Responsibilities," to clarify the union's policy for the general public as well as its members. AFSCME leaders and members were keenly aware that strikes in the public sector differed from strikes in the private sector. Not only were the laws governing the two types of strikes different; winning the public's approval was even more critical for a union's success when public employees were involved. The employers were governments, and the workers could only win if they had substantial favorable public support that pressured their government employers.

Despite this national labor upsurge, AFSCME's Memphis affiliate had difficulty getting firmly established in the "right-to-work" state. From 1964 on, the city steadfastly refused to recognize Local 1733, and its president, T. O. Jones, had to collect dues from the workers as best he could. The result was that the local's finances were sparse and its dues-paying membership small. The city aborted a strike by the garbage men in 1966 by obtaining an injunction that later cast a shadow on the 1968 stoppage because it was still in effect.

The sanitation men's decision to strike in 1968 took place during an era of singular rising expectations and increasing social frustration among African Americans. Congressional passage of the Civil Rights Act of 1964 and the Voting Rights Act of 1965, combined with the relatively peaceful, voluntary desegregation of many of Memphis's public institutions, promised hope for the city's African-American residents. However, the realities of "token" desegregation, ongoing racial discrimination in employment, and the demeaning paternalistic attitudes of the city's white power structure produced a general sense of anguish. According to U.S. government reports, about 40 percent of Memphis's population of 550,000 were black, with many of them living below the poverty line. Meanwhile, white Memphis proudly congratulated itself on its "good race relations" after major urban riots erupted in *other* American cities in 1967.

Two specific incidents in Memphis sparked the strike. One involved the Department of Public Works' traditional policy for paying workers on rainy days when work had to be halted. On one such day, January 31, 1968, twenty-one black sanitation workers were sent home while white workers were allowed to remain on the job. The men mistakenly thought they should—and would—be paid for the whole day but were disgruntled later when they only received "call up" pay for two hours of work. Then, on February 1, a gruesome accident resulted in the deaths of two black garbage men who were ground to pieces because of faulty equipment in the truck, where they had taken shelter from the rain. That no city official attended the men's funerals and the city only reluctantly paid the relatives of the "unclassified" men a month's wages and $500 for their funerals further fueled anger.

In an attempt to resolve these issues, P. J. Ciampa, AFSCME's international union field staff director, and T. O. Jones met with Charles Blackburn, Memphis's Director of Public Works, on February 1. Ciampa outlined the union's requests verbally and, then again, in writing, on February 8. The sanitation men were asking for a no-discrimination policy toward union members, union recognition, a dues checkoff, a grievance procedure, and a procedure that allowed for an ongoing discussion with the city about wages, hours, and working conditions. Blackburn told them that he did not have the authority to make such decisions. In fact, in January, Memphis had established a form of government that left responsibility for major municipal decisions solely in the hands of the newly elected mayor, Henry Loeb. On February 11, Blackburn refused to explain the city's position to a union meeting of 700 sanitation workers. AFSCME Local 1733 then voted to go on strike the next day and to march downtown so that the city would take their plight seriously.

The Memphis strike took place at a fortuitous time for labor when various public unions, including those representing sanitation workers in other cities throughout the nation, were striking and winning contracts. Indeed, a victorious walkout by New York City's garbage collectors had immediately preceded the local walkout. In the midst of this public union upsurge, Mayor Loeb greeted the effective walkout in his city with firm opposition. He emphasized that Memphis was not New York and that the strike was not only illegal but also a danger to the public. On February 14, he issued this ultimatum: "If work is not resumed by 7 a.m., Thursday, February 15th, 1968, we will immediately begin replacing those people who have chosen to abandon their jobs and their rights."[2] When the sanitation men did not return to work, he hired strikebreakers and had the police escort the garbage trucks. He made it clear that he was not going to be the first southern mayor to recognize a public union, allow a dues checkoff, or sign a written contract with workers. In fact, the city had a long history of *never* signing contracts with *any* unions.

Loeb viewed his adamant stance against the black union as a principled one. He was personally convinced that AFSCME could not possibly represent the men and was only interested in collecting their dues money. He had come to power in a city with a history of weak unions and virulent opposition to militant groups that the Memphis power structure frequently labeled as "communist." According to Loeb's friends and enemies alike, the former Commissioner of Public Works believed he understood African Americans, and knew what was in their best interest better than they did, even though he had received less than 2 percent of their vote in the 1967 mayoral election. When he insisted on sending an open letter directly to the strikers on February 29, rather than negotiate with their representatives, the union and the African-American community ridiculed his paternalistic "plantation mentality."

From the outset, Loeb's position was applauded by the city's white power structure and the vast majority of its white residents but simultaneously deplored by the black community. On February 16, the city council reconfirmed its support of the mayor. Memphis's two major newspapers were already openly and aggressively siding with him against the strikers. *The Commercial Appeal* even questioned the "patriotism" of the union in a scathing editorial on February 16. The one-sided nature of the two newspapers' strike coverage quickly led the Memphis National Association for the Advancement of Colored People (NAACP), which had endorsed the strikers' cause, to call for a boycott of them.

Meanwhile, church groups and other organizations in the African-American community had begun to collect money and food for the strikers. AFSCME was disappointed that white trade unionists in Memphis contributed only minimal support to the strikers but happy that labor support from outside Memphis was more substantial. From February 18 to 23, AFSCME President Jerry Wurf took part in negotiations with Loeb, negotiations arranged by a third party—a neutral white Ministerial Association. When the talks failed over the issue of union recognition and the dues checkoff, the stage was set for a long and bitter racial and labor conflict.

Four key events stand out for their importance in shaping the subsequent course of the strike. Among these events are: (1) the macing of strike supporters by Memphis police on February 23; (2) the strikers' success in gaining national publicity in mid-March; (3) the violence that marred a march led by Dr. King on March 28; and (4) King's assassination on April 4.

The macing grew out of preceding events. On February 22, after a hearing during which 700 sanitation workers held a classic sit-in, a city council subcommittee on public works passed a resolution urging the city to recognize the union and approve a dues checkoff. But, on February 23, when the full council met, it heard neither the resolution nor the strikers. Instead, it hastily convened, passed a preconceived substitute measure that endorsed all the strikers' demands except those for union recognition and a checkoff, the key obstacles to a settlement, and then adjourned. To deal with the strikers' anger after the debacle, strike organizers got permission from city officials to allow them to march down Main Street to a meeting hall.

What happened next proved to be a turning point in the strike. Police forcibly broke up the march after a minor incident occurred between one police car and some of the marchers. Moving in en masse, the police clubbed and indiscriminately maced *all* marchers—union leaders, strikers, black ministers, government officials. The Reverend Ralph H. Jackson, a strike supporter and negotiator for the African-American community, was one of the many maced marchers who later described the significant impact this event had on his life. From February 23 on, AFSCME Local 1733's cause became *the* cause of the black community, and the city's refusal to meet the union's demands was viewed as an assault on the community itself. On February 24, the city obtained an injunction to prohibit picketing or demonstrating, and 150 black ministers met to found COME, the Community on the Move for Equality, to mobilize support for the strikers. One of COME's immediate actions was to launch a boycott of the two Memphis newspapers, downtown businesses, and enterprises that carried the Loeb family name.

"I Am A Man," was a sign the strikers carried thereafter in their daily marches downtown. The phrase epitomized the meaning of the strike for both the union and the sanitation men. The strike had become a *movement for dignity*. The city's refusal to recognize the union and allow it a dues checkoff, even though checkoffs were allowed for other purposes, combined with its refusal to recognize the human dignity of its black garbage men, was taken as an affront to the African-American community as a whole.

The strikers' morale rose on March 4, when 500 white unionists joined them in a daily march for the first time. Meanwhile, the boycott was having an impact, and downtown business was reported to be off by about 35 percent. But the city was also hiring more and more strikebreakers and picking up garbage in the white areas. COME decided to enlist national support and invited Roy Wilkins, executive director of the national NAACP, and Bayard Rustin, a prominent civil rights leader and an official of the A. Philip Randolph Institute, to come to speak. On March 14, the two leaders spoke to a crowd of over 9,000 at Mason Temple. Rustin called the strike "one of the great struggles for the emancipation of the black man today" and added: "This becomes the symbol of the movement to get rid of poverty. The record here shows that in Memphis this fight is going to be won because the black people in this community and the trade unions stand together."[3] COME also invited Dr. Martin Luther King, Jr., to come to speak, a move that further tied the Memphis strike in with important national issues.

Throughout the 1960s, racism and poverty stood out as two prime social concerns. The publication of Michael Harrington's *The Other America* in 1962 had brought the problem of poverty to the nation's attention, and President Lyndon B. Johnson had launched a series of government programs in a War on Poverty from 1964 to 1966 to try to alleviate it. But poverty remained after the civil rights movement successfully won passage of the Civil Rights Act in 1964 and the Voting Rights Act in 1965, and the urban riots that erupted in Watts in Los Angeles and other major cities in the mid-1960s exposed the severe structural problems that underlay racism and poverty in U.S. society. In 1968 the struggle of poor black Memphis sanitation workers thus took on a symbolism of national importance. It represented the deepest concerns of a growing social movement concerned with racism and poverty.

It is no accident that King was deeply engaged in planning the Poor People's Campaign, a new crusade to get the federal government to take serious steps to end poverty as well as racism, when he came to Memphis. In a speech there on March 18, he called upon an audience of thousands to take part in a general work stoppage if the city did not agree to recognize the union and accept the checkoff. "Along with wages and other securities, you're struggling for the right to organize. This is the way to gain power. Don't go back to work until all your demands are met," he told them. "There is a need to unite beyond class lines. Negro haves must join hands with Negro have-nots. Our society must come to respect the sanitation worker."[4] He promised to come back to Memphis and lead a march for the strikers.

The white power structure of Memphis disliked the critical national attention that began to be focused on the city after the appearances by Wilkins, Rustin, and King. But the criticism did lead *The Commercial Appeal* to advocate, for the first time, that the city council take action to resolve the dispute. The council's response was to bring in Frank Miles, a skilled labor mediator, who reestablished negotiations. Miles even got city and union representatives to approve a compromise that contained a carefully worded form of recognition, a demand Ralph Jackson insisted upon. But Loeb rejected recognition in any form, and the talks ended.

The media could no longer avoid the racial dimensions of the strike or the threatening racial climate. Still, *The Commercial Appeal* blamed *all* racial tensions on irresponsible "Black Power" advocates and illegal strikers and had no criticisms whatsoever of Loeb, questionable police actions, broad-scale injunctions, or the strategic encampment of state troops in the city on March 4. In fact, throughout the strike, Federal Bureau of Investigation agents spied on strike leaders as well as on King. The city was racially polarized and on the verge of an explosion.

In this context, on March 28, King arrived, belatedly, to lead the only march he ever joined in which some of the demonstrators became violent. Soon after the march began, black youths, including members of a Memphis "black power" group called the Invaders, began to throw rocks at store windows, and the police intervened with clubs and tear gas. Lawson insisted that King leave the march, and the riot led to looting, 280 arrests,

and the death of one black youth. The governor sent in the National
Guard. No one focused on the strike or its issues. *The Commercial Appeal*
questioned King's credibility and intimated that he was a coward. Senator
Robert Byrd and others demanded that King and the Southern Christian
Leadership Conference (SCLC) call off plans for the forthcoming Poor
People's March on Washington. After meetings with his advisers and with
the Invaders, King insisted on returning to Memphis to lead a genuinely
peaceful march on April 5. The city went to court to try to block the
march, and the night before his assassination, King gave his famous and
prophetic "I've Been to the Mountaintop" speech. He was shot to death
on April 4. The rioting that occurred in Memphis afterwards was minor in
comparison with the riots that erupted in other major American cities.

On April 8, King's widow, Coretta Scott King, led an impressive coalition of national civil rights and labor delegations in a peaceful memorial
march in Memphis to honor King and the sanitation workers. Jerry Wurf
told the large crowd, "Until we have justice and decency and morality, we
will not go back to work." Ralph Abernathy, the new head of the SCLC,
vowed that "We are bound for the promised land . . . we ain't gonna let
nobody turn us around." And, before presenting the strikers with a
$50,000 check, Walter Reuther, UAW president, proclaimed, "We're gonna
drag you [Mayor Loeb] into the 20th century somehow."[5]

Ultimately, it took federal intervention and considerable federal pressure to get a strike settlement, and it is highly significant that such intervention and pressure came about only *after* King's death. Loeb had never
wanted nor sought federal mediation, and in the past, the government's
policy had been to provide mediation services during such conflicts only
after both sides formally requested it. On April 4, President Johnson
superseded that policy and issued a direct order to the Under Secretary of
Labor, James Reynolds, to go to Memphis and settle the strike. Reynolds
flew to Memphis on April 5 and quickly met with the union and with the
mayor. He and Frank Miles then joined forces. As Loeb continued to
maintain his old position, *Newsweek* and the national media began to
report on the backwardness of the city's racial and labor relations, and to
single out the mayor as the major obstacle to a settlement. After King's
death and the national publicity, segments of the local white community,
including businesses, dropped their support of the mayor. Finally, on
April 16, the city council approved a compromise agreement similar to the
one Loeb had rejected earlier in March.

The final settlement, a written "Memorandum of Understanding," formally recognized the union, granted it a voluntary checkoff through the
employees' credit union, established a formal grievance procedure, and
provided mechanisms for equalizing city benefits and merit promotions.
It also included a no-discrimination clause and a no-strike clause. The
strikers were to be rehired, and an attachment to the agreement provided

for a gradual pay increase that totaled 15 cents an hour. The strikers, AFSCME, and the civil rights community rejoiced at the settlement.

In both the short term and the long term, the Memphis strike has captured the imagination of those who share a commitment to ending racism and poverty in the United States. Because the strike occurred in a year filled with many traumatic events and crises, it is very difficult, if not impossible, to isolate its subsequent specific impact from that of other happenings. Nonetheless, in the wake of the strike and King's assassination, a previously hesitant U.S. Congress passed the Civil Rights Act of 1968 to establish guidelines for ending racial discrimination in housing; the National Council of Churches and other organizations passed an "Economic Bill of Rights" for all Americans; and the SCLC went ahead and launched a modest but precedent-setting Poor People's Campaign from Memphis. The Memphis strike had brought into life a progressive labor and civil rights coalition that was committed to continuing the difficult struggle to achieve greater racial and economic justice.

"Memphis is the beginning of an era and not the end of a strike,"[6] proclaimed A. Philip Randolph, the elder statesmen of black unionists. The strike prompted AFSCME and the civil rights movement to join forces to try to organize the South, both black and white. Public employees in Charleston, Atlanta, and other places took heart from the Memphis movement and sought collective bargaining rights. Some were successful, others were not, but public unions gained an important foothold in the South.

It is easier to assess the impact of the strike in Memphis itself. Afterwards, local businesses pledged to hire more blacks, the city established a Human Relations Commission, and *The Commercial Appeal* finally dropped "Hambone," its racially demeaning cartoon strip. Within a year, AFSCME successfully organized public employees in Memphis hospitals, schools, and the federal housing authority. And when the "Memorandum of Understanding" expired in 1969, the once "invisible" sanitation workers secured a better and more generous three-year contract. In the 1970s, Local 1733's membership grew to over 6,000.

Without question, the sanitation strikers' unprecedented victory established important rights for labor and racial minorities in the public sector, produced economic gains for poor workers, and provided a means for negotiating racial conflict. Yet, it was a costly victory, if only because of King's death. Tragically, the progressive civil rights and labor coalition that came into being during the strike with a determination to end two of the nation's most serious problems—racism and poverty—never fully developed, and a rare historic opportunity for fundamental social change was missed. Today, the Memphis sanitation strike stands out as an especially meaningful example and inspiration for those who share those values and continue that struggle.

NOTES

1. *New York Times*, March 18, 1968, p. 28.
2. *The Commercial Appeal*, February 15, 1968, p. 1.
3. *The Commercial Appeal*, March 15, 1968, p. 23.
4. *The Commercial Appeal*, March 19, 1968, p. 1.
5. *The Commercial Appeal*, April 9, 1968, p. 10.
6. *The Commercial Appeal*, April 27, 1968, p. 3.

DOCUMENTS

**10.1.   AFSCME, "Public Employee Unions: Rights and
          Responsibilities," July 26, 1966**

> *In 1966 the International Executive Board of AFSCME issued
> this important statement to clarify the union's policies for the
> general public as well as its members. Especially noteworthy fea-
> tures include the union's rationale for public employee rights,
> the reference to dignity, and the limitations on strikes.*

In recent years, there has been a substantial growth in the number of
public employees who have joined unions. This trend seems certain to
continue at an accelerated pace as public employment—already the
largest single work force in the United States—expands still further and
as the labor movement intensifies its efforts to organize public employees.

As this growth continues, the necessity for logical, orderly methods of
settling labor-management disputes in the public sector becomes more
and more evident. Progress has been made in this area. President John F.
Kennedy, in his historic Executive Order 10988, established a basic approach toward collective bargaining procedures in the field of Federal employment. Several states and local governments have, through statute,
ordinance, or executive order, set up collective bargaining procedures for
their employees. Some of these attempts have been highly successful.
Others have been at least partial failures, primarily because they represented gestures in the right direction but, in practice, amounted to form
more than substance.

PUBLIC EMPLOYERS occasionally tried to hide behind the "sover-
eignty concept" of government, a concept rooted in English law dating
from the period when the right of kings, i.e., of government, was considered Divine. The concept has long since been abandoned in this nation—except occasionally where public employees are concerned. The
attempt to invoke this outmoded doctrine in situations which cry out for
democratic procedures and mutual understanding is to single out these
workers as unworthy of dignity.

Government's refusal to bargain with its employees carries with it a
substantial threat to the entire democratic concept which marks labor-
management relations in the United States. It is absurd to believe that a

governmental unit which signs contracts for buildings, for supplies, for services, for the purchase of real property, and for a thousand and one other things, virtually all of them secured under conditions regulated by the generally-applicable rules of labor-management relations would seek to deny equal treatment to its own employees. The use of public funds is the same in either case.

WE BELIEVE THAT good labor-management relations in government, as in the private sector of the economy, must be concerned with fundamental problems and fundamental relations. The certification and collective bargaining processes used in private industry have worked well, where tried, in the public area. They can be improved and expanded in the public employment field by the continued application of sound principles. Public officials must recognize that they must deal with the problems of their employees, not sweep them under the rug and hope they will stay out of sight. If public officials and public employee unions approach the problem responsibly, sound solutions will be found. Collective bargaining does work in the public interest.

Inevitably, in any discussion of the right of public employees to bargain collectively, the question of their right to strike is also raised. Because we believe that the position of this Federation should be perfectly clear, we adopt and announce the following policy:

AFSCME INSISTS upon the right of public employees—except for police and other law enforcement officers—to strike. To forestall this right is to handicap free collective bargaining process. Wherever legal barriers to the exercise of this right exist, it shall be our policy to seek the removal of such barriers. Where one party at the bargaining table possesses all the power and authority, bargaining becomes no more than formalized petitioning.

The right to strike, however, is not something to be exercised casually. It should be exercised only under the most extreme provocation or as a final resort if an employer acts in an irresponsible manner. Further, let it be clearly understood: It is beyond the authority of any officer of this Federation or of the International Executive Board to call a strike. The decision to strike or to accept an agreement to end a strike can be made only by the members of a local union involved in a dispute.

WE POINT OUT, further, that the prohibition on the use of the strike weapons by police and other law enforcement officers is, in this union, absolute. . . .

IT IS NOT the policy of this union to make mere strikes to achieve our objectives. We look upon collective bargaining as the most democratic— and the most realistic—method of settling disputes over the substance of agreements between organized workers and their employers. We welcome the use of outside mediators and of genuine third-party fact finding processes as means of resolving impasses in bargaining. But efforts of this kind can be successful only if both the union and the employer enter into bargaining in good faith. The will to reach an agreement must be present at the table.

It is for this reason, as well as because of our unwillingness to turn over to strangers the final voice in determing [sic] the wages and working conditions of our membership, that we reject the concept of compulsory arbitration to resolve bargaining disputes.

BARGAINING IS, by its nature, a give-and-take process in which compromise and flexibility are frequently important features. . . .

We believe there is a place for arbitration of disputes, but that place is the voluntary use of such procedures to settle disputes over the meaning or the application of the provisions of an existing collective bargaining agreement or in the final settlement of grievances which may arise under the terms of an agreement.

Source: AFSCME, "Public Employee Unions: Rights and Responsibilities," *The Public Employee*, vol. 31, no. 8 (August 1966): 10. Used with permission of the American Federation of State, County, and Municipal Employees.

10.2.   "Loeb Takes Right Course," *The Commercial Appeal*, February 16, 1968

This editorial is typical of those the newspaper ran against the strike. It impugned the patriotism of the union representatives, and after correctly noting that the strike was illegal, it also suggested, incorrectly, that there was something illegal—or sinister—about union recognition and dues checkoffs.

THE BLUSTER, swagger and insolence of the men purporting to represent city garbage workers cannot be construed as "bargaining." They "negotiate" with Mayor Henry Loeb and the City of Memphis somewhat like the Viet Cong and Hanoi do with South Vietnam and the United States.

Mayor Loeb has proceeded through this city crisis with proper firmness, and yet has listened to the most brazen and abusive language from union leaders without losing his well-known temper.

Since the strike is illegal, under a standing court injunction, Mayor Loeb has gone more than halfway in even talking with the union men. Furthermore, this is a union which is not recognized by the city, and in fact that is the prime goal of the strike—to win union recognition by a municipality through a walkout that paralyzes garbage pickup and endangers the health of the citizens. The ultimate aim, supported from the top level of the union, is to collect dues from workers.

Memphians, struggling with uncollected garbage, should not be intimidated either. The city is making every possible effort to handle emergency pickups.

Meanwhile, the individual family can help in other ways, and thus help itself. Any "wet garbage" that cannot be flushed through a sink disposer should be heavily and tightly wrapped and compressed to the smallest possible size. Garbage cans should be used for food waste and lids kept tight to keep animals out. Paper can be bundled with string so it won't blow about. Bottles and cans can be sacked and set beside cans unless there is a way of keeping them indoors until the strike ends, or until new crews are hired by the city and pickups return to normal.

Reason has not worked in dealing with this wildcat strike. Strong measures have had to be taken. Citizens can add to the strength of their city by managing as best they can to protect the public health and to regain the service they pay for in taxes.

Source: "Loeb Takes Right Course," *The Commercial Appeal*, February 16, 1968, p. 6. Copyright, *The Commercial Appeal*, Memphis, TN. Used with permission (http://www.commercialappeal.com).

10.3.   Mayor Henry Loeb's Letter to Striking Sanitation Workers, February 29, 1968

Loeb, who believed that he and not the union understood the black sanitation workers, insisted on writing this letter directly to them to tell them that the strike had to end before he would negotiate. The strikers took this letter, in which he offered a small pay raise without union recognition and a dues checkoff, as an insult and as evidence of the mayor's "plantation mentality."

For four years while I was Commissioner of Public Works we got to know each other well. You know that I keep my word. Certain employees of the Sanitation Department have been off the job for over two weeks, and I am writing to restate the City's position.

A strike of public employees is illegal. We are a nation governed by laws and as Mayor I have given my oath to uphold the law. As a precondition to any rearrangement of wages and working conditions, the strike must end.

After this condition is met, I will again sit down with representatives of employees of the Public Works Department.

Once these representatives have been named, we welcome their advice to make our meaningful grievance procedure even more meaningful. I have and will recommend to the Council a salary increase of 8c. This appears to me eminently fair and equitable, considering the City's financial condition, and the needs of other employees of the City who are also entitled to fair salary increases.

In answer to a question, I thoroughly respect and recognize the right of each of you to join and pay dues to a union of your choosing, and whether you pay these dues with private funds or money borrowed by you from a credit union is strictly your personal business.

In other areas present City policy will continue. The City offers health, hospitalization and life insurance to all employees, including the sanitation workers, and this policy will be continued. On July 1, 1968, according to an ordinance already on the books, all employees of the City will receive two-weeks paid vacation, after one year of service. After the tenth year, each employee will receive three weeks paid vacation; and after the fifteenth year of employment, each employee will receive four weeks paid vacation. Uniform sick leave should be made standard for all City employees.

I will also recommend to the Council that the City's pension fund again be made available to all City employees, on a voluntary basis. Also, I will suggest that all sanitation workers be placed under Civil Service rules to govern promotions, hiring, and dismissal procedures, with a hearing on request. The standard work week at the Sanitation Department has been 40 hours, and this will continue.

I again say that the strike must end and I assure you fair, dignified treatment. As I have said many times there will be no reprisals. In fairness I should remind you that some of the regular jobs have been filled and others are being filled daily. Your jobs are of the utmost importance to you and your family and I am sincerely interested in your welfare.

Source: Text quoted in *The Commercial Appeal*, February 29, 1968, p. 16.

10.4.   Dr. H. Ralph Jackson, Interview by Arvil Van Adams, July 21, 1969

In this oral history, Dr. Jackson, Director of the Department of Minimum Salary of the African Methodist Episcopal Church and representative of COME, explained the significant impact the macing of February 23 had on him and on other marchers. He also stressed the African-American community's views on the importance of the demand for recognition and the significance of "I Am A Man."

How did you become involved in the dispute?
The dispute to start with was really between the sanitation workers
through their union and the City. I was contacted for permission to use
my name as a member of the community on the committee to raise funds
for the strikers. I stated that they could use more than my name; I would
be out of town, but when I got back I would also actively help them raise
funds for that purpose. When I returned, I found out that they were to
have a meeting with the City Council. When we got to this meeting, instead of a meeting, the City Council came in and read a statement that
they would have nothing to do with it [the subcommittee's resolution ap-
proving recognition and the checkoff], and they were leaving it [the
strike] in the hands of the mayor and adjourned the meeting without giving anybody a chance to say anything. The union officers decided that all
the members representing the union and some of the community would
return to Mason Temple where they would hold a meeting and discuss
where they were going to go from there.

   We started marching for Mason Temple and were told that if we
marched on the right hand side of the center line we could go in the street.
Within about two blocks, a disturbance started behind me. There was a
debate as to what started it, but, anyway, the police started indiscriminately to mace the folks in the line, including me. This made me mad as
it did several others. We then went to Mason Temple where we got all of
the details involved with the sanitation strike and the workers' grievances. Once we had heard their grievances and the inhumane conditions
under which they were working at that time, it was a natural sequence
that we decided that this was something that we had to commit ourselves
to obtain fully. From that, a vast source of information was brought out
about the overall conditions in the city. It had been so easy for all of us
to lose sight of what was happening around us. I and others had become
unaware of conditions in trying to make it under the system. We had really gotten away from the things that go on and the conditions under
which people live and work, the types of wages and salaries they receive,
the types of homes they live in. All of these things were unfolded to us,
and we had to look at these and the sanitation strike in light of the needs
of the folks. The need for a commitment to change these things is what
actually got me involved.

What was the impact of this strike in the black community?
The same day that the strikers marched, or I guess it was the next day,
we called the ministers together and explained to them the conditions
that the sanitation men faced, and they immediately rallied along with
leaders of the city, the NAACP with Mr. Jesse Turner, and members of the
community in support of the sanitation workers in their demands for
recognition for the union so that the workers would have somebody there

really to represent them and try to change these conditions. I think that since the workers are on the low end of the economic scale and could not support themselves, many of us just launched in and tried to help them out.

How were you brought into the negotiations that were conducted by Frank Miles?
When the community became involved with mass meetings, I was elected as finance chairman to raise money for the men. We made speeches at various meetings, and I guess from this that certain ones of us evolved as spokesmen for the community. When it was time for the negotiations, Mr. Wurf, who was president for the International, felt that the community had become so involved then that someone should be in the negotiations representing the community as well as those representing the union. The union officials decided to ask me to sit in on the negotiations. So I went in as a representative of the community.

How did you see the parties in the negotiations? What was your assessment of both parties, the union and the City?
The first item that we had to deal with was recognition. It was obvious to me from the start that the men there who represented the City were not there with the authority to make any kind of a decision. They came there with instructions, and, if anything further had to be done, they had to adjourn and go back and get instructions. To me, the whole thing seemed like a waste of time because we were getting nowhere real fast.

It seemed to me that by this time things were polarized. The City was determined not to recognize the union, to meet the demands of the workers. It was obvious; they were coming in saying we can't do this and we can't do that, the same old malarkey they always come up with. So this was what we were confronted with. It was not a case of someone coming in and saying, "all right, we have a problem, so let's solve it." It was kind of "we want you to understand our position of why we can't do this or that. We've got a lot of people in the East end of town who are a large number of votes, and they would never understand it or appreciate it if we did this or that. The mayor must save face, and the mayor has a number of telegrams, 200, from folks who want him to stand pat, and he must stand pat because these are the folk who elected him." All of this kind of thing was what we had to face.

The discussion of recognition at this time was dealing with ways of skirting the use of the word recognition. Frank Miles was suggesting that recognition be spelled out [deleted], but you objected to this. Why?
I took the position that when we went to the table and the City was on the other side, that until the City recognized who we were there could be no further negotiations. Otherwise, they were talking to us as though we

had no name. "We recognize the right of the people to organize," this is what they said; "We recognize the right of the people to organize." But they stopped right there, and they did not say, "We recognize the obligation of the City to recognize and deal with the person that this organization says we want to deal with them." I don't know if that covers too clearly what I was trying to say there, but what I'm trying to say is that it was one thing to say "we recognize the right of people to organize and to select certain persons to speak for them," but that is not saying "we recognize *you* [italics added] as the persons selected by these people." That was the point. They were willing to stop right there, and I was not willing to stop until they were ready to say that these people had the right to organize and select someone to represent them, and the City had the obligation to recognize the persons the people had selected. This is recognition. The argument over exclusive recognition was not a problem with me. The agreement that we finally came to satisfied the point that I had raised. Otherwise I would not have agreed to it. I use the illustration to you that if we are not recognized here as representatives of the union, then you might as well say "hey you" and not call my name or say Dr. or Mr. Jackson, but when you say Dr. Jackson or Mr. or whatever you choose, then you recognize me as a person. Until that was done, then there could be no further discussion. They finally got it worded a way that was satisfactory. [But the mayor rejected the wording, and the talks ended.] . . .

How do you assess the impact of black identity on the black community as represented by the sign carried in the march, "I Am A Man"?
The creation of that sign came from this office as we were getting ready for the marches and deciding on the different signs and placards we should have. The sign "I Am A Man" really came up from the idea that this is what the men are really saying when we say these men have the right to plan for what they feel is the best interest of their families. You have to keep in mind that Mayor Loeb was saying that he was fighting the union because he didn't feel it was best for the men. What we were saying was that it was not Loeb's responsibility to decide what was best for a man. If I feel what I should have is an endowment policy for my children, mortgage insurance on my house, whatever I feel is the best way to help me to provide for my family, which is my responsibility as a man, I have that right to decide for myself and not Loeb. These men had the right to decide for themselves what was best, and if they decided that a union was best, even if the union was not the best, they have a right to decide that. And the City had the obligation to recognize that they had this right. This goes back to my original argument about recognition. This is what these men were saying, "I am a man, I don't need any Great White Father. I am a man, this is what I've decided I want in the best interest of my family, and as a man I have the right to make that decision." While the sign was new to a lot of people,

it was not new to the black people because this is what we were steadily saying in our speeches at the mass meetings: "This is a man and not a child, and he has the right to decide for himself." So we had built this up, and when the man came out on the street with the sign, this was what he needed, it was backbone for him, and it was instant communication to the black community because we had been discussing it.

Source: F. Ray Marshall and Arvil Van Adams, "Memphis Public Works Employees Strike," in *Racial Conflict and Negotiations: Perspectives and First Case Studies*, edited by W. Ellison Chalmers and Gerald W. Cormick (Ann Arbor: Institute of Labor Relations, University of Michigan and Wayne State University, 1971), pp. 169–72, 177–78. Used with permission of Hattie Jackson and the Institute of Labor and Industrial Relations, University of Michigan.

10.5.   James Reynolds, Interview by Arvil Van Adams, June 9, 1969

In this oral history, the former Under Secretary of Labor described how he became involved in the strike, and the situation he found upon his arrival in Memphis.

How did you become involved?
After Dr. King's assassination on the fourth, I was in my office on April 5, where I received a phone call from President Johnson. He asked me why I wasn't down in Memphis trying to settle that strike. I explained to him that the Department of Labor doesn't normally get involved with a strike unless both parties request this, and then it is the Federal Mediation and Conciliation Service that would be involved. The only other cause would be a national emergency for the federal government to get involved. Johnson told me, "I regard this as a matter of great danger as it has implications far beyond the issues of the strike. The urban problems facing our nation could be enlarged by the events of Dr. King's death. I want you to get down there and help settle that thing."

I first contacted Governor Buford Ellington of Tennessee and told him that I had been directed by the President to try and bring the strike to a settlement. He welcomed me and offered his cooperation. I caught the first plane out of Washington for Memphis. As the plane took off, I could see fires in Washington from the disturbances there. I arrived in Memphis Friday evening, April 5. I contacted the mayor and explained to him that the President had sent me and why. I told him that I wasn't here to impose a solution or to circumvent his position but that I was here to try and bring the parties to some form of agreement that they could live with.

Loeb explained that he was desperately tired from having been up all the previous night and asked if I could come see him the next morning.

I got a pass the next morning so that I could get out on the street. As I approached City Hall, I was met by armed guards. I entered and went up to the mayor's office where I was again met by armed guards. When I saw the mayor, I again explained to him that I recognized his position and responsibility but that this thing *had* to be settled. After discussion, he agreed to my entrance in the case.

What was the state of negotiations when you entered them?
On March 27, the Mayor had gone on television and made some statements about the union and reiterated his position against the union. This made it harder for him to back down. The union also made some charges. Thus, the lines were pretty well drawn.

How well did Loeb understand the racial issues?
Loeb really thought he understood the racial issue. He cited his history in business with a predominantly Negro labor staff as a basis for his understanding. His outlook was a part of his whole makeup, which had been the product of generations. He viewed the matter as having been encouraged by radical civil rights people. At heart, he didn't feel the men really wanted the union.

I talked with men on the picket lines who didn't know who I was. I sensed a deep frustration in them. Black dignity was definitely an issue to them.

Source: F. Ray Marshall and Arvil Van Adams, "Memphis Public Works Employees Strike," in *Racial Conflict and Negotiations: Perspectives and First Case Studies*, edited by W. Ellison Chalmers and Gerald W. Cormick (Ann Arbor: Institute of Labor Relations, University of Michigan and Wayne State University, 1971), pp. 203–5. Used with permission of the Institute of Labor and Industrial Relations, University of Michigan.

10.6.   Memorandum of Understanding, City of Memphis and Local 1733, AFSCME, AFL-CIO, April 16, 1968

In this excerpt from the settlement, the city formally granted the strikers union recognition and a dues checkoff, plus their other demands. In return, the workers gave up the right to strike. That the final agreement was in the form of a Memorandum of Understanding, not a contract per se, allowed Loeb to save face.

1.
RECOGNITION

The City of Memphis recognizes the American Federation of State, County and Municipal Employees, AFL-CIO, Local 1733 as the designated representative for certain employees in the Division of Public Works, for the purpose of negotiations on wages, hours and conditions of employment to the full extent and authority provided by the Charter of the City of Memphis and the laws of the State of Tennessee.

The term "certain employees" as used herein places no limitations or restrictions on the right of any employee to belong and be represented by the Union.

2.
PAYMENT OF DUES

In the past it has been the established policy of the City to permit employees to authorize payroll deductions to be paid to their Credit Union. Employees may contine [sic] to make arrangements with their Credit Union for the availability of funds for any lawful purpose, including payment of union dues. The manner in which such funds are paid out by the Credit Union is a matter exclusively between the employees and their Credit Union.

The City has no control over the relationship between the employees and their Credit Union on the disbursements of funds by the Credit Union.

The City has not in the past and will not in the future attempt to exercise any control over the activities of employees' Credit Unions, which are wholly separate corporations operating under Federal statutes.

Therefore, the City of Memphis recognizes that any employees of the Public Works Division who desire to make arrangements with the Credit Union in order to pay their dues to Local 1733 may do so and that the City will honor procedures for the deduction of sums payable to the Credit Union by reason of such arrangements, provided that the arrangement between the Credit Union and the employee is based upon full compliance with Federal statutes under which it operates.

3.
PRESENT BENEFITS

The City will formally list the present benefits available and currently in force for unclassified employees, with the understanding that continuing discussion will be held for the purpose of providing for equitable changes therein.

4.
PROMOTIONS

The City shall make promotions on the basis of seniority and competency.

5.
GRIEVANCE PROCEDURE FOR THE PUBLIC WORKS
DIVISION

1. The City recognizes and will deal with representatives of the Union in all matters relating to grievances upon request of an aggrieved employee or employees.

2. The representatives of the Union may be the officers of the Union or Union Stewards, provided the Union Stewards shall be employees of the City and their names shall be furnished to the City by the Union.

3. Officers of the Union and Union stewards shall be granted reasonable time off during working hours to investigate and settle grievances, upon approval of their immediate supervisor, without loss of pay.

4. The number of stewards and the areas in which they are to be representatives of the Union shall be determined upon by mutual agreement.

5. Any grievance or misunderstanding which may arise concerning the interpretation or application of City rules and procedures, working conditions, suspension, discharge and discipline, shall be acted upon in the following manner: . . . [It then outlined, in some detail, a four step grievance procedure culminating in arbitration, if needed.]

6.
NO STRIKE CLAUSE

The Union agrees that neither it nor any employee member thereof covered by this Agreement will engage in a strike against the City of Memphis or any Department or Division thereof.

7.
NO DISCRIMINATION

No member of the Union shall be discriminated against or discharged because of the present work stoppage or subsequent Union activities, including the utilization of the grievance procedure outlined herein, and there shall be no discrimination against any employee because of age, sex, marital status, race, religion, national origin, or political affiliation. Nothing herein, however, shall provide immunity of any employee of the Public Works Division for the violation of any law, statute, or ordinance.

Source: Memorandum of Understanding Between Memphis and Local 1733, AFSCME, April 16, 1968, 1968 Sanitation Strike Collection, Special Collections, University of Memphis Libraries, MS 178, Box 7, Folder 38.

10.7.   "The Mess in Memphis," *Newsweek*, April 22, 1968

*This article, written a day or two before the April 16 settle-
ment, accurately described the situation at that time. It also
shows how negatively the national media had come to view the
city of Memphis and Mayor Loeb.*

In almost any other American city it would have been hard to imagine
a similar labor dispute—a major municipality taking a stand against recognizing an established municipal union. But it was precisely this issue
that first locked the city of Memphis in conflict with its sanitation workers—a dispute that led first to a bloody riot and ultimately set the stage
for the slaying of Martin Luther King Jr. The strike was still on last week.

There is no question that the responsibility for the city's adamant stand
rests with 47-year old Mayor Henry Loeb, a native Memphian who got
his wealth from his family's laundry business and his segregationist politics from the traditional white plantation paternalism that still permeates
Memphis at every level. From the moment the Negro sanitation workers
struck last February—seeking union recognition and a dues-checkoff system along with a pay raise and nondiscriminatory merit promotion—
Loeb insisted that he would approve no agreement with them so long as
the "illegal" strike continued. Even after the trouble and tragedy that this
rigidity precipitated, Loeb stuck stubbornly to his position. By late last
week, with Under Secretary of Labor James Reynolds on-scene in Memphis to help arrange a settlement, Loeb still stood against formal recognition of the union, but had given the nod to some kind of undefined de
facto recognition and to a form of dues deduction. At the weekend, however, he was still unwilling to agree to more than an 8-cent-an-hour increase for the 1,480 sanitation men, which they rejected. The lowest-paid
worker now earns $1.60 an hour.

Source: "The Mess in Memphis," *Newsweek*, April 22, 1968, p. 33. From *Newsweek*,
April 22, 1968. © 1968 Newsweek, Inc. All rights reserved. Reprinted by permission.

10.8.   "Monument to King" [Editorial], *New York Times*, April 17, 1968

*This brief editorial in one of the nation's leading newspapers
considered the strike settlement an important breakthrough and*

a worthy monument to Dr. King that had brought into being the
viable progressive civil rights and labor coalition he sought.

The settlement of the Memphis garbage strike marks a constructive end of the specific mission that led Martin Luther King to his death. The pact makes the predominantly Negro sanitation local the first civil service union in Memphis to win formal recognition from the city—an elementary right accepted long ago in many other cities. The Memphis workers also get an orderly grievance and promotion system and a modest increase in their wretchedly low pay.

Out of this overdue advance for a single small group of exploited Southern workers can come a renewed effort to forge the kind of coalition between organized labor and the civil rights movement that was a constant goal of Dr. King. At the 1961 A.F.L.-C.I.O. convention he urged united activity by these "two most dynamic and cohesive liberal forces" to erase the separate identification of Negroes and labor. The degree to which such unity was established in the Memphis strike long before Dr. King's assassination makes the breakthrough there much more than a symbolic monument to the murdered leader.

Source: "Monument to King" [Editorial], *New York Times*, April 17, 1968, p. 46. Copyright © 1968 by The New York Times Co. Reprinted with permission.

SELECTED ANNOTATED BIBLIOGRAPHY

Books

Beifuss, Joan Turner. *At the River I Stand*. 2nd ed. Memphis: St. Luke's Press, 1990. Best comprehensive narrative of the strike.

Fairclough, Adam. *To Redeem the Soul of America: The Southern Christian Leadership Conference and Martin Luther King, Jr.* Athens: University of Georgia Press, 1987. Analytical account of the SCLC from its founding in 1957 to post-Memphis events.

Goulden, Joseph C. *Jerry Wurf: Labor's Last Angry Man*. New York: Atheneum, 1982. Timely biography of Wurf contains a good brief description of the strike.

Honey, Michael Keith, ed. *Black Workers Remember: An Oral History of Segregation, Unionism, and the Freedom Struggle*. Berkeley: University of California Press, 1999. Collection of valuable oral histories of black men and women workers who document their lives and struggles in Memphis during the Jim Crow and industrial eras.

———. "Martin Luther King, Jr., the Crisis of the Black Working Class, and the Memphis Sanitation Strike." In *Southern Labor in Transition, 1940–1995*. Edited by Robert H. Zieger. Knoxville: University of Tennessee Press, 1997, pp. 146–75. Excellent essay with important analysis of the strike's broader impact and meaning.

————. *Southern Labor and Black Civil Rights: Organizing Memphis Workers*. Urbana: University of Illinois Press, 1993. Important account of the civil rights and labor movements in Memphis during the 1930s and 1940s.

Kramer, Leo. *Labor's Paradox: The American Federation of State, County, and Municipal Employees AFL-CIO*. New York: John Wiley and Sons, 1962. Classic study of the union from its founding in 1932 to 1960.

Marshall, F. Ray and Arvil Van Adams. "The Memphis Public Employees Strike." In *Racial Conflict and Negotiations: Perspectives and First Case Studies*, edited by W. Ellison Chalmers and Gerald W. Cormick, 71–107, 161–216. Ann Arbor: Institute of Labor and Industrial Relations, University of Michigan and Wayne State University, 1971. Essential essay and analysis of the strike; appendix contains good documents.

McAdory, Jeff. *I Am a Man: Photographs of the 1968 Memphis Sanitation Strike and Dr. Martin Luther King, Jr.* Foreword by Joan Turner Beifuss. Memphis: Memphis Publishing Company, 1993. Beautiful photographic overview of the strike.

Stanfield, J. Edwin. *In Memphis: More Than a Garbage Strike*. Atlanta: Southern Regional Council, March 22, 1968. The first of three valuable contemporary strike reports by the author. See also his *In Memphis: Tragedy Unaverted*. Atlanta: Southern Regional Council, April 3, 1968; and *In Memphis: Mirror to America?* Atlanta: Southern Regional Council, April 28, 1968.

Web Sites

The single best site on the strike, by far, is AFSCME's "Memphis: We Remember," at http://www.afscme.org/about/memphist.htm. Students, teachers, and researchers will find photographs; a day-to-day chronology of events; three articles from the 1968 issues of *The Public Employee*, the union's monthly newsletter; the transcript of King's "I've Been to the Mountaintop" speech; a number of King's little-known statements on labor; Stanfield's first report; four recent retrospective articles written by sanitation workers who took part in the strike; and useful multiple links to sites on African-American history and events.

The National Archives and Records Administration provides strike-related documents online. Teachers might note "Teaching with Documents Lesson Plan: Court Documents Related to Martin Luther King, Jr., and the Memphis Sanitation Workers," located at http://www.archives.gov/digital_classroom/lessons/memphis_v_mlk/memphis_v_mlk.html. Other useful information on King, the civil rights movement, and the Memphis strike appears in the *Report of the Select Committee on Assassinations of the U.S. House of Representatives*, at http://www.archives.gov/research_room/jfk/house_select_committee/committee_report_mlk_findings.html.

Videos

Appleby, David, Allison Graham, and Steven John Ross. *At The River I Stand*. Produced by Memphis State University, Department of Theatre and Communication Arts. San Francisco: California Newsreel, 1993. VHS. 59 minutes. Powerful documentary.

PBS Video. *The Eyes on the Prize II, The Promised Land (1967–1968)*. Alexandria, VA: PBS Video, 1990. VHS. 60 minutes. This volume in the important documentary series on the civil rights movement covers King's final year and the Memphis strike.

11

The Professional Air Traffic Controllers Organization (PATCO) Strike of 1981

The Professional Air Traffic Controllers Organization's strike of 1981 proved to be a watershed event in U.S. labor relations. By engaging in an illegal work stoppage, the professional union of federal employees challenged the U.S. government and lost. With strong support from the media and the general public, President Ronald Reagan fired the striking air controllers, ordered the Justice Department to take action to decertify the union, and refused ever to rehire or return the strikers to their former positions. PATCO was the biggest loser, by far, of the conflict, but, in many ways, organized labor, the government, the general public, and select business interests were hurt by it as well. Underlying the relatively simple story of what happened—of what some have termed a "suicidal" or "kamikaze" action by an "arrogant" labor union—lay critical issues of immediate and lasting importance.

The strike was the result of years of deep frustrations and troubled relations between the Federal Aviation Administration (FAA), the government agency responsible for overseeing the safe operation of the nation's air system, and PATCO, the professional union of air traffic controllers that had been founded in 1968. As air travel greatly expanded in the 1970s, the government issued reports that documented serious labor-related problems within the agency, problems that impinged on safety. As early as 1970, a prestigious Department of Transportation study known as the Corson Committee Report criticized the FAA for its reliance on obsolete equipment and for work schedule and mandatory overtime policies that led to controller "burnout." In addition, it found the agency's internal communications ineffective and labor relations in "an extensive state of disarray." Although mildly critical of the union for making attacks on the FAA, it reserved much harsher judgment for the FAA's management. Most significantly, the report concluded, the agency did not seem "to understand and accept the role of employee organizations."[1]

Another valuable study, the Rose Report, commissioned by the FAA and conducted by the Boston University School of Medicine, came to similar conclusions in 1978. The pioneering Rose Report is noteworthy both for its documentation of the nature of the controllers' health problems and for the serious criticisms it made of FAA management in the process. One of its major findings—that the controllers suffered from hypertension in greater numbers than other population groups—linked this illness directly to the work they did. However, another major finding—that the controllers' serious stress-related health problems did not emanate from the work itself but from their distinctive work *environment*—was possibly of even greater significance. The researchers warned that dissatisfaction among workers was widespread, relations between employees and the agency were strained and adversarial, and alienated workers were at risk for serious health problems. Improving the work environment was essential, and they recommended that the FAA make substantial democratic managerial changes, including, above all, the adoption of policies oriented toward joint union–management cooperation.

Throughout successive administrations in the 1970s, the FAA ignored such trenchant criticisms and made no apparent efforts to remedy the problems noted. It simply refused to acknowledge the existence of stress, obsolete equipment, poor working conditions, and questionable labor relations. FAA critics, before and after the strike, cited the agency's military mind-set, along with its monopolistic position as the sole employer of air controllers, for sustaining what they termed its "autocratic" style of management.

Meanwhile, during the 1970s, PATCO was earning a controversial reputation of its own. It is significant that the professional union came to life in the late 1960s during a turbulent era of domestic social and political unrest. President John F. Kennedy's Executive Order 10988 had guaranteed federal employees the right to unionize and engage in collective bargaining, and public unions were busily expanding at all levels of government. Although strikes were expressly outlawed, teachers, firefighters, and other government workers throughout the nation were taking part in illegal strikes to protest conditions, gain higher wages, and secure collective bargaining rights. In 1970 the postal workers set a historical precedent when they became the first federal employees in U.S. history to launch an illegal strike against the federal government.

It was in this context that PATCO grew and developed and became increasingly militant. Because the professional union was mindful of the strictures against strikes by federal employees, it initiated lesser "job actions"—slowdowns and sickouts—on six different occasions from 1968 to 1981, to express concerns over working conditions, benefits, and safety issues. In one such slowdown in 1970, a U.S. district court in Brooklyn ruled that these "job actions" were tantamount to strikes and illegal. It fined PATCO heavily and issued a permanent injunction that remained in effect in 1981. But, overall, the government refrained from exercising severe measures against the union, and PATCO survived and prospered. By 1981 it had won exclusive recognition as the controllers' representative, negotiated several contracts with the FAA, and grown to a membership of about 14,500.

Who were these air traffic controllers? Virtually all were male and high school graduates. Many were young and Vietnam veterans. All had undergone rigorous training for years. Most claimed they loved their jobs but were highly critical of their working conditions. In general, they proudly considered themselves skilled and essential professionals, a "breed apart" from ordinary working people. That the controllers were more highly paid than other federal employees (the average—not the median—controller's salary was $33,000 in 1981) was a fact that the FAA and the media would use against the union repeatedly throughout the strike.

These proud, disaffected controllers became increasingly militant after PATCO reluctantly approved a three-year contract it disliked in 1978. PATCO President John Leyden immediately led an effort designed to win members a better contract and a greater role in running the nation's airways in 1981 but without a strike. The union formed various committees, established a strike contingency fund, and elected "choir boys" to serve as conduits of communication between the disparate centers. Meanwhile, the controllers' dissatisfaction with the FAA continued to mount. Langhorne M. Bond, the FAA administrator under President Jimmy Carter's administration, reneged on a contract provision that protected controllers who reported on unsafe incidents. Many controllers viewed the issues of safety and working conditions as interlinked, and labor relations were so poor that the FAA and PATCO appeared to be on a collision course. Bond predicted a strike and, in 1980, ordered the preparation of a plan, subsequently published in the *Federal Register*, to keep the nation's air system operating in the event of a strike.

PATCO's disenchantment with their conditions, and the response of the Carter administration, was such that it became one of the few U.S. trade unions to endorse Ronald Reagan for the presidency in 1980. Members of the Republican candidate's campaign staff sought out and met with PATCO officers, and Reagan expressed a sympathetic concern for the controllers' working conditions in a letter he sent to Robert Poli, PATCO president, on October 20. The endorsement followed. Reagan's controversial letter—much cited during the strike—subsequently led the union to mis-judge its situation seriously and to believe it would have a friend in the White House during contract negotiations in 1981.

In reality, as a public- rather than a private-sector union, PATCO was caught in a paradoxical position at negotiating times. Although the FAA had the responsibility of negotiating the agency's contracts, only Congress had the authority to approve major contract items such as the controllers' pay, hours, and working conditions. Because of this anomalous situation, PATCO decided to draft a bill, H.R. 1576, "The Air Traffic Controller Act of 1981." The legislative measure contained the comprehensive program on hours, wages, retirement, working conditions, and more that PATCO was seeking, and Rep. William Clay, a Missouri Democrat and PATCO supporter, introduced it into Congress on February 3. By bringing the bill to Congress at this time, PATCO hoped to have the administration's support and to be able to pressure the FAA during the talks.

In fact, both the U.S. government and PATCO were preparing for a showdown. On the one hand, PATCO was adamantly determined to pursue and win its optimal demands in 1981 and had elected Robert Poli president in 1980 because of his militancy. On the other hand, the new administration was claiming that the 1980 election had given it a mandate to change and reduce the role and size of government. As he took office, President Reagan announced a program that entailed severe budget cuts in social programs, tax cuts for the wealthy, and greater support for business interests. He also made key appointments of people who were considered "union busters" in labor circles. Two of those who subsequently played an important role in the strike were the new FAA administrator, J. Lynn Helms, a former president of the Piper Aircraft Corporation, and Helms's boss, the new Secretary of Transportation, Drew Lewis, a Republican campaign manager and management consultant. Immediately upon assuming office in February, Lewis went outside the FAA and the Department of Transportation to hire a noted anti-union law firm to represent the government in the negotiations. Meanwhile, the Reagan administration sided with the Congressional Budget Office—not PATCO—when it denounced H.R.1576 because of its cost—an estimated $13 billion in five years.

Negotiations began on February 12 and continued after the old contract expired on March 15. PATCO had come to the bargaining table with ninety-nine items or articles to negotiate. More than half pertained to working conditions. From the outset, Robert Poli stressed that the union's goal was to create a "survivable career." The union claimed that about 85 percent of the controllers never made it to retirement because they had to leave the job for medical reasons. It considered three issues of prime importance: (1) a $10,000 across-the-board raise for all controllers; (2) a reduction in the work week from 40 to 32 hours; and (3) a more generous retirement program for those who had been controllers for twenty years.

It was a costly package. By contrast, the FAA was insisting on an economic wages-and-benefits package that totaled no more than $40 million, far less than the PATCO demands. Although the FAA offered the controllers a substantial pay raise as part of its offer, it angered the union by its steadfast refusal to talk about, let alone alter, existing policies regarding hours, overtime, sick leave, working conditions, and retirement. By the time PATCO broke off talks on April 28, only four of the ninety-nine articles had been resolved, and all were minor ones.

Serious efforts to get the two parties talking again occurred only after May 22, when PATCO publicly announced a strike deadline of June 22, if no agreement had been reached by then. Senators and representatives quickly reacted by warning the controllers not to strike, and Rep. Newt Gingrich, a Republican from Georgia, compared PATCO's strike threat to Iran's seizure of American hostages, a recent "hot" issue. Then, on June 18 and 19, a subcommittee of the House Public Works and Transportation Committee convened hearings to investigate the crisis. The hearings exposed PATCO's immense dissatisfaction with the FAA as well as the government's commitment to keep the nation's airways operating if a strike occurred. As part of the FAA's preparations, Helms had sent a taped message to supervisors at all FAA facilities. His audio description of the government's strike policy indicated a general disdain for unions, especially PATCO; unlike previous administrations, the Reagan one had made its last offer and would remain firm. For Helms, the foremost issue of the potential strike was to determine who—the government or PATCO—would run the FAA. Many in PATCO would have agreed that the broad issue of "workers' control"—over how to run the nation's airways safely—was a primary issue underlying their specific grievances.

Meanwhile, the strike threat captured the media's attention, unfavorably for PATCO. The union had done a poor job in presenting its case. Arrogant rhetoric such as Poli's statement that "the only illegal strike is an unsuccessful strike," along with the union's demands for a $10,000 pay raise, had already alienated much of the public. But the country rejoiced when the June 22 strike was unexpectedly averted at the last minute after Poli agreed to accept a contract, contingent on approval by union members, that basically mirrored the government's earlier proposal. He had only accepted the contract because the union's policy forbade it to initiate a strike unless 80 percent or more of the members endorsed one, and only 75 percent had approved the June strike.

But, on July 29, PATCO announced that 95 percent of its members had rejected the proposed contract, and the union requested a renewal of negotiations that failed. About 13,000 controllers began the long anticipated walkout on August 3.

On that date, the FAA's newly revised and strengthened strike contingency plan also went into effect. Four hours after the strike began, President Reagan went on national television to denounce it and issued an ultimatum to the strikers to return to work within 48 hours or lose their jobs permanently. By stressing the walkout's illegality, the controllers' failure to honor their oaths not to strike, and the union's privileged economic status, he successfully limited the terms of subsequent debate. His decisive action presaged the ending of the strike and was hailed throughout the media.

PATCO's misjudgments about the strike were fatal. It had naively believed in its "uniqueness" and in its friend in the White House. As a union of highly skilled professionals, it believed its members' talents were irreplaceable and that their absence would halt or seriously affect the nation's air traffic. But the government's contingency plan worked. It proved possible to keep 50 percent, and then more, of the nation's air traffic flying safely. It did so by prioritizing and cutting flights severely; by using nonstrikers, retirees, supervisors, and military controllers to do the controllers' work; and by adopting "flow control," one of PATCO's previously ignored proposals, to even out flights so that there weren't hectic "peak periods" of traffic in which accidents were more likely to occur. PATCO had underestimated the repressive measures the government would actually take. On the day the strike began, the government went to court to begin the process of getting PATCO decertified, district judges were already citing union leaders for contempt, and courts were fining PATCO, heavily, by the hour.

Outside of mobilizing its own members, the professional union proved woefully inadequate in mobilizing support. Its amateurish strike preparations had ignored the importance of the media, the general public, and organized labor as interested parties in such a major illegal work stoppage. It had not prepared or educated the public; it had not consulted with, or informed, other unions about its plans beforehand. Consequently, when the AFL-CIO was taken by surprise at a meeting in Chicago as the strike began, its executive council issued a strong statement of support but took no major action.

Nevertheless, PATCO members remained proud, defiant, and devoted to their cause. The vast majority—nearly 11,345—disobeyed Reagan's ultimatum and did not return to work. Only 1,300 returned. Many of the strikers interviewed stressed that money was not as important a demand as stress and safety issues. They produced a brochure, "Why We Were Forced to Strike," to emphasize the working conditions that led them to act, and the discontinuities that existed between the rights of employees in the public sector and the rights of those in the private sector. On August 4, Rep. John Conyers, Jr., a Democrat from Michigan, introduced into Congress an ill-fated bill that would have granted public employees the same collective bargaining, and the same right-to-strike rights as workers in private industry enjoyed.

After it became clear that the air traffic control system was operating, albeit at a diminished level, the union began to question the safety of the system and the qualifications of the working controllers. The FAA's claim that the system was safe was bolstered by the fact that no major accident occurred during the critical weeks following August 3, and by a widely publicized statement from the president of the pilots' union, the Air Line Pilots Association, that the system was safe.

PATCO was one of the featured causes during massive protests organized by the AFL-CIO against Reagan's policies on Labor Day, September 7. By then, the president of the autoworkers' union, Douglas Fraser, and others were beginning to voice concern that the defeat of PATCO might have serious consequences for the labor movement as a whole. Intermediaries tried unsuccessfully to get the government to reopen negotiations, and there was talk of possible mediation, but only talk. The administration's hard-line approach left no way for the union to save face and back down. It not only humiliated PATCO but allowed no room for impartial fact-finding or other remedies for legitimate grievances. And as attention focused on the question of rehiring the controllers in the fall of 1981, AFL-CIO president Lane Kirkland apparently made a little-known, behind-the-scenes, effort to avoid decertification and permit rehiring, but could not convince PATCO to accept the terms that would be involved. On October 22, 1981, the Federal Labor Relations Authority decertified the union.

As the months passed, the failure of air traffic to reach pre-strike levels, along with the human misery inherent in the massive firings, increased public support to rehire the strikers, at least selectively. On December 1, 1981, Reagan issued a directive that allowed the discharged strikers to apply for other government jobs but prohibited them from ever working again as controllers. The strikers ridiculed the gesture. Soon many were charging that the government was blacklisting them and preventing them from obtaining employment in either the private or public sectors. Poli resigned as president in January 1982, and the new union officers focused on the rehiring issue, but to no avail. In July 1982, decertification was finalized, and PATCO declared bankruptcy.

The lost strike hit PATCO members and their families hard economically, and the controllers soon became a classic example of downward mobility. Yet, according to interviews, few controllers regretted their decision to strike. Their pride in the 1981 "job action" was bolstered by subsequent evidence that confirmed the validity of their criticisms of the FAA. Reports by the National Transportation Safety Board in October 1981, the Lewis-commissioned Jones Report in March 1982, another Jones Report in 1984, and a congressional investigation in 1985 were unanimous in their scathing findings: The FAA *was* an autocratic and poor employer, and controller complaints about alienation, stress, horrible labor relations, and working conditions were just as rampant as they had been before the strike. Consequently, by the mid-1980s, the controllers were once again trying to unionize, and, in 1987, they formed a new union, the United States Air Traffic Controllers Association, to replace PATCO.

The strike's impact was long term and costly to the public, select businesses, and airlines. Year after year, the government issued plans to improve the safety and quality of the air traffic system, but, despite technological changes, the controllers remained understaffed and unable to handle the amount of traffic that had existed before the strike. At labor's request, President Bill Clinton lifted Reagan's ban on rehiring the PATCO strikers in 1993, but not many returned. The critical problem of controller shortages remains today.

Organized labor was a big loser of the PATCO strike in the short and long terms. With Reagan's union-busting and the economic recession in mind in 1981 and 1982, public unions like the postal workers, and private unions such as the Brotherhood of Railway and Airline Clerks, hastily settled contracts without considering the strike option. In fact, the PATCO debacle signaled a sharp decline in long-term strike activity in the United States. From 1947 to 1980, the average annual number of strikes in the nation was 300; from 1981 to 2000, it fell to 47. The labor movement has always considered the strike its last and most potent weapon for securing economic and social justice, and after PATCO, its diminishing ability to wield this weapon successfully not only weakened unions but hurt broader social efforts to combat rising economic inequality in the United States.

"Not since the infamous 1892 Homestead strike undermined unionism in the emerging mass production industries has any single defeat cast such a long historical shadow over organized labor," declared the award-winning historian Joseph A. McCartin.[2] PATCO's demise ushered in an era of new assaults on labor by business and government. The 1980s were marked by employee givebacks, plant closings, and the deindustrialization of the nation's industrial heartland—once a union bastion. After PATCO, with government acquiescence, employers felt freer to adopt hard-line tactics that disrupted union organizing, violated collective bargaining rights, and undercut wages in both the union and nonunion sectors. After PATCO, with government acquiescence, employers felt freer to abandon the social compact that prevailed after the New Deal. Before PATCO, few employers exercised their legal right to hire permanent replacement workers during a strike; after PATCO, that taboo was gone. The PATCO strike underlines the critically important role of the state in labor relations.

Perhaps the greatest tragedy of the PATCO debacle is that the important ongoing labor relations issues the strikers raised were overshadowed by media and other presentations that cast the conflict in simplistic terms, focusing only on the strike's legality, the union's arrogance, and the government's decisive actions. A deeper analysis reveals that the strikers were highlighting concerns that many working people and other Americans share today. Along with the workers' perennial questions pertaining to wages, hours, working conditions, retirement, and other benefits, the controllers took part in a career life-and-death struggle that brought forth contentious issues such as the viability of collective bargaining; the right to strike in the public sector in a democratic society; the problems of stress and other occupational health hazards; the role of technology in the workplace; and the rights of workers as well as management to make decisions in running an industry.

From contrary perspectives on these unresolved issues, both business and labor continue to emphasize the importance of the PATCO strike as a determinant of labor relations today. In a speech on April 9, 2003, Alan Greenspan, chairman of the Federal Reserve System, singled out Reagan's firing of the controllers as a welcome watershed event that bolstered capitalism by giving American employers in the *private* sector as well as the public sector greater flexibility to discharge workers. A few years earlier, George Becker, the president of the steelworkers' union, stressed the strike's lasting significance in a different way: "Busting PATCO sent a message to some corporate leaders that the parameters of acceptable behavior had changed."[3] Indeed, they had changed.

NOTES

1. Arthur B. Shostak and David Skocik, *The Air Controllers' Controversy: Lessons from the PATCO Strike* (New York: Human Sciences Press, 1986), p. 54.

2. Joseph A. McCartin, "The Anniversary Everbody Forgets," History News Service, August 14, 2001, http://hnn.us/articles/199.html (accessed March 28, 2004).

3. George Becker, "Restoring Respect After the PATCO Strike," *New Steel* (August 2000): 36.

DOCUMENTS

11.1.   Robert M. Rose, C. David Jenkins, and Michael W.
         Hurst, *Air Traffic Controller Health Change Study*,
         1978

This important FAA-commissioned study, conducted by the Boston University School of Medicine before the strike, documented the controllers' serious health problems—an underlying issue of the strike. As can be seen in this excerpt, the Rose Report found a direct relationship between such problems and the agency's managerial policies.

The main goal of the study was to determine the nature and extent of health changes in the air traffic controllers and by what characteristics these health changes might be predicted. . . .

We did find that the controllers had more hypertension than other groups, and possibly some forms of psychiatric problems were also more prevalent. . . .

Our findings are in many ways different from our expectations, especially with regard to the predictors of psychiatric illness and mild to moderate physical health problems. However, despite the fact that different men had different illness problems and relatively few had no problems at all, several themes emerged from our data. One cannot help but be impressed that controllers who perceived their work environment negatively, who were dissatisfied with work, with their co-workers, or with the FAA, showed a significantly increased risk for developing either psychological disorders or mild medical illness. We did not find that those men who developed more physical or psychological problems spent less time working, nor were they rated less competent by their peers. We did find that they felt estranged or alienated from their work and this occurred despite the fact that they said they enjoyed air traffic controller work. They were usually more invested in doing a good job, even though they could not discharge their tensions well after work, and too often they used alcohol as a way of coping.

These findings suggest that it was not so much what they were doing but the context in which they were doing it and the attitudes and feelings they had about their situation that influenced their risk for health change. We were surprised by the relative importance of attitudes about work in predicting health change. We had expected that the work load itself during field studies would have stronger predictive power than it turned out to have. The consistency of these results, which might be summarized as the alienation controllers experience from their work environment, suggests that changes should be made in this environment and in the way it is experienced. We believe that dissatisfaction with FAA management policies are a significant problem and represent part of the negative set associated with an increased risk for health change.

We also believe that some of the divisiveness that the controllers experience may in part derive from union-management interactions. Thus, despite controllers' perceptions of many positive benefits derived from the growing strength of PATCO, some of the alienation and divisiveness controllers often experience may be an unexpected and unwanted side effect of the adversary relationship between union and management. One of the recommendations for change coming from this study is that attempts be made to improve the work environment, to diminish the degree of dissatisfaction or alienation that controllers feel. Our interpretation is that this is not solely a matter of working hours or of pay, but that there is a need to improve the communication between management and individual controllers and to attempt to limit the adversary nature of their relationship. It is our view that this could be accomplished by a cooperative effort between the FAA and union management and that individual controllers would significantly benefit from such a reduction of controversy in their work environment.

The predictors of hypertension are in a different cluster and have different implications from those predicting psychological problems and mild or moderate illnesses. Air traffic control work *per se* has a closer relationship to development of hypertension than for other illnesses. . . .

By the time an individual becomes a journeyman controller, he has undergone three to five years of training as a developmental. There has been a considerable investment of time and money to help him acquire his controlling skills. Our data support the notion that controllers are concerned with burning out and being less able to control aircraft efficiently. The period of maximum productivity as controller is a limited one, perhaps 10, 15, but not more than 20 years. Medical disqualification is a problem for the individual controller and represents a significant burden financially to the agency and the government. It is one of our conclusions that interventions be attempted to maximize the period of time that controllers can function productively. . . .

Our data also suggest another intervention not oriented toward the individual but toward the relationship of the controller to management and the agency. There seems to be considerable general dissatisfaction among the controllers with FAA management. Those who showed the most dissatisfaction towards work, co-workers, and the FAA had a significantly increased risk for health change. We feel that some union activities may inadvertently have contributed to the alienation and divisiveness many controllers experience in the ongoing adversarial relations with the agency. We therefore suggest that an organizational development program be undertaken with joint union management cooperation to improve work life. If successful, such a change might be most beneficial for reducing the risk for future health change among controllers.

Source: Robert M. Rose, C. David Jenkins, and Michael W. Hurst, *Air Traffic Controller Health Change Study: A Prospective Investigation of Physical, Psychological and Work-Related Changes* (Washington, DC: Department of Transportation, Federal Aviation Administration, Office of Aviation Medicine, 1978), pp. 2, 14–16.

11.2.   Ronald Reagan, Letter to Robert E. Poli, October 20, 1980

During the 1980 presidential campaign, candidate Reagan sent this letter to Robert Poli, PATCO president. The letter was instrumental in securing him PATCO's endorsement and in leading the union to believe it would have a friend in the White House during negotiations in 1981.

Dear Mr. Poli:

I have been thoroughly briefed by members of my staff as to the deplorable state of our nation's air traffic control system. They have told me that too few people working unreasonable hours with obsolete equipment has placed the nation's air travellers in unwarranted danger. In an area so clearly related to public safety the Carter administration has failed to act responsibly.

You can rest assured that if I am elected President, I will take whatever steps are necessary to provide our air traffic controllers with the most modern equipment available and to adjust staff levels and work days so that they are commensurate with achieving a maximum degree of public safety.

As in all other areas of the federal government where the President has the power of appointment, I fully intend to appoint highly qualified individuals who can work harmoniously with the Congress and the employees of the government agencies they oversee.

I pledge to you that my administration will work very closely with you to bring about a spirit of cooperation between the President and the air traffic controllers. Such harmony can and must exist if we are to restore the people's confidence in their government.

Sincerely,
Ronald Reagan (signed)
RONALD REAGAN

Source: U.S. Congress, House, Committee on Public Works and Transportation, Subcommittee on Investigations and Oversight, *Aviation Safety, Air Traffic Control (PATCO Walkout): Hearings*, 97th Congress, 1st and 2d sess., June 18, 19, and 25, July 8, and December 16, 1981, and March 25, 1982, p. 84.

11.3.   Tape-Recorded Message from J. Lynn Helms to FAA Supervisors, June 1981

In anticipation of a strike on June 22, FAA Administrator Helms sent a taped message to the supervisors (all males) at regional offices. As this excerpt suggests, underlying the administration's policy was a deep-rooted hostility toward PATCO and other unions, along with a belief that only management—not workers or union—should run the FAA.

Good Afternoon Gents:

This is the Administrator and I felt what I oughta do is talk with ya' for a few minutes, both to bring you up to date as where we see things as regards the possibility of a controller strike, but even more important, to try to put this thing into perspective for you....

. . . Let us talk a little bit about where the FAA is, what we're doing, what the overall strategy is as regards why I cannot go along, or at least even accept the possibility of these people telling us how we're going to run our business.

First, there was a major message on November 4th that came to this town of Washington. An awful lot of people here didn't truly understand it at first. They knew there was a different political party, but they didn't understand the subconscious message which the American people were sending. And in all frankness, I must say that I'm not even 100 percent sure I did myself until perhaps the middle of December or late December. But by the early part of January there wasn't any question in my mind and what the American people said was first, there's gonna be a change. And these are the three things we want changed: There's got to be a reduction in cost of government, there's got to be an improvement in productivity, and there's got to be a deregulation effort. You gotta get out of our lives in the federal government. . . .

So fundamentally, what we're looking at is for the first time in perhaps a little over a quarter of a century this town of Washington is now undergoing a change in its mental thinking. . . .

Now if you take that, and then take a look at the FAA, and if I ask oh, say, fifty people—and I've done it over the last two months to all kinds of people—they start to tell me then what they say are our major problems in the FAA. And then if I ask each of you gents, why you'd have your idea also. And it runs the gamut. But the first one is usually "we've got a terrible problem with the controllers' union or labor". Over on the Hill, talking to some Senators and Congressmen. And I did it again today. And I said, "Well, let me ask you. What was the major labor issue of the last three years in the United States?" And no one can really remember. They hum and haw a little bit and say "Well, I don't recall exactly." And I say "well, if you recall it's practically three years ago exactly . . . there were statements by the leadership in the coal miners' union to the effect "By golly—they're going to shut this nation down." That we know you've got coal piled up for three weeks—maybe four—we're prepared to stay out five weeks—even six weeks—forty/forty-five days because this time we're going to have things go our way.

Then I ask these same people "How long did that strike last?" And you know, none of them can remember. . . . And in fact, it was the 111th day that that strike was settled. Now, during that time period there were no shutdowns of any power plants. As far as I know, not a single kilowatt of power was lost. There was nothing to bring this nation to a halt. And what that really says is that this nation has tremendous resilience. It has tremendous capabilities to absorb adversity and respond. And the American people just don't like to be threatened. They don't like to have some small group or some other special interest group working in their own behalf telling them "You're going to do this or else."

If you put that in perspective then, I would daresay that even six months from now, but certainly a year from now, none of you will even be thinking about this confrontation that exists between the union itself and the FAA. A year from now people won't even remember it. Two years from now they won't. But they will remember what the FAA did to provide safe and efficient transportation in the air transportation system as regards new equipment, and new capability to handle more traffic. . . .

Now, the reason that I wanted to talk with you personally is that they're two things that are uppermost in my mind. And I wanted to talk with ya a little bit about those.

The first is . . . my position on the offer that we've made to the union is firm. We're not going to make any more offers. We're not going to make any more changes. If they want to work the numbers around a little bit, that's fine. But this is a final decision. It's not something which is going to be bandied about. . . .

In addition . . . I absolutely do intend to go ahead with the Justice Department for legal action. And I recognize that to some extent the people feel they've heard this before. All I can say is they haven't heard it under this management team. . . . I want to emphasize to you that I am absolutely serious and I do not intend to back off. I do intend to take all the legal action, including civil and criminal action as is necessary. I will not go along with violation of law on the premise by people that they think "Don't worry, it will be forgiven later." That is absolutely not the case. . . .

. . . The second is I really have no desire to degrade our employees or make them feel bad. Now there's always a tendency, and when you have a confrontation, one side thinks they won and the other side thinks they lost. Or both sides think they've won. I want to get that out of your mind. In fact, any time you have a strike and employees get hurt by it or the organization does, both sides lose. But more importantly, the employees still believe some way that they're going to be saved by this magic thing called the union. And I want them to recognize that as they're let down that they're let down easily. I would far rather you meet with those people that do show up on Monday morning [the first day of the proposed strike] and give one of 'em a pat on the shoulder and say "Bob, I'm glad you came on in." . . .

Let's don't get around the fact that these people helped us build this system. What we've gotta do is protect them from what they're being led into. But we're going to do so with an absolute firmness that we run the FAA. Our management team runs the FAA. We make the decisions. We're not going to abdicate that. We're not going to let anybody take that away from us. And you gents can't either.

Source: U.S. Congress, House, Committee on Public Works and Transportation, Subcommittee on Investigations and Oversight, *Aviation Safety, Air Traffic Control (PATCO Walkout): Hearings*, 97th Congress, 1st and 2d sess., June 18, 19, and 25, July 8, and December 16, 1981, and March 25, 1982, pp. 427–34, 440.

11.4.   Ronald Reagan, Statement on the PATCO Strike, August 3, 1981

President Reagan was on firm legal ground when he issued this ultimatum to the strikers only four hours after the strike began.

This morning at 7 a.m. the union representing those who man our air traffic control facilities called a strike. This was the culmination of 7 months of negotiations between the Federal Aviation Administration and the union.

At one point in these negotiations, agreement was reached and signed by both sides granting a $40,000,000 increase in salaries and benefits. This is twice what other government employees can expect. It was granted in recognition of the difficulties inherent in the work these people perform.

Now, however, the union demands are 17 times what had been agreed to—$681 million. This would impose a tax burden on their fellow citizens which is unacceptable.

I would like to thank the supervisors and controllers who are on the job today helping to keep the nation's air system operating safely. In the New York area, for example, four supervisors were scheduled to report for work and 17 additionally volunteered. At National Airport a traffic controller told a news person he had resigned from the union and reported to work because, "How can I ask my kids to obey the law if I don't." This is a great tribute to America.

Let me make one thing plain; I respect the right of workers in the private sector to strike. Indeed as president of my own union I led the first strike ever called by that union. I guess I'm the first one to ever hold this office who is a life-time member of an AFL-CIO union. But we cannot compare labor-management relations in the private sector with government. Government cannot close down the assembly line, it has to provide without interruption the protective services which are government's reason for being.

It was in recognition of this that the Congress passed a law forbidding strikes by government employees against the public safety. Let me read the solemn oath taken by each of these employes:

I am not participating in any strike against the Government of the United States or any agency thereof, and I will not so participate while an employee of the Government of the United States or any agency thereof.

It is for this reason I must tell those who failed to report for duty this morning they are in violation of the law and if they do not report for work within 48 hours they have forfeited their jobs and will be terminated.

Source: U.S. Congress, Senate, 97th Cong., 1st sess., *Congressional Record* (August 3, 1981), vol. 127, pt. 15, 19299–300.

11.5.   **"Holding up America" [Editorial], *New York Times*, August 4, 1981**

This New York Times *editorial is representative of how the major American media viewed the strike and Reagan's action.*

"Maybe we are crazy," said Michael Fermon, a vice president of the striking Professional Air Traffic Controllers Organization. Then again, maybe the controllers, like most everyone else, would just like to work shorter hours for higher pay.

Whatever the merits of their case—and they appear to be dubious—the air controllers have no right to hold up the nation. President Reagan's tough threat to fire workers who are not back at work by Wednesday is appropriate. A settlement that rewards them for illegally withholding vital services would be a serious mistake.

The 15,000 union controllers currently earn an average of $34,000 a year. They had been negotiating with the Government for some months, asking for pay and fringe increases that would more than double their compensation. In June, hours before a threatened strike, union leaders backed down. They accepted a package that would have raised their income by about 10 percent a year.

But the aroused rank-and-file members were not to be bought off so cheaply. Air controllers bear responsibilities as great as those of airline pilots; so they feel they deserve salaries comparable to those won by the tough pilots' union. The controllers overwhelmingly rejected the settlement proposed by their union leaders and set the stage for yesterday's walkout.

Although their work certainly requires discipline and creates stress, it is hard to feel much sympathy for the controllers. There is no evidence that the work is debilitating. At a time when other Federal employees are asked to accept a 4.8 percent raise, there is little justification for giving them more than twice that much.

But beyond that, the equities here are really beside the point. The controllers have no legal right to promote their interests by damaging the national economy. If President Reagan were now to sweeten the deal already cut in June, he would only be inviting other Government employees in key positions to exploit their leverage. Living temporarily without regular air service is a heavy burden. Restoring it on the controllers' terms could be a disaster.

Source: "Holding up America" [Editorial], *New York Times*, August 4, 1981, p. A14. Copyright © 1981 by The New York Times Co. Reprinted with permission.

**11.6.   PATCO, "Why We Were Forced to Strike,"
            August 1981**

PATCO found it difficult to make its case about working conditions heard. After Reagan fired the controllers, the union pro-

*duced this brochure to educate the public about its basic griev-
ances. The bold-faced and oversized print is as it appeared in
the original document.*

Did you know?   **Our union had 38 negotiating meetings with the
FAA** in seven months and they refused to resolve one
significant issue.

   Finally, a strike was the only choice left to us. We
would not have placed our jobs, our families and our
homes in jeopardy if we thought there was any other
chance to reach a decent, dignified settlement with
the FAS [*sic*]. Some of our problems with the FAA go
back 10 years.

Did you know?   **Job stress for air traffic controllers** produces hypertension, ulcers, heart disease, high blood pressure
and other medical and psychological difficulties at a
much higher rate than the rate for the average working population.

Did you know?   The rate of sickness for air traffic controllers is so high
that insurance companies will not issue disability in-
surance for our union.

Did you know?   **U.S. Government statistics show that 89% of air
traffic controllers do not last on the job long
enough to reach retirement age.** The tremendous job
stress causes early "burn-out" and medical disabili-
ties. Many controllers are forced to quit early to preserve their health. **Nine out of ten controllers cannot
last long enough to retire on a normal pension.**

Did you know?   The government recognizes the hazards of the job
and keeps it a young person's profession. No one
over 30 can be hired, no one can work as an air controller past 55.

Did you know?   **Only American air traffic controllers work a forty
hour week.** In France they work 32 hours a week,
West Germany 33, Canada 34, Eurocontrol 29, Aus-
tralia 35. These nations recognize the extraordinary
stress of the job. Also these nations give far more vacation and paid sick leave to their controllers.

   France, for instance, gives 56 vacation days, up to
90 paid sick days a year. YET ABOUT HALF THE
WORLD'S TOTAL AIR TRAFFIC IS HANDLED BY

AMERICAN CONTROLLERS—THE MEMBERS OF
OUR UNION.

Did you know? **The main improvements we are trying for are in
working conditions. Our demands are for a reduced
workweek and a more realistic retirement program
as well as wage increases.**

The FAA has always been insensitive to the legitimate on-the-job needs of air traffic controllers. The
heads of FAA are political appointees whose attitudes towards professional employees have always
been negative and "take it or leave it." Even Secretary of Transportation Drew Lewis admitted that
"The FAA is a bad employer."

Did you know? The air traffic controllers were fired for going on a
strike. Our union was fined millions of dollars and
union leaders were jailed. Yet if the pilots who fly the
planes were to strike and close everything down,
they would not be fired, their union would not be
fined.

Same with the airplane mechanics. They could
stop all flights and not be fired and penalized as the
controllers were.

The law to prohibit strikes by government employees is unjust and obsolete. It imposes severe
penalties on the workers but no responsibility on the
political appointees who can force a strike by refus-
ing to negotiate legitimately.

And did you know what President Reagan wrote to our union on October 20, 1980 when he was a candidate for election?

These are Ronald Reagan's exact words:

"I have been throughly [sic] briefed by members of my staff as to the
deplorable state of our nation's air traffic control system. They have told
me that too few people working unreasonable hours with obsolete equipment placed the nation's air travellers in unwarranted danger."

**Now President Reagan is out to break our union—and set a pattern
to bust every other union that refuses to take whatever management
offers.**

If our union is defeated it will be a signal to corporations and politicians all over the country to go to war against the unions of their employees.

The members of PATCO want to resume negotiations—our differences
can be settled at the bargaining table. We are asking for open, honest col-

lective bargaining and the chance to return to our jobs with a reasonable contract.

Source: "Why We Were Forced to Strike," Professional Air Traffic Controller Organization, Southern Labor Archives, Special Collections Department, Georgia State University Library, copyright owned by Georgia State University, a unit of the Board of Regents of the University System of Georgia. Atlanta, GA, Series IV, Box 19, folder 17. Used with permission.

11.7.   John Conyers Jr., Letter to the Editor, *New York Times*, August 13, 1981

In response to the strike, Rep. Conyers, a Michigan Democrat, introduced a bill into Congress to grant public employees the same collective bargaining and right-to-strike rights as private-sector employees. In this letter to the New York Times, *he defended the bill (it failed later), and harshly criticized Reagan's actions in the strike.*

President Reagan's response to the air-traffic controllers' strike is without parallel in U.S. history. Never before has there been such a deliberate effort to eliminate a national union.

The firing and jailing of striking controllers, the move to impound the union's $3.5 million contingency fund and the attempt to decertify the union amount to nothing less than a strategy to destroy Patco. The Administration has ignored constructive avenues for resolving the conflict, such as fact-finding, mediation and voluntary arbitration.

The idea that Government employees are different from other types of workers is without foundation. Utility companies, A.T.&T., the railroads and others provide services no less essential than those of air-traffic controllers, postal workers and other governmental employees. Yet employees in these private-sector industries have the right to strike under Federal law.

The air-traffic controllers' strike should be considered in the context of the growing number of strikes by other public-sector employees, such as policemen and firemen. Court injunctions and criminal penalties have not proved a deterrent to such strikes by state and local or Federal employees. In fact, between 1978 and 1979 the number of strikes in the public sector rose 23 percent, the number of workers on strike grew by over 30 percent and the number of working days lost jumped 75 percent. The size and duration of the average strike in the private sector diminished while it increased in the public sector.

In an effort to find a way out of the present impasse, I have introduced legislation (H.R. 4375) to extend to Federal employees the full range of collective-bargaining rights now provided under law to private-sector employees, including the right to strike. It would apply retroactively to the air-traffic controllers' action.

Federal employees should be protected from arbitrary governmental intervention to the same extent as their counterparts in private industry. There is no countervailing bargaining power if a union does not have the right to strike. In providing Federal employees with such power, we can reverse the trend toward more public-sector strikes and, in the process, remove the double standard that has become so embarrassing to the nation.

The Government, as an employer, should be no more sovereign than other employers.

Source: *New York Times*, August 13, 1981, p. 22.

11.8.   Congress, House, Committee on Public Works and Transportation, Subcommittee, *Rebuilding of the Nation's Air Traffic Control System*, 1985

In 1985, after a number of fatal plane crashes aroused safety concerns, a subcommittee of the House Committee on Public Works and Transportation investigated the rebuilding of the nation's airway system. Its report was a scathing critique of FAA management and its post-strike policies. This excerpt highlights its devastating conclusions.

Little tangible progress has been made in the area of management and human relations since the 1981 strike. The same human relations problems that existed before the strike—an adversarial relationship between labor and management, ineffective communication between labor and management, management's failure to acknowledge problems that have been identified, and management's giving a higher priority to supporting administration than to supporting actual air traffic control operations—continue to exist.

Although some FAA managers have maintained that "The trouble walked out on August 3, 1981," the adversarial relationship between FAA and PATCO has been replaced by an almost identical employee-management polarity which followed a brief post-strike "honeymoon period." Layers of communication filters between top management and the work force have resulted in those at the top of the organizational structure and those at the bottom having different views of the air traffic control world. Top management is often unaware or misinformed about what is happening "in the trenches." Controllers have great difficulty understanding management initiatives or programs. Ineffective communication continues to be a great source of frustration, and to play a significant role in perpetuating the adversarial labor-management relationship in Air Traffic Control.

The Jones Report, contrary to FAA's contention, has been implemented cosmetically. . . .

An autocratic management style still thrives within FAA. . . .

FAA's public assurances that the system has returned to normal has created poor morale among controllers, who feel that overtime, increased traffic, lack of input into decisions affecting them, continued training of developmentals, and denial of sick leave and annual leave are anything-but-normal and should be faced and addressed by management. . . .

. . . FAA has a propensity to dance around its problems by either not implementing the study recommendations, as in the case of the Rose Report, or cosmetic implementation, as with the Jones Reports. In the management area, FAA contends that the system has returned to normal and asserts that the problem left with PATCO; but the Jones studies have shown that the management problems created by FAA continue to exist, and only FAA can rectify them—with major surgery. The studies to identify the stress and management problems have been conducted; the problems are real and are major. FAA should stop waltzing around its problems, stop sponsoring additional studies that waste tax dollars and start implementing the recommendations.

Source: Congress, House, Committee on Public Works and Transportation, Subcommittee on Investigations and Oversight, *Rebuilding of the Nation's Air Traffic Control System: (Has Safety Taken a Back Seat to Expediency?)*, 99th Cong., 1st sess. (Washington, DC: GPO, August 1985), pp. 82–83.

SELECTED ANNOTATED BIBLIOGRAPHY

Books

AFL-CIO. *Proceedings of the Fourteenth Constitutional Convention of the AFL-CIO: Daily Proceedings and Executive Council Reports, New York, New York, November 16–19, 1981*. Washington, DC: AFL and CIO, 1982. Contains Poli's speech before the convention and the convention's resolutions on the strike.

Geoghegan, Thomas. *Which Side Are You On? Trying to Be For Labor When It's Flat on Its Back*. New York: Farrar Straus Giroux, 1991. PATCO's importance emerges in a labor lawyer's passionate memoir of organizing in the 1980s.

Industrial and Labor Relations Review (ILRR). For an important and contested
scholarly exchange about the strike's motivations and meaning, see Herbert R. Northrup's "The Rise and Demise of PATCO," *ILRR* 37 (January
1984): 167–84; Richard W. Hurd and Jill K. Kriesky, "'The Rise and
Demise of PATCO' Reconstructed," *ILRR* 40 (October 1986): 115–22; and
Northrup's "Reply," *ILRR* 40 (October 1986): 122–27.

Jones, Lawrence M., David G. Bowers, and Stephen H. Fuller. *Management and
Employee Relationships within the Federal Aviation Administration: An Analysis of Management-Employee Conflict within the Air Traffic Control System of
the Federal Aviation Administration and a Program of Action to Improve Working Relationships Throughout the Organization*. 2 vols. Washington, DC: FAA,
1982. Excellent primary source.

Newman, Katherine S. *Falling from Grace: Downward Mobility in the Age of Afflu-
ence*. Berkeley: University of California Press, 1988. Excellent study traces
the human impact of the strike on controllers and their families.

Nordlund, Willis J. *Silent Skies: The Air Traffic Controllers' Strike*. Westport, CT:
Praeger, 1998. Only scholarly book-length account of the strike to date.

Poli, Robert. "How Not to Do It." In *Management and Labor: Must They Be Adversaries?* Edited by Robert M. Cooper. Memphis: Southwestern at Memphis,
1982, pp. 1–24. Essential memoir of the strike from the PATCO president.

Reagan, Ronald. *An American Life*. New York: Simon and Schuster, 1990. Contains
Reagan's explanation of his position on the strike and other events.

Rose, Robert M., C. David Jenkins, and Michael W. Hurst. *Air Traffic Controller
Health Change Study: A Prospective Investigation of Physical, Psychological and
Work-Related Changes*. Washington, DC: Department of Transportation,
Federal Aviation Administration, Office of Aviation Medicine, 1978.
Critical primary source.

Round, Michael. *Grounded: Reagan and the PATCO Crash*. New York: Garland Publishing, 1999. Useful exploration of public policy and the strike's contradictions.

Shostak, Arthur B. and David Skocik. *The Air Controllers' Controversy: Lessons from
the PATCO Strike*. New York: Human Sciences Press, 1986. Important pro-
labor account of the strike by a former PATCO consultant and a former
controller, contains excellent interviews and a strike chronology.

U.S. Congress. House. Committee on Public Works and Transportation. Subcommittee on Investigations and Oversight. *Aviation Safety, Air Traffic Control
(PATCO Walkout): Hearings*. 97th Congress, 1st and 2d sess., June 18, 19,
and 25, July 8, and December 16, 1981; and March 25, 1982. Excellent primary source.

———. *Rebuilding of the Nation's Air Traffic Control System (Has Safety Taken a Back
Seat to Expediency?)*. Washington, DC: GPO, 1985. Critical post-strike report.

Web Sites

Two online historical articles of special value. See Joseph A. McCartin's "The
Anniversary Everybody Forgets," August 14, 2001, at http://hnn.us/articles/
199.html, History News Service; and Rebecca Pels's "The Pressures of PATCO:

Strikes and Stress in the 1980s," *Essays in History*, vol. 37 (1995), at http://etext.
lib.virginia.edu/journals/EH/EH37/Pels.html.

Reagan's public papers can be found at the Reagan Presidential Library site.
See http://www.reagan.utexas.edu/resource/speeches/1981/80381a.htm. Alan
Greenspan's remarks about PATCO on April 9, 2003, are online at the Federal Re-
serve Board's site, http://www.federalreserve.gov/boarddocs/speeches/2003/
200304092/default.htm. George Becker's "Restoring Respect After the Patco
Strike" can be found at http://www.newsteel.com/2000/NS0008sf.htm.

Sound Recording

The PATCO Strike—Varying Views. [New York]: Encyclopedia Americana/CBS
News Audio Resource Library, 1981. Cassette. 30 minutes. Valuable recording of
speeches, statements, interviews of Reagan, Poli, Lewis, and others during strike.

Selected Bibliography

BOOKS

American Social History Project. *Who Built America? Working People and the Nation's Economy, Politics, Culture, and Society*. 2nd ed. 2 vols. New York: Worth Publishers, 2000.

Babson, Steve. *The Unfinished Struggle: Turning Points in American Labor, 1877–Present*. Lanham, MD: Rowman & Littlefield, 1999.

Baron, Ava, ed. *Work Engendered: Toward a New History of American Labor*. Ithaca, NY: Cornell University Press, 1991.

Bernstein, Irving. *The Lean Years: A History of the American Worker, 1920–1933*. Boston: Houghton Mifflin, 1960.

———. *Turbulent Years: A History of the American Worker, 1933–1941*. Boston: Houghton Mifflin, 1969.

Boris, Eileen and Nelson Lichtenstein, eds. *Major Problems in the History of American Workers*. Lexington, MA: D.C. Heath and Company, 1991.

Boyer, Richard Owen and Herbert Montfort Morais. *Labor's Untold Story*. 3rd ed. New York: United Electrical, Radio & Machine Workers of America, 1976.

Brecher, Jeremy. *Strike!* Rev. ed. Cambridge, MA: South End Press, 1997.

Brody, David. *Workers in Industrial America: Essays on the Twentieth Century Struggle*. New York: Oxford University Press, 1980.

Buhle, Paul. *Taking Care of Business: Samuel Gompers, George Meany, Lane Kirkland, and the Tragedy of American Labor*. New York: Monthly Review Press, 1999.

Commons, John R., Ulrich B. Phillips, Eugene A. Gilmore, Helen L. Sumner, and John B. Andrews, eds. *A Documentary History of American Industrial Society*. Preface by Richard T. Ely and introduction by John B. Clark. 11 vols. Cleveland: Arthur H. Clark Company, 1910–1911.

Commons, John R., David J. Saposs, Helen L. Sumner, E. B. Mittelman, H. E. Hoagland, John B. Andrews, and Selig Perlman. *History of Labour in the United States.* Introduction by Henry W. Farnam. 4 vols. New York: Macmillan Company, 1918–1935.

Dubofsky, Melvyn. *The State and Labor in Modern America.* Chapel Hill: University of North Carolina Press, 1994.

Dubofsky, Melvyn and Warren Van Tine, eds. *Labor Leaders in America.* Urbana: University of Illinois Press, 1987.

Filippelli, Ronald L. *Labor in the USA: A History.* New York: McGraw-Hill, 1984.

Filippelli, Ronald L., ed. *Labor Conflict in the United States: An Encyclopedia.* New York: Garland Publishing, 1990.

Fink, Gary M. *Biographical Dictionary of American Labor.* Westport, CT: Greenwood Press, 1984.

———. *Labor Unions.* Westport, CT: Greenwood Press, 1977.

Foner, Philip S. *History of the Labor Movement in the United States.* 2nd ed. 10 vols. New York: International Publishers, 1975.

———. *Women and the American Labor Movement.* 2 vols. New York: Free Press, 1979.

Foner, Philip S. and Ronald L. Lewis, eds. *The Black Worker: A Documentary History from Colonial Times to the Present.* 8 vols. Philadelphia: Temple University Press, 1978.

Forbath, William E. *Law and the Shaping of the American Labor Movement.* Cambridge, MA: Harvard University Press, 1991.

Fossum, John A. *Labor Relations: Development, Structure, Process.* 8th ed. Boston: McGraw-Hill/Irwin, 2002.

Green, James R. *The World of the Workers: Labor in Twentieth-Century America.* Illini Books ed. Urbana: University of Illinois Press, 1998.

Gross, James A. *Broken Promise: The Subversion of U.S. Labor Relations Policy, 1947–1994.* Philadelphia: Temple University Press, 1995.

Gutman, Herbert G. *Power & Culture: Essays on the American Working Class.* Edited by Ira Berlin. New York: Pantheon Books, 1987.

———. *Work, Culture, and Society in Industrializing America: Essays in American Working-Class and Social History.* New York: Vintage Books, 1976.

Jones, Jacqueline. *American Work: Four Centuries of Black and White Labor.* New York: W. W. Norton, 1998.

———. *Labor of Love, Labor of Sorrow: Black Women, Work, and the Family from Slavery to the Present.* New York: Vintage Books, 1985.

———. *A Social History of the Laboring Classes: From Colonial Times to the Present.* Malden, MA: Blackwell Publishers, 1999.

Kessler-Harris, Alice. *Out to Work: A History of Wage-Earning Women in the United States.* Oxford, Eng.: Oxford University Press, 1982.

Kochan, Thomas A., Harry Charles Katz, and Robert B. McKersie. *The Transformation of American Industrial Relations.* 1st ILR Press ed. Ithaca, NY: ILR Press, 1994.

Laurie, Bruce. *Artisans into Workers: Labor in Nineteenth-Century America.* Urbana: University of Illinois Press, 1989.

Mantsios, Gregory, ed. *A New Labor Movement for the New Century.* New York: Garland Publishing, 1998.

Milkman, Ruth, ed. *Women, Work and Protest: A Century of Women's Labor History.* London: Routledge, 1985.

Montgomery, David. *The Fall of the House of Labor: The Workplace, the State, and American Labor Activism, 1865–1925.* Cambridge, Eng.: Cambridge University Press, 1987.

———. *Workers' Control in America: Studies in the History of Work, Technology, and Labor Struggles.* Cambridge, Eng.: Cambridge University Press, 1979.

Nelson, Daniel. *Managers and Workers: Origins of the New Factory System in the United States, 1880–1920.* Madison: University of Wisconsin Press, 1975.

———. *Shifting Fortunes: The Rise and Decline of American Labor, from the 1820s to the Present.* Chicago: Ivan R. Dee, 1997.

Ray, Douglas E., Calvin William Sharpe, and Robert N. Strassfeld. *Understanding Labor Law.* New York: M. Bender, 1999.

Taylor, Benjamin J. *U.S. Labor Relations Law: Historical Development.* Englewood Cliffs, NJ: Prentice Hall, 1992.

Tomlins, Christopher L. *The State and the Unions: Labor Relations, Law, and the Organized Labor Movement in America, 1880–1960.* Cambridge, Eng.: Cambridge University Press, 1985.

U.S. Bureau of Labor. *Report on Condition of Women and Child Wage-Earners in the United States.* 19 vols. Washington, DC: GPO, 1910–1913.

Weir, Robert E. and James P. Hanlan, eds. *Historical Encyclopedia of American Labor.* 2 vols. Westport, CT: Greenwood Press, 2004.

Yates, Michael. *Power on the Job: The Legal Rights of Working People.* Boston: South End Press, 1994.

———. *Why Unions Matter.* New York: Monthly Review Press, 1998.

Zaniello, Tom. *Working Stiffs, Union Maids, Reds, and Riffraff: An Organized Guide to Films about Labor.* Ithaca, NY: Cornell University Press, 1996.

Zieger, Robert H. and Gilbert J. Gall. *American Workers, American Unions: The Twentieth Century.* 3rd ed. Baltimore, MD: Johns Hopkins University Press, 2002.

WEB SITES

"AFSCME Laborlinks: Women's Labor History," http://www.afscme.org/other lnk/whlinks.htm.

"The Baltimore Railroad Strike & Riot of 1877," *Documents for the Classroom*, Maryland State Archives, http://www.mdarchives.state.md.us/msa/educ/html/sc2221.html.

"Born in Slavery: Slave Narratives from the Federal Writers' Project, 1936–1938," Federal Writers' Project, Works Progress Administration, American Memory, http://memory.loc.gov/ammem/snhtml/.

"A Curriculum of United States Labor History for Teachers," Illinois Labor History Society, http://www.kentlaw.edu/ilhs/curricul.htm.

Documents on the New Deal, The New Deal Network, Franklin and Eleanor Roosevelt Institute, http://newdeal.feri.org.

"The Dramas of Haymarket," Chicago Historical Society and Northwestern University, http://www.chicagohistory.org/dramas/.

"The Flint Sit-Down Strike," Michigan Department of Education, Michigan Education Portal for Interactive Content, http://www.michiganepic.org/flintstrike/.

"The Great Flint Showdown," the Reuther Library, Wayne State University, http://www.reuther.wayne.edu/exhibits/sitdown.html.

History Matters, the U.S. Survey Course on the Web, George Mason University, http://historymatters.gmu.edu/.

Labor History Curricula and Related Materials, American Labor Studies Center, http://www.labor-studies.org/.

"Labor History on the Web," AFL-CIO, http://www.aflcio.org/trivia/links.htm.

Labor Laws, Cornell University, Legal Information Institute, http://www.law.cornell.edu/topics/labor.html.

"Lawrence Textile Strike," Ohio State University, History Department, http://1912.history.ohio-state.edu/labor/lawrence.htm.

"Memphis: We Remember," American Federation of State, County, and Municipal Employees, http://www.afscme.org/about/memphist.htm.

"Pamphlets in the Fight Against Taft-Hartley 1947–1948," Holt Labor Library, http://www.holtlaborlibrary.org/tafthartley.html.

"Remembering the Flint Sit-Down Strike, Audio Gallery," Michigan State University, http://www.historicalvoices.org/flint/strike.php.

"The Rise of Big Business & Labor," College Board, U.S. History Advanced Placement, http://www.historyteacher.net/AHAP/Weblinks/AHAP_Weblinks16.htm.

"Seattle General Strike Project," University of Washington, Harry Bridges Center for Labor Studies, http://faculty.washington.edu/gregoryj/strike/.

"The Story of Cesar Chavez," United Farm Workers of America, http://www.ufw.org/cecstory.htm.

"Teaching with Documents," National Archives and Records Administration, http://www.archives.gov/digital_classroom/teaching_with_documents.html.

"Women and Social Movements in the United States, 1775–2000," Center for the Historical Study of Women and Gender at the State University of New York at Binghamton, http://womhist.binghamton.edu/about.htm.

VIDEOS AND FILMS

A. Philip Randolph: For Jobs and Freedom (1995, 86 minutes, California Newsreel).

American Dream, (1992, 98 minutes, HBO Video).

At the River I Stand (1993, 58 minutes, California Newsreel).

Black Fury (1935, 92 minutes, First National and Vitaphone Pictures).

Bound For Glory (1976, 149 minutes, MGM/UA Entertainment Co.).

Bread & Roses (2000, 110 minutes, Parallax Pictures, Road Movies Filmproduktion, and Tomasol/Alta Films).

Daughters of Free Men (1987, 30 minutes, American Social History Project).

Doing As They Can (1987, 25 minutes, American Social History Project).

1877, The Grand Army of Starvation (1987, 30 minutes, American Social History Project).

El Norte (1983, 141 minutes, CBS/Fox).

Eugene Debs and the American Movement (1977, 44 minutes, Cambridge Documentary Films).

The Eyes on the Prize II, The Promised Land (1967–1968) (1990, 60 minutes, PBS Video).

The Fight in the Fields: Cesar Chavez and the Farmworkers' Struggle (1996, 115 minutes, Paradigm Productions).

The Global Assembly Line (1986, 60 minutes, Los Angeles: Educational TV and Film Center).

Golden Lands, Working Hands (1999, 172 minutes, California Federation of Teachers).

The Grapes of Wrath (1940, 115 minutes, Twentieth Century-Fox).

The Great Depression: (1) A Job at Ford's. (2) The Road to Rock Bottom. (3) New Deal/New York. (4) We Have a Plan. (5) Mean Things Happening. (6) To Be Somebody. (7) Arsenal of Democracy. (1993, each 60 minutes, Blackside, Inc., WGBH, Boston, and PBS Video).

Harlan County U.S.A. (1976, 103 minutes, Cabin Creek Films).

Harry Bridges: A Man and His Union (1992, 60 minutes, Cinema Guild).

Harvest of Shame (1960, 60 minutes, CBS News).

Heaven Will Protect the Working Girl (1993, 28 minutes, American Social History Project).

The Inheritance (1964, 35 minutes, Amalgamated Clothing Workers of America).

The Killing Floor (1984, 119 minutes, Public Forum Productions, Ltd.).

Labor History in Massachusetts: Collective Voices: The Textile Strike, 1912 (1990, 22 minutes, Capital Services, Inc.).

The Life and Times of Rosie the Riveter (1980, 60 minutes, Clarity Productions).

Memorial Day Massacre of 1937 (1980–89?, 17 minutes, Illinois Labor Society).

Miles of Smiles: Years of Struggle (1983, 60 minutes, California Newsreel).

NAFTA: A 3-Way Tie For Last (1993, 28 minutes, Paper Tiger Television).

Norma Rae (1979, 117 minutes, Twentieth Century-Fox).

Out at Work: A Documentary (1996, 56 minutes, Frameline).

Out of Darkness: The Mine Workers' Story (1990, 100 minutes, Labor History and Cultural Foundation).

Out of the Depths: The Miner's Story (1984, 58 minutes, PBS Video).

The Pullman Strike (1985, 20 minutes, Multi-Media Productions and Zenger Video).

The Richest Man in the World [Andrew Carnegie] (1997, 117 minutes, American Experience, PBS Video).

The River Ran Red (1993, 58 minutes, WQED Productions).

The Rockefellers (2000, 210 minutes, American Experience, PBS Home Video).

Roger & Me (1989, 87 minutes, Dog Eat Dog Film Production).

Salt of the Earth (1953, 94 minutes, International Union of Mine, Mill, and Smelter Workers).

The Struggle for an American Way of Life: Coal Miners and Operators in Central Pennsylvania, 1919–1933 (1992, 56 minutes, Indiana University of Pennsylvania, Folklife Documentation Center).

Struggles in Steel: A Story of African-American Steelworkers (1996, 58 minutes, California Newsreel).

Taylor Chain, 1: A Story of a Union Local (1980, 33 minutes, Kartemquin Films Pro-

duction); *2: A Story of Collective Bargaining* (1984, 30 minutes, Kartemquin
    Films Production).
Tea Party Etiquette (1987, 30 minutes, American Social History Project).
The Triangle Factory Fire Scandal (1979, 98 minutes, Alan Landsburg Productions).
Union Maids (1976, 50 minutes, New Day Films).
Up South: African-American Migration in the Era of the Great War (1996, 30 minutes,
    American Social History Project).
The Uprising of '34 (1995, 87 minutes, First Run/Icarus Films).
With Babies and Banners: Story of the Women's Emergency Brigade (1978, 45 minutes,
    New Day Films).
The Wobblies (1979, 89 minutes, Center for Educational Productions).

Index

97; and railroad strikes (1877), 62,
64, 73–75; and sit-downs, 181, 191–
92; and Taft-Hartley Act, 13, 197–98,
200, 203, 208, 214–15, 218; and Truman, 200, 205–7; and women's
rights, 15; and World War I, 10
"The Labor War at Lawrence," (O'Sullivan), 117
LaFollette committee on labor and violations of civil rights, 177
Laissez-faire, 60, 72
Laissez-faire capitalism, 82, 89, 129
"The Late Riots" (*The Nation*), 72–73
Latta, Robert, 62, 68
Law of supply and demand, 60, 82,
90, 92
Lawrence, Massachusetts, 10, 102–3,
111, 119; description of, 102; reputation of, 106; strike actions defended,
115–17; strike arrests and trials, 105,
107; transport of children from, 105–
6, 112–14, 116
Lawrence Citizens' Association, 104;
"A Reign of Terror in an American
City," 115–16
Lawrence Manufacturing Company,
22, 31
Lawrence mill owners, 102–4, 106–7,
109–10
Lawrence strike (1912), 10, 101–19;
and arrests, 105–6; beginning of,
103; as "Bread and Roses," 10, 101,
107, 119; cause of, 102; and children,
101–2, 105–6, 112–14, 116; and Citizens' Association, 104, 115–16; and
deaths, 105; demands of strikers,
103–6, 109–12; ending of, 106; grievances of strikers, 102–3, 105, 109–12;
as highest ideal of labor movement,
107; as hope and impetus for reform, 101, 106; and IWW, 101, 103–
9, 113, 115–16, 118; and public, 101–
2, 106; as reign of terror, 115–16; results of, 106–7; as social revolution,
102, 116; and tactics of strikers, 104–
6, 115–16; turning point of, 105–6; as
warning, 102, 117; and women, 101,
103, 105–6, 111–14, 116–17, 119

"The Lawrence Strike" (Beal), 108–9
Lawrence, Massachusetts, textile
workers, 101–3, 106–7
Lawson, James M., Jr., 223, 229
Layoffs, 151, 161–63, 174
League for Industrial Democracy, 128
Legislation, protective, 9, 102–3, 109–
12
Lever Act (1917), 125
Lewis, Drew, 252, 255, 267
Lewis, John L., 11–12; assumes UMWA
presidency, 126–27; and CIO and in-
dustrial unionism, 175, 191; and GM
sit-down strike (1936–1937), 173,
175, 180–81, 189–92; opposition to
Miners' Program, 11, 126–30, 137–38,
144; and "Speech Delivered at the
Fifth Annual Convention of the In-
ternational Union, United Auto
Workers of America," 189–90; and
Taft-Hartley Act, 199, 203
Leyden, John, 251
Lincoln, Abraham, 5; speech at New
Haven, Connecticut, March 6, 1860,
54–56
Lists, price (wage), 42, 44, 47, 51–52
Lo Pizza, Anna, 105
Local 1733, AFSCME, 223–26, 228, 231,
236, 242–44, 246
Lockouts, 197–98, 205, 207
Loeb, Henry, 226–30, 239–40, 242, 245;
letter to striking sanitation workers,
236–37; supported by *The Commer-
cial Appeal*, 235–36
"Loeb Takes Right Course" (*The Com-
mercial Appeal*), 235–36
Los Angeles, California, 229
Louisville, Kentucky, 26, 34, 61; reso-
lution of workers on slavery, 34–35
Lowell, Massachusetts: "[Proclamation
of Lowell Women Strikers]," 31–32;
textile strike, 5, 22–23, 31–34
Lowell Female Reform Association, 6
Lynn, Massachusetts, 5, 22, 41–54
Lynn Light Infantry, 43, 48–49
Lynn Mechanic's Association, 42, 47
Lynn Weekly Reporter, "Cordwainers'
Song," 47–48

cal shift, 151; in Lawrence, 102; and
trade associations, 151; and Winant
board, 154–55, 167–69; and workers'
complaints against code authorities,
153, 161–63. *See also* General Textile
Strike (1934)
Textile National Labor Relations
Board, 156, 167
Textile workers: and cotton textile
code, 152–53, 158, 160–63; and de-
pression (1920s and 1930s), 151. *See
also* General Textile Strike (1934)
"The Textile Workers Lose" (*The New
Republic*), 168–70
Textile Workers Union of America,
104, 117
Textile World, 156
Thirteenth Amendment, 3, 27
Thomas, Norman, 166
Tilden, Samuel, 60
Title VII, 15
"To All Employes of General Motors
Corporation" (Sloan), 186–87
Toledo, Ohio, 175
Trade associations, 11, 151; Cotton
Textile Institute, 151, 153, 165
Trade unions, 4; and 1830s, 5, 20–25;
and 1970s, 15; and AFL, 8, 86; and
capitalism, 8, 85; as citadels of democracy, 201–2, 214; and civil rights,
8, 14–15; as criminal conspiracies, 5,
22–23; formation of national, 6, 22;
growth after railroad strikes (1877),
63; and impact of GM strike on, 174;
impact of nineteenth-century depressions on, 7, 24, 27, 60; and IWW, 9;
as "labor monopolies," 200, 207–8,
210; and Lawrence strike (1912),
103–4, 106–7, 117; as legal entities, 6,
24; and NAM, 9; and NCF, 8; and
New Deal, 12; and PATCO strike
(1981), 16–17, 249, 254–57, 267; and
postwar accommodation, 13; and
public unions, 14–15; and Pullman
strike (1894), 79, 80–85, 89–90; and
sit-downs, 176, 181, 190–91; and social value of, 16; and Taft-Hartley
Act, 13, 197–99, 201–3, 207–19; and

Truman, 200, 202–3, 205–7; as un-
American, 62, 72; and women, 8–9,
15; and World War I, 10; and WTUL,
9. *See also* Industrial unionism; Labor
movement; Labor relations; *names of
individual unions*; Taft-Hartley Act
Trainmen's Union, 61, 65–66
Tramps, 60, 63, 74
Travis, Robert, 175, 178
Tredegar Iron Works, 26; and strike
(1847), 26
Tresca, Carlo, 105
Troops, federal: in Pullman strike
(1894), 79, 83, 93, 95, 97; in railroad
strikes (1877), 59, 62, 75; in textile
strike (1934), 155
Truman, Harry S., 13; and 1946
strikes, 200–201; proposal to draft
strikers, 200; "State of the Union"
speech (1947), 205–7; and Taft-
Hartley Act, 197, 200–203, 205–8,
214–15
Turner, Jesse, 238
Turner, Nat, 25
Turn-outs (strikes), 22; Lowell women,
22–23, 31–34

"Unclassified" workers, 224, 226, 243
Unemployment and unemployed, 7,
10, 15, 42, 203; and auto industry,
174, 176; depression of 1873, 60, 63,
71, 74; and textile industry (1920s
and 1930s), 151, 158, 162–63, 166;
after World War I, 125, 139
Unfair practices, 177, 199, 212, 219
Unfree labor, 4, 19. *See also* Slave
labor; Slave-labor system; Slavery;
Slaves
Union membership: and 1920s, 11;
and 1930s, 12; and CIO, 14; and
CLUW, 15; and decline of, 16; and
UMWA, 124; and World War I, 10
Union recognition, 10, 125; and GM
sit-down strike (1936–1937), 173–74,
176–78, 180, 182–87; and Memphis
sanitation strike (1968), 224, 226–27,
229–30, 235–40, 242–43, 245–46; and
New Deal policy, 164–65; signing

About the Author

MILLIE ALLEN BEIK is an independent labor historian who currently works as a reference librarian at Georgia Perimeter College. She earned her doctorate at Northern Illinois University and has taught history at Emory University and the Georgia Institute of Technology. The International Labor History Association honored her book, *The Miners of Windber: The Struggles of New Immigrants for Unionization, 1830s–1930s* (1996), as the Best Book of the Year in 1996.